Information Systems Project Management

Second Edition

Information Systems Project Management

Second Edition

How to Deliver Function and Value in Information Technology Projects

Jolyon Hallows

AMACOM

American Management Association

New York • Atlanta • Brussels • Chicago • Mexico City • San Francisco
Shanghai • Tokyo • Toronto • Washington, D.C.

Special discounts on bulk quantities of AMACOM books are available to corporations, professional associations, and other organizations. For details, contact Special Sales Department, AMACOM, a division of American Management Association, 1601 Broadway, New York, NY 10019.
Tel.: 212-903-8316. Fax: 212-903-8083.
Web site: www.amacombooks.org

This publication is designed to provide accurate and authoritative information in regard to the subject matter covered. It is sold with the understanding that the publisher is not engaged in rendering legal, accounting, or other professional service. If legal advice or other expert assistance is required, the services of a competent professional person should be sought.

Library of Congress Cataloging-in-Publication Data

Hallows, Jolyon
     Information systems project management : how to deliver function and value in information technology projects / Jolyon Hallows.— 2nd ed.
          p.   cm.
     Includes bibliographical references and index.
     ISBN 0-8144-7273-7 (hardcover)
     1. Project management.   2. Management information systems.   I. Title.

HD69.P75H35   2005
658.4'038'011—dc22

                                                                    2004019139

Printing number

10   9   8   7   6   5   4   3   2   1

To Sandra

My loving wife, best friend, and biggest supporter

Contents

List of Exhibits

Preface to the Second Edition

In the seven years since *Information Systems Project Management* was published, the discipline of project management has matured and has faced new challenges, particularly in information technology. Part of the maturation has been the broader acceptance of project management as an essential contributor to the success of projects. Consider just a few trends.

A few years ago, I had to start seminars on project management with a rationale for the subject; why it was important, and how to overcome the objections that it constituted nothing more than a layer of bureaucracy. Today, seminar attendees rarely need to be sold on the value of the discipline.

A few years ago, project management was often an afterthought in assembling a project team, and organizations turned to project managers only when their projects turned sour—as they usually did. Today, project managers are in demand, and few organizations would initiate projects without ensuring that they are managed.

A few years ago, information systems projects, particularly those that developed new applications, tended to be monolithic, spanning a year or more before the customer ever laid eyes on the results. Today, projects emphasize delivery of interim results, providing value in phases and responding more nimbly to business requirements.

A few years ago, projects tended to be isolated, treating what little user contact there was as a nuisance. Today, projects emphasize user involvement, from initial planning through review of deliverables to project closeout.

And, on a personal note, a few years ago, when I was asked what I did for a living and replied that I was a project manager, I would get blank looks or a noncommittal "That's nice." Today, I still get much the same response, except from people in the IT industry. That's progress.

However, with the growth of project management have come some challenges to it. In an attempt to speed up or streamline the systems development process, new approaches or life cycles have arisen, which celebrate what is seen as the democratization of projects and a corresponding decline of process, including the processes of project management. In many cases, it seems as if the old project-management-as-bureaucracy fear is resurfacing and, once again, needs to be slain.

Just as project management has changed, so too has *Information Systems Project Management*. This second edition has been updated to include new material, and to remove other material that is less relevant now. In particular, the chapter on management skills has been deleted, not because these skills are unimportant but because information on them is available from the general management literature. This change allows the second edition to focus exclusively on the concerns of project management.

So what is new in this second edition?

In chapter 1, "Introduction," you will find two new sections. "The Role of a Project Management Office" deals with an emerging component of project management and how it can promote the project management discipline. The section "Managing and Participating" describes how to avoid the traps in managing projects when you are not only the project manager but also a team participant. This section also deals with the issues in managing multiple projects.

Chapter 2, "Understanding the Project," has a new section, "Project Initiation." Getting a project started properly is one of the keys to managing it properly, and this section describes what a good project initiation process should entail.

In chapter 3, "Defining the Project," the section "Defining the Scope" has been expanded to include a checklist of items that you need to consider when you are preparing a scope statement. Chapter 3 also includes a major new section, "Systems Development Life Cycles," which describes several SDLCs and the approach that project managers need to take when they are faced with each one.

Chapter 4, "Planning the Project," contains three new sections. The first, "Planning for Implementation," describes how to plan your project so that implementation is smooth. The section "Planning for Completion" discusses that crucial question "How do you know when you're finished?" and gives some activities to ensure that the project closes cleanly. The third section, "Communications," presents a set of communications mechanisms and typical stakeholder groups and discusses how to plan the project so that everyone is involved at the right level.

In chapter 5, "Running the Project," the section "Managing Scope Changes" has been expanded to include a discussion of the four types of scope change and how to manage each. In addition, chapter 5 has two new sections. The major section "Earned Value" presents a proven method of determining where you are in your project and, if the current trends continue, where you'll likely end up. "Closing the Project" deals with the steps needed to complete a project, from capturing lessons learned to administrative closeout.

I would like to thank my readers for their many helpful and kind comments. I hope that you find the second edition as useful, usable, and valuable as you've told me the original was. I invite you to send your comments to me at jhallows@westwindconsulting.com.

Acknowledgments

This book arises from my own personal studies of project management, my many years of working in and managing projects, and the scars I have accumulated to prove it. However, I owe a great debt to the numerous colleagues and associates I have worked with along the way. Many of them I remember with fondness; others I remember. But all of them taught me fresh ideas and new principles about the fascinating, frustrating, and critical discipline of project management. I am indebted to them all.

Of course, some people stand out more than others: Russ Crosby, who was the first to demonstrate to me that managers can be supportive; Grant Gisel and Ian Reid, who built a strong consultancy by respecting their people; Jim Hayward, who confirmed that managing projects is more about people than technology; Harvey Gellman, for his exceptional knowledge of project management; and Bruce Burgetz, for his outstanding passion for his staff and his clients.

A special thanks to my colleagues who took the time to review my manuscript. It is better because of them: Stella Skerlec and her consummate professionalism; Alan King, who actually keyed the first draft of my introductory section into his word processor, ran the grammar checker, and wryly commented that my book required postgraduate education to understand; and Bea Cunningham, whose enthusiasm for this book at times exceeded my own.

Finally, I give special thanks to my wife, Sandra, to whom this book is dedicated, for her support and love during the many times over the years that I questioned whether being a project manager was worth it.

1

Introduction

Introduction

Congratulations. You have been given your own project to run. If you are like most project managers, part of you is elated that your company has entrusted you with an important assignment, while the rest of you is petrified that it will soon discover the magnitude of its error. Whether the project is your first and you are being "tried out," or you have been doing this for years but never on a project this big, this book is designed for you. I hope you find it valuable.

Project management is management. Its context and constraints are different from those of line management, but its concern is the same: to direct a group of people to achieve an objective. Therefore, project managers need to know how to manage budgets, people, and processes.

Why, then, do so many companies assign senior technical people—who usually have little interest in or aptitude for management—to head up projects? More critically, why are there so few trained project managers in an industry that is project driven? One reason is that companies tend to regard project management as secondary, not as important as line management or technical skills, and certainly not a career goal for ambitious souls.

The result is that projects founder, destroying schedules, shredding estimates, derailing careers, and delivering results that are accepted out of desperation rather than design. In the longer term, those who have managed these commonplace disasters retreat from project management and either return to the technical world or move into "real" management. So project managers are not developed, and the cycle continues.

It is to those corporate managers, project managers, and technical staff who understand that project management is a special discipline that this book is directed.

*   *   *   *   *

THE PROJECT MANAGEMENT CONTEXT

Project management is management, but five characteristics make it unique: responsibility without authority, its source of power, project transience, the observation that you get what you get, and the need for specialized tools and techniques.

Responsibility Without Authority

As a project manager, you are responsible for a project. If it does not meet its budget, schedule, or expectations, you are the one who will be held accountable and who will, at a minimum, suffer the scowls of management and receive an unflattering performance appraisal.

Bringing a project in on target requires resources: people, equipment, and support services. But, with rare exceptions, project managers do not command resources. You cannot arbitrarily assign staff to your projects, purchase equipment as you require it, hire people, or place your needs at the top of the corporate priority list. You cannot even promote or demote staff. Those prerogatives belong to supervisors and line managers.

To acquire resources, you must make a case to someone who does have authority. All too often, that person regards such requests as evidence of incapacity or poor judgment.

The Source of Power

Despite the project manager's lack of formal authority, the position carries with it considerable power for those project managers who are prepared to exercise it. The source of that power is the reality that the project manager is the only one able to make the project deliver value; without a project manager, the project is in extreme jeopardy. The exercise of that power is the project manager's willingness to withdraw from a project under extreme conditions. Bluntly, you have the right, and the obligation, to say to a client or to your management, "This project cannot succeed under these conditions, and until they change, I will not continue."

Obviously, this is a stand that requires unusual circumstances; you will not use it for the day-to-day frustrations that accompany most projects. Equally obviously, you will want to consider the personal and professional consequences of taking such a strong position. Nevertheless, you are not obligated to accept passively all conditions that clients or management impose, and, in most reasonable organizations, a blunt refusal to accept unnecessarily difficult demands serves as a shock treatment, indicating that a problem exists and must be addressed.

Project Transience

Teams, not managers, execute projects. Hence, one of your major tasks is team building. This is also true of line management, but the difference is that while departments endure, projects are temporary. You must apply team-building skills to a group of people who may have no commitment to the project or to you and who will soon move on to another assignment. You do not have the luxury of allowing a team to evolve. You must actively construct one.

You Get What You Get

Some project management theorists emphasize the importance of selecting a good project team, of matching skills to activities, and even of ensuring that personalities mesh. Unfortunately, companies do not have large, idle pools of technical expertise waiting to be chosen as if for a sandlot baseball game. The problem most project managers face is not choosing the right people but getting people who are even remotely qualified. Your job is not to select a project team but to build one from the people who are available.

Specialized Tools and Techniques

Project management has its own set of tools and techniques. Concepts such as work breakdown structure, resource leveling, and estimates at completion are largely unknown outside the discipline. Even techniques, such as Gantt charts or critical-path analysis, that have become commonplace in business are not used as richly in general business practice as they are in formal project management. It is not easy to learn these concepts or to understand how to apply them, particularly since few companies implement them consistently. The tendency to regard project management as being of secondary importance means that few companies will train people like you to master them.

Furthermore, since project management is management, it requires the same tools and techniques used by all good managers. Whether you are a project manager or a line manager, you need to know how to listen, frame outcomes, manage meetings, gather information, build teams, communicate, and manage your time. However, project managers seldom receive management training, nor are they selected, as line managers are, because of any promising management aptitudes or behaviors.

These five characteristics mean that managing projects requires, if anything, more management skill than most line management. Project management is a distinct discipline requiring its own aptitudes, standards, and training. Anything less will ensure that systems projects continue to suffer overruns, delays, and the increased antipathy of users and corporate management who are weary of regarding "systems service" as an oxymoron.

* * * * *

WHAT IS A SUCCESSFUL PROJECT?

A successful project is one that delivers expected results. These traditionally include a budget, a schedule, and a scope—the "triple constraints" of project management. Any project that meets these measures is, by this definition, a success. In fact, many project managers are regarded as successful if they can hit two of the three.

However, budget, schedule, and scope are technical metrics that define how well the project was managed. They bear little relation to the real concerns of the client.

A project is executed because the client expects some benefit, such as lower inventory levels, reduced staff, or increased annual sales. The project may be executed perfectly, coming in on time and on budget and doing what it is supposed to, but if the company does not actually reduce inventory, cut staff, or increase sales at least enough to cover the cost of the project, then the money the client spent is wasted. For example:

A company with a $10 million inventory budgeted $100,000 for an inventory control system, expecting to cut inventory by 20 percent, or $2 million. At 10 percent interest, the system would cut carrying costs by $200,000 per year. The project suffers a 100 percent cost overrun.

If the company does not implement the system or does so but fails to reduce its inventory, it has wasted $200,000—the budgeted cost plus the overrun. But if the company does implement the system and cuts inventory as expected, it will recover the cost of the overrun *in just six months,* and it will pay for the entire system in one year. This is not unusual: The benefits from a system normally exceed even devastating overruns. The catch is that the system must be implemented and the benefits realized.

This is not an argument for ignoring the project budget; it is an appeal that you accept the responsibility of helping the client realize the benefits that justify the project. You must be as concerned with the delivery of benefits as you are with the delivery of the system.

* * * *

WHY DO PROJECTS FAIL?

Stories of spectacular failures abound. A project that was budgeted at $10 million is finally killed when it passes $100 million. A system that was due at the end of July is delivered at the end of September—two years later. Why do these and less extreme but equally frustrating failures haunt the industry?

The most commonly cited culprit is bad estimating. It is the conventional wisdom that technical people cannot estimate the cost of lunch, even given a menu to work from, but this explanation is a myth. Of course, there are poor estimators, but even if the entire estimate were off by 100 percent, the total cost would do no more than double. This is not desirable, but neither is it comparable to the industry's celebrated overruns—the ones that we speak of in hushed tones, thankful that we were not involved.

In fact, most people can estimate reasonably well, and, in the sweep of a large project, the optimism of some estimators is fairly well balanced by the pessimism of others. In fact, there are three recurring reasons that projects fail: scope changes, poor project planning, and technology.

Scope changes are probably the major cause of failures. The problem with scope changes is not simply that they add cost but that they add cost out of proportion to their apparent effort. For example, a project estimated at $1 million grows into a project that, had it been planned that way from the start, would have been estimated at $2 million. It is tempting to believe that the final cost of the project will be about $2 million, but it will be closer to $4 or $5 million, because scope changes disrupt planning and development that has already been completed.

Scope changes are a problem for two reasons. Either the scope was not clearly established at the start of the project (see the section "Defining the Scope" in chapter 3) or scope changes are poorly managed (see the section "Managing Scope Changes" in chapter 5). However, scope changes are a fact of life. They are detrimental only when they are not properly handled, that is, when they are not adequately defined, tracked, and managed.

The second major cause of project failure is poor planning and, in particular, the overlooking of project activities during planning. Such activities are not part of the estimates, they do not appear on the schedule, and they have no effect on the plan. When they do appear, they can cause chaos. This topic is discussed in chapter 4, in the section "Defining Project Activities."

The third major reason that projects fail is technology and the plethora of tools in a typical project development environment. All of these tools must fit within a particular operating system, all come with a multiplicity of options and versions, and all are provided by different vendors. Those companies that select a development environment and stick with it for a reasonable period will find that they are rewarded by increased productivity and predictable projects. Unfortunately, many companies become sold on the idea that their development environment has become archaic and that this one tool will be the silver bullet that will solve their problems. The result is twofold. First, productivity suffers because developers never develop deep expertise in an environment. Second, projects suffer because, inevitably, the new pieces do not work with some of the older ones or with one another, and simply trying to get the environment functioning can take months.

Projects do not have to fail. When project and corporate managers and development teams take seriously the planning and running of projects,

projects usually succeed. This book is intended for those who prefer to work quietly on successful projects and are happy to leave the disasters to others.

＊　＊　＊　＊

THE PROJECT CONTROL ENVIRONMENT

This book is about managing projects. But one measure of the potential success of any project is the environment for project management within the organization. Many companies simply hand projects over to somebody to run and hope that things will work out—or at least that they will have a convenient scapegoat. The companies in which projects are most likely to succeed are those that have established structures and procedures, similar to the following, that support their project managers.

Reporting and Escalation Structures

What requirements for reporting project status are laid upon project managers? To whom do status reports go? How frequently? What must they say? What follow-up will be done on issues raised in the status reports? By whom?

Until these questions are answered, status reporting will be ad hoc and inappropriate. While many project managers dislike having to prepare status reports, any environment that does not require them is one in which management has disavowed any interest in the project and will not intervene except to assign blame when things go wrong. The existence of good reporting standards is an indication that management cares about the progress of projects and, by implication, is willing to help when needed.

Another component of reporting structures is escalation procedures. When issues need to be escalated, what is the procedure for doing so? To whom should the issue be addressed? How? With what expectations?

Companies that have defined escalation procedures recognize that some issues need senior-level intervention and have defined a mechanism for providing it. Any management that does not welcome escalation from its project managers is saying, "Don't bother me."

Project Management Career Paths

Companies that regard project management as important nurture the people who are responsible. They ensure that project managers have a clear and desirable career path that includes training, promotion criteria, recognition of achievement, and the opportunity to progress to the highest executive levels in the organization. Furthermore, such companies, by their recognition of project management, acknowledge that project management is a discipline, that it is needed, and that it is worthy of fostering. These are the companies that, in turn, attract, develop, and retain the best project management practitioners and skills available.

✳   ✳   ✳   ✳

HOW DO YOU KNOW YOU HAVE A PROJECT?

When people speak of projects, they normally mean the large, expensive, visible, cast-of-dozens projects that characterize systems development. Few will argue that these do not require some level of management. But what about the smaller activities, the ones that are not so obviously risky or critical to the organization? When do these become projects requiring the attention of a project manager?

For example, the hardware is being upgraded with additional memory, additional disk capacity, and, coincidentally, a new version of the operating system. Is this a project, or can it be left to the systems people to simply do the work without imposing a project structure on them?

There is a gray area between activities that are part of someone's daily responsibilities and activities that constitute a project. As a consequence, many organizations have wrestled with the question "How do we know when we have a project?" Exhibit 1.1 provides a set of criteria and a checklist that should help provide an answer.

If two or more boxes are checked, particularly those that involve coordination or risk, then the activities are a project. It may not be large, nor might it occupy much of the time of an experienced project manager, but if it is not properly managed, the company is at some degree of risk.

Exhibit 1.1. Project Definition Criteria

The activities will involve more than two people.	❏
The activities will require more than two weeks of effort.	❏
The activities will require more than one month elapsed time.	❏
The activities involve substantial risk.	❏
If the activities fail, there will be a significant impact.	❏
The activities will require coordination of two or more departments.	❏
The activities will involve outside partners.	❏
The activities will involve new technology.	❏
The activities fall outside the scope of normal operations.	❏

One of the barriers to defining simple sets of activities as a project is the overhead that a project imposes. The temptation is to say, "Let's skip the bureaucracy and let the people get on with the work." This appeal to action is attractive, and it is true that in most cases, small sets of activities get done more or less unobtrusively. However, consider the risks and the costs in these examples:

- A hardware upgrade was scheduled for installation before month-end processing. The upgrade was needed in order to complete month-end reports on time, but installation of the new hardware required shutting down the system, and nobody had cleared this with the users. The user manager refused to permit the shutdown without two weeks' notice for rescheduling staff time. The result was that the month-end reports were delayed because of insufficient capacity and the company lost business.

- A new version of the operating system was being installed. Since the application had been successfully tested, the new version was installed at night, ready for the next day, but this version required changes in network system tables, and nobody had notified network support. By the time the problem was fixed, production had experienced four hours of downtime.

The purpose of project management is to reduce risk and ensure timely delivery. As these examples illustrate, problems are not restricted to projects with a six-figure price tag. Anything that could go wrong deserves to be managed.

❋ ❋ ❋ ❋ ❋
THE ROLE OF A PROJECT
MANAGEMENT OFFICE

Until recently, most organizations treated project management as if managing projects were a matter of individual preference. They would send their project managers on a course or, more ambitiously, to a certification program, but, upon returning, the project managers would be left on their own to manage projects as they chose, using as much or as little formality as their inclinations dictated. Organizations have come to appreciate that there are two main problems with this approach:

1. Project management is a discipline. Those who do not exercise the principles of that discipline will see their projects struggle and often collapse. Therefore, the effectiveness of project management is as spotty as the variations in formality.

2. When project managers leave the organization or are transferred to another project, it is extremely difficult for their replacements to step in and take over because all of the project documentation conforms to the departing project manager's personal preferences, instead of to an organizational standard.

Some organizations, in an attempt to create standards, purchase methodologies that are supposed to provide structure and consistency to projects. Again, however, good intentions fall prey to three problems:

1. Most of these methodologies are focused on project activities themselves, such as development, instead of on how the projects are to be managed. As such, their usefulness in establishing project management standards is minimal.

2. The methodologies deal primarily with applications development projects, ignoring projects in other IT areas such infrastructure or strategic planning.

3. Any methodology is only as good as the degree of its use. When managers do not enforce the use of a methodology, project managers adopt it inconsistently, if at all.

So how is an organization to create and enforce standards? The answer that is gaining wide acceptance is the project management office, or PMO, a corporate department responsible for the practice and discipline of project management within the organization or at least within that part of the organization that falls under its control.

PMOs vary across organizations. Some are little more than support groups that provide assistance and guidelines but that have no authority, while others are full-blown departments with management control over project managers and responsibility for project success. A PMO may report to an IT or to an engineering department or, in organizations in which project management is regarded as strategic, all the way up to the executive level and even to the CEO.

The functions of a PMO may vary, but they generally fall into three categories:

1. Development functions are those that build a cadre of effective project managers. They include activities such as recruiting staff, defining project management career and training paths, providing support and assistance to project managers, and evaluating project managers at the end of a project.

2. Support functions are those that help project managers become more effective in managing their projects. They include such activities as time gathering and reporting, defining standards for project documents, establishing priorities among projects, establishing procedures for such issues as scope control or review and approval, creating standards for initiating and closing projects, implementing project management methodologies and software, and providing a mediation forum for resolving disputes.

3. Control functions are those that deliver line management to project managers. They include overseeing employee promotion, providing discipline and direction, defining mandatory standards such as the frequency of status reports or team meetings, and reviewing projects in progress.

Organizations that have implemented effective PMOs have found that their consistency of project success improves and that their ability to provide their project managers with incremental career growth and training allows them to build a group of experienced, qualified people who are committed and able to provide value to their organizations by ensuring that their projects succeed.

There are resources to help organizations that wish to set up their own PMO. One is *The Project Management Office Toolkit* (AMACOM, 2002, ISBN 0-8144-0663-7), by Jolyon Hallows.

* * * * *

SOME COMMENTS ON PROJECT LIFE CYCLES

Most textbooks on project management deal extensively with the author's preferred systems development life cycle (SDLC) or development approach. They spend chapters describing the phases of the SDLC, the interrelationships among phases, and the project management needed to produce the SDLC deliverables. They therefore introduce three problems: They intertwine project management with the development life cycle, they implicitly reject other approaches to projects, and they ignore projects that do not produce code.

The development life cycle deals with how the work is done; project management deals with doing it. The life cycle is analogous to a construction blueprint that shows, for example, where water pipes are to run. Project management ensures that the work crews place the pipes properly so that when the toilet is flushed, the right things happen.

Project management does not depend on any particular SDLC or development approach. As a project manager, it is certainly your job to ensure that you know how you are going to reach the end goal of the project, and a workable SDLC can help, but good project managers can handle any proven approach.

Furthermore, to associate project management with a particular SDLC is to ignore (or reject) evolving ways to develop systems. The conventional "waterfall" approach is being supplanted by concepts such as rapid applications development, evolutionary prototyping, iterative design refinement, and the "spiral" approach. Even conventional SDLCs are being used more flexibly.

Finally, SDLCs are aimed primarily at systems development projects— those that produce code. To focus on them is to ignore other types of projects, such as defining application requirements, implementing major packages, upgrading hardware, designing a technology architecture, or developing a systems strategic plan. These are projects as well, and they also need to be managed.

This book does not advocate any particular SDLC, nor does it require that projects be conducted with any specific approach. Project management is a discipline that applies to any project, regardless of its SDLC, irrespective of its technical approach. See the section "Systems Development Life Cycles" in chapter 3 for a discussion of how the discipline of project management applies to various approaches such as rapid applications development or "extreme programming."

* * * * *
MANAGING AND PARTICIPATING

In many organizations, the "project manager" is also a team participant, expected to produce project deliverables as well as manage the project. As if that burden were not enough, the project manager is also expected to participate in, and often manage, several projects at once. (In this discussion, I differentiate between being a technical team member responsible for project deliverables such as design documents or code and being a project manager responsible for managing the project. I do not mean to imply that project managers are not team members or participants in the broader sense.)

The problem with asking a technical person to manage a project as well as to participate as a team member is that people tend to do what interests them, and what interests technical people is technology. Given a choice between collecting and analyzing time sheets or solving some fascinating technical problem, which is the person more likely to do? When the project hits snags and the team is starting to put in extra time to keep up with the schedule, how can a line manager criticize an employee for not preparing a status report when that person is putting in sixty hours a week on technical development?

Being a Project Manager and a Team Participant

If you are asked to manage a project as well to produce project deliverables, you will need some guidelines to ensure that you have the time to devote to your new responsibility.

First, understand the time demands of project management. Typically, a project manager will need about 15 percent of the total project technical effort. This will vary depending upon the complexity of the project and the experience of the project manager, but, overall, if the project technical effort is 1,000 hours, the project management effort will be 150. Therefore, you need to know the total project effort so that, when you assign work to yourself, you leave enough time to carry out your project management tasks.

Second, although project management effort is 15 percent of technical effort, that work is not evenly distributed throughout the project. It is higher at the start of the project, when you're doing the planning, and at the end, when you're closing the project out. Therefore, plan to devote all of your time to project management during the planning and closeout stages. Do not assign yourself any technical work.

In the middle of the project, the time you'll need to monitor the ongoing activities will be lower, about 10 percent of the total project effort. So, for example, if the project has three people producing project deliverables, including you, that's a total of 120 hours a week. You will need to devote 10 percent of that time—twelve hours or a day and a half a week—to managing the project. If the project team size reaches ten full-time people, they will work a total of 400 hours each week, and you will need to set aside 40 hours to manage them. That's full time with no availability for working on project deliverables. You may object that this means that a project team can never exceed ten people. In practice, however, larger projects are broken into smaller project teams, each with a team leader or project leader. The point is that any project with this many people on the team requires a full-time project manager.

Managing Multiple Projects

Experienced project managers can manage several smaller projects concurrently without affecting the quality of their work. The principles that apply to managing individual projects apply to managing multiple ones. These projects still need proper initiation, planning, management, and closeout. The only additional problem you'll face in managing more than one project is determining which one on which to spend your time. In other words, you will need to be able to set priorities among your projects and to work that prioritized list.

Nevertheless, the advice given earlier for managing and participating applies to managing multiple projects. In particular, if the sum of the technical efforts of the projects you are being asked to manage exceeds about 400 hours a week, you have reached the limit of your availability, and you have the responsibility to decline if you are asked to take on another project.

However, there are some other considerations in managing multiple projects. First, remember that you will be extra-busy during project planning and project closeout. Therefore, you need to ensure that these stages will occur at different times in the various projects you are managing. That is, if the planning stage of one project coincides with the execution stage of the others, then you should have no difficulty in managing them, but be cautious if you are required to plan more than one project at the same time. Try to get one of them deferred.

All of this discussion assumes that, in managing multiple projects, you are not also required to produce project deliverables for any of them. If that's not the case, you will need to ensure that your daily project management tasks—10 percent of the sum of the total effort on all projects during execution and full time during planning and closeout—leave you enough time to act as a technical participant as well. Because this is unlikely, it's dangerous to commit to managing concurrent projects and also to producing project deliverables.

* * * * *

SOME NOTES ON TERMINOLOGY

In this book, I use the following terms.

The *client* is the company or department that specifies what the project is to accomplish, pays the bill, and accepts delivery of the system. The client may be an external customer, such as that of a consulting company, or an internal department.

The client is represented by client staff. Among them are client managers or decision makers and users. When this book refers to a client as a person, it is referring to the former.

The *project manager* is the person responsible for the schedule, budget, functionality, and implementation of a project or subproject. Many organizations differentiate between project managers and project leaders, but the difference is one of nomenclature and sometimes project size. It is not one of responsibilities.

A *project* is a set of activities that has a clearly defined start and end and that produces a tangible product. A project can produce a new application system or a major enhancement. It may also provide an implemented software package, upgraded hardware, reports and analyses such as application requirements, a technology architecture, a strategic technology plan, or a reengineering plan. By contrast, ongoing activities such as regular maintenance, help, or consulting do not constitute a project.

Users are the people who will actually use the results of a project. For most projects, users form part of the client team, responsible for specifying the project requirements.

*   *   *   *   *

ABOUT THIS BOOK

Any project has four distinct stages: understanding the project, defining it, planning it, and running it. In all of these stages, you must exercise both general management skills and specialized project management skills within the project management context described earlier. A picture of project management would look similar to what you see in Exhibit 1.2.

This book consists of the following five sections.

1. "Introduction" sets the framework and the context for the book.

2. "Understanding the Project" describes what you need to understand about a project that you are about to manage and what role you can take in shaping a project from the start.

3. "Defining the Project" lists the things that you need to define, including deliverables, scope, and how you will manage the project.

4. "Planning the Project" deals with the techniques of project management planning, including how to break down a project into activities; how to prepare an estimate, a budget, and a schedule; how to plan resources; and how to identify the risks.

Exhibit 1.2. Project Management Overview

Specialized Project Management Skills

General Management Skills

Project Management Context

Understanding the project

Planning the project

Defining the project

Running the project

5. "Running the Project" presents the day-to-day activities needed to keep the project on track, including how to build effective teams, how to track progress and manage schedule slippages, and how to handle scope change requests. It also deals with how to manage sub-contractors and client teams.

Many sections of the book include a set of "What If" questions about issues that can arise from the topic of the section. Each What If question represents a problem or risk that, if it actually arises, must be addressed. For each question, there is a brief description of the consequences of not resolving the issue and a set of actions that can help.

In the ideal project, you would move sequentially through the stages of understanding, defining, planning, and running the project. In reality, these stages overlap; until the project is over, you are never finished with any of them. Nevertheless, a project roadmap can be drawn (see Exhibit 1.3). In it, the heavy arrows mark the normal flow of your work, and the smaller ones indicate that the process is iterative. Throughout the entire project, you will always be returning to previous stages as project conditions change.

The roadmap also acts as a checklist. If you can answer yes to all of the questions it presents, you have your project well under control. Any no's are flags indicating where some pitfalls may lie and where you may want to dig deeper.

This book follows the roadmap. It offers a methodology and serves as a reference guide for managing systems projects. It is a tool kit whose pieces are to be used as the situation requires.

The book is not intended to be a theoretical academic text on project management; there is no final examination. It is a practical discussion of topics and issues that you will encounter every day in your real job of managing a successful project. Each topic is restricted to a few pages so that you can treat the book as a reference guide, rather than a textbook. However, the wise reader will at least skim the subjects to understand the context of what is being recommended.

To further help you apply the concepts that are presented, chapters 2, 3, and 4 on understanding the project, defining the project, and planning the project include detailed checklists.

Finally, I hope that you find the book useful, usable, and readable. I invite your comments, and I wish you every success in one of the most demanding roles in systems projects.

Exhibit 1.3. Project Management Roadmap

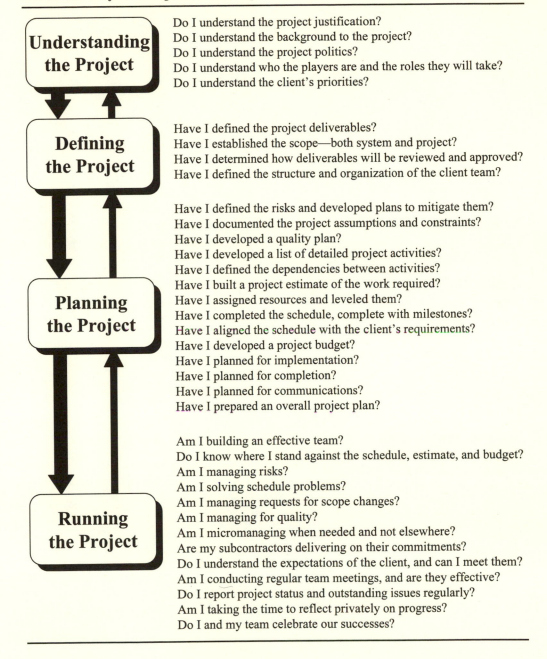

Understanding the Project
Do I understand the project justification?
Do I understand the background to the project?
Do I understand the project politics?
Do I understand who the players are and the roles they will take?
Do I understand the client's priorities?

Defining the Project
Have I defined the project deliverables?
Have I established the scope—both system and project?
Have I determined how deliverables will be reviewed and approved?
Have I defined the structure and organization of the client team?

Planning the Project
Have I defined the risks and developed plans to mitigate them?
Have I documented the project assumptions and constraints?
Have I developed a quality plan?
Have I developed a list of detailed project activities?
Have I defined the dependencies between activities?
Have I built a project estimate of the work required?
Have I assigned resources and leveled them?
Have I completed the schedule, complete with milestones?
Have I aligned the schedule with the client's requirements?
Have I developed a project budget?
Have I planned for implementation?
Have I planned for completion?
Have I planned for communications?
Have I prepared an overall project plan?

Running the Project
Am I building an effective team?
Do I know where I stand against the schedule, estimate, and budget?
Am I managing risks?
Am I solving schedule problems?
Am I managing requests for scope changes?
Am I managing for quality?
Am I micromanaging when needed and not elsewhere?
Are my subcontractors delivering on their commitments?
Do I understand the expectations of the client, and can I meet them?
Am I conducting regular team meetings, and are they effective?
Do I report project status and outstanding issues regularly?
Am I taking the time to reflect privately on progress?
Do I and my team celebrate our successes?

2

Understanding the Project

Do I understand the project justification?
Do I understand the background to the project?
Do I understand the project politics?
Do I understand who the players are and the roles they will take?
Do I understand the client's priorities?

Have I defined the project deliverables?
Have I established the scope—both system and project?
Have I determined how deliverables will be reviewed and approved?
Have I defined the structure and organization of the client team?

Have I defined the risks and developed plans to mitigate them?
Have I documented the project assumptions and constraints?
Have I developed a quality plan?
Have I developed a list of detailed project activities?
Have I defined the dependencies between activities?
Have I built a project estimate of the work required?
Have I assigned resources and leveled them?
Have I completed the schedule, complete with milestones?
Have I aligned the schedule with the client's requirements?
Have I developed a project budget?
Have I planned for implementation?
Have I planned for completion?
Have I planned for communications?
Have I prepared an overall project plan?

Am I building an effective team?
Do I know where I stand against the schedule, estimate, and budget?
Am I managing risks?
Am I solving schedule problems?
Am I managing requests for scope changes?
Am I managing for quality?
Am I micromanaging when needed and not elsewhere?
Are my subcontractors delivering on their commitments?
Do I understand the expectations of the client, and can I meet them?
Am I conducting regular team meetings, and are they effective?
Do I report project status and outstanding issues regularly?
Am I taking the time to reflect privately on progress?
Do I and my team celebrate our successes?

Understanding the Project

Managing projects requires that you make decisions, which, in turn, requires that you understand the project environment, background, and people. In other words, you need to understand the cultural and political context of the project. If you have been appointed project manager because of your technical seniority, one of the temptations you will have to overcome is to focus on technical issues rather than on those you consider "political" and therefore the responsibility of others. Hard though it may be to admit, the people side of projects is more important than the technical side.

To manage a project, you need to understand four things:

1. **Why is this project being done?** What does the client expect to get from it?

2. **What is the background to this project?** How did we get to where we are?

3. **Who are the players?** Who has fought for this project? Who has fought against it? Who is the executive sponsor?

4. **What are the client's priorities for this project?**

These questions overlap; they all reflect different ways of acquiring an understanding of the project, but they are not exhaustive. Projects involve a dynamic mix of people with different interests, philosophies, values, approaches, and priorities. One of your main functions as a project manager is to ensure that this mix becomes coherent and drives the project forward. The alternative is chaos.

On Fiduciary Responsibility

Project management is not gentle, nor does it depend upon uncritically pleasing the client. At times, the good of the project requires that you challenge client decisions or actions and oppose those that put the project at risk. As the project manager, you are the representative of the project: If it could speak, what would it say? This role is common in business—executives and board members can be held legally accountable for exercising their "fiduciary responsibility" to act on behalf of their company. As project manager, you must also accept that you have a fiduciary responsibility to act on behalf of the project.

* * * * *

WHY ARE WE DOING THIS?

There is only one valid reason to spend money on a project: It will generate or save more money than it costs. Unfortunately, there is confusion between a project's *objective* and its *justification*. The objective of a project (see the section "Defining the Project Objective" in chapter 3) is a general statement about why the project is being carried out. Such a statement might be:

The purpose of this project is to create a state-of-the-art, on-line, real-time inventory system that will allow us to manage our inventory more closely while continuing to meet the demands of our customers.

This objective statement, despite the high-tech buzzwords, is clear: We are going to build a system that will manage inventory. What it does not tell us is whether the project is justified—that is, whether it will save or earn more than it will cost.

A justification is an analysis of the costs versus the benefits showing that the benefits are greater. (If the analysis shows that the costs are greater, then it is a justification for scrapping the project, not for proceeding.) A justification describes exactly where the improved savings or revenues will arise.

Many justifications are filled with such vague notions as flexibility, customer service, integration, state-of-the-art, and other motherhood values that remain both unchallenged and undefined. But a true justification has two necessary characteristics: It is dollar quantified, and it is treated as a target or goal.

Justifications Are Dollar Quantified

A justification describes the returns that will accrue from doing a project—the benefit side of a cost-benefit analysis. It must be quantified; if it is not, nobody will know in the beginning if the project is worthwhile or in the end if it was successful.

Consider the justification "to increase customer service." This could mean reducing response time to customer inquiries, improving the accuracy or quantity of information available, adding to the services that are offered, or simply smiling at customers. Without more detail, nobody will understand what is expected.

Furthermore, if the justification is not quantified, then any improvement, however slight, in any area that affects customers will allow the company to claim that service has been increased. For example, if the system reduces an average two-minute customer waiting time by five seconds, service has been improved, but few companies would expend effort to achieve such a trivial result, and, more important, no customers will notice.

Justifications are quantified only when they are expressed in terms of dollars (or some other currency). They might involve payroll savings, increased sales, or reduced costs in areas such as inventory or finance charges. However they are expressed, justifications must be quantified so that they can be assessed and projects can be approved based on real—financial—benefits.

Some observers have noted that there is one other justification: to fulfill a legal requirement or mandate. For example, if the legislature imposes a new type of tax that will require modifications to systems in order to implement, companies that are affected have no choice. Similarly, a government department may be required to conduct a project in order to meet a legislative mandate. Nevertheless, the ultimate justification, even in projects of this type, is financial. For a private company, the benefit is that it gets to stay in business, which, one assumes, is more financially beneficial than the alternative. For a government department, while there is no option on conducting the project, the financial factor is determining how to do so in the most cost-effective manner.

Justifications Are Goals, Not Predictions

Assume that a project is justified by an expected sales increase of 15 percent. When the project is being evaluated, nobody can state with certainty what the increase will be; it can simply be said that one is expected. A 15 percent increase is an estimate, subject to the vagaries of all estimates. Whether this figure is realized depends on whether it is treated as a goal or as a prediction.

A prediction is a guess about what will happen; a goal is a target to be achieved. The difference is startling. With a prediction, the outcome of the project is left to the fates, who, the client hopes, will be kind. With a goal, the justification becomes a matter of policy, planned within the overall project. It becomes part of the system implementation plan, enters your purview, and becomes a discrete set of activities rather than an idle hope. Your job is to ensure that justifications become goals that management accepts the responsibility for achieving.

Intangible Benefits

Justifications for projects usually include a long, predictable list of "intangible benefits." The problem is that there is no such thing; all benefits are realized in terms of costs or revenue. To call a benefit "intangible" simply means that nobody has been able—or has bothered—to attach hard numbers to it. For example, consider flexibility. (This word, like most words used to label intangible benefits, lacks a consistent definition. Here, I use it to describe a system that can be easily modified.) With a flexible system, enhancements take less effort, producing the tangible benefits of lower maintenance costs and faster delivery of enhancement requests. Furthermore, client departments will realize the tangible benefits that arise from enhancements sooner. Flexibility is a benefit because it leads to real results. The problem is how to measure what those results will be.

Some will argue that, even though certain benefits cannot be quantified, they should still be identified. Indeed they should, but only if they are used to set targets. For example:

- The system will be flexible. We intend to reduce maintenance costs by 15 percent, which will save us $24,000 per year.

- The system will be developed with state-of-the-art tools. We plan to increase development productivity by two function points per work-month, which will save us an average of $100,000 per year in development costs at current levels.

- The system will be integrated. We plan to lever the greater access to customer information into a 5 percent increase in sales, which will boost our revenues by $200,000 per year.

The point of setting targets is to ensure that a real—that is, tangible dollar—benefit emerges from the flexible, state-of-the-art, or integrated nature of the system.

The best way to quantify an intangible benefit is to ask three questions: "So what?"; "How much?"; and "What does that work out to in dollars?" (Your actual phraseology may not be as blunt, but the intent is the same.) Keep asking these questions until you get an answer with a dollar value in it. Ultimately, the slipperiest project advocate will be forced into giving numbers, however imprecise, or admitting that none can be stated, in which case the "benefit" has evaporated.

Here's a brief example:

Client: The system will be flexible.

Project Manager: So what?

Client: So we'll be able to modify it more easily.

PM: So what?

Client: Well, that means that our maintenance time will be cut.

PM: How much?

Client: That's hard to quantify.

PM: Make a guess. (How much?)

Client: Well, perhaps by 15 percent.

PM: And what does that work out to in dollars?

Client: Well, we have three maintenance programmers at $60,000 per year. That's $180,000 per year total, so we could probably save about $27,000 each year.

You have just shifted the benefit from an intangible wish to a real target.

If a benefit is not capable of being quantified—as opposed to having highly uncertain results—then it is not a benefit, it carries no implicit target, and it does not belong in any list of justifications.

Beware the Phantom Justification

Consider a project that is justified by a reduced time to process business transactions. The numbers indicate that each of five people will have his or her workloads reduced by an average of an hour a day, which, at a salary (plus benefits) rate of $30 an hour, will save the company $150 per day, or $37,500 per year. Here are just three things that could go wrong with this justification:

1. A reduction of five hours a day is less than one full-time person, which makes it difficult to reduce staff. It is true that because of the resulting slack time, the company will be able to assign extra work to the people, but the benefit comes from a redistribution of work, not from staff cuts.

2. The people are currently overloaded and have to cut corners. The reduced workload means that they can do a more thorough job, which may lead to improved quality but not to staff cost savings.

3. The people may have specialized skills, which means that they are not interchangeable. Nobody can be cut, and there is no real benefit.

The problem with the apparent cost saving is that it is an *effect,* not a *benefit.* Certainly, the five people will each have an extra hour, but that hour does not automatically translate into returns for the company.

An effect differs from a benefit in that it does not *directly* lead to reduced costs or increased revenue. Reducing the staff time required to perform some task saves nothing unless the payroll is actually reduced. Making customer information more accessible to the sales staff achieves nothing unless the information leads to increased sales. Improving quality is pointless unless sales are increased or service costs are reduced. Effects may lead to benefits, but only benefits constitute justification for the costs of a project.

The best way to smoke out effects is to ask questions until you are satisfied that the "benefit" is real. Here's a simple example:

Client: The staff workload will be cut by five hours per day.

Project Manager: How does that help?

Client: We'll be able to cut our costs.

PM: How?

Client: Uh, good question. We don't have enough of a savings to cut staff.

PM: What else could these people do with their extra time?

Client: Well, right now they complain of being rushed. More time would enable them to do a better job, which could cut rework. If we could reduce that by just 10 percent, it would save us, let's see, more than $200,000 per year.

PM: Would the improved quality get you more customers?

Client: Perhaps, but I know that it would improve goodwill among existing customers. There's an intangible benefit!

PM: So what?

By the time this dialogue is over, not only will you have helped the client identify where the real benefits of the system are to be sought; you will also have increased the benefits far beyond what could be realized from simply laying off staff.

In reviewing project justifications, ensure that the effects of the system lead to real benefits that are capable of being realized.

Payback Period

Some companies insist on knowing the payback period before they will approve an expenditure. This is the period in which the benefits will fully recover the project costs. Payback periods are easy to compute: Divide the project costs, including operations costs, by the annual benefits. Adjust for months, and you will have the number of months required to recover the project costs.

The payback period is a powerful indicator of how desirable a project is. If the costs can be recovered in under a year, few companies will decline to proceed. If it will take four or five years, few will approve the project. Most companies that ask for a payback period in a project proposal have guidelines indicating what periods are acceptable and what are not.

When you are computing a payback period, do not concern yourself with calculating future costs of money unless your company requires it. For most projects, the payback period is short enough that inflation is not a significant factor.

Cost Components

When you review your project's cost-benefit analysis, examine the costs to ensure that they are complete. Many projects have run into trouble because a major item, such as software licenses or consulting fees, was not included in the costs. The costs should also identify operating expenses during the payback period.

Exhibit 2.1 is a checklist that identifies costs that your project may include and that should be part of the cost-benefit analysis.

What If?

The Client Will Not Identify Benefits

If the client will not identify benefits, you will find it difficult to make project decisions that enhance the project justification and you will find it harder to keep the project in scope.

Actions

Create a "working benefits statement," a set of benefits that arise from your understanding of the project and that seem reasonable to you. This will be your private benefits statement; it will not have the force of a real statement, but it will allow you to act day-to-day as if benefits were clearly defined.

(continues)

Exhibit 2.1. Potential Cost Components

Systems Development Labor Costs

Labor costs to define system requirements ❑

Labor costs to design the system ❑

Labor costs to design the system infrastructure such as network costs ❑

Labor costs to code, unit test, integrate, and systems test the system ❑

Labor costs for documentation including training materials ❑

Labor costs for project management including such functions as configuration management, quality control, and support ❑

Hardware Costs

Labor costs to scope, configure, and order hardware ❑

Capital costs to purchase hardware ❑

Labor costs to install hardware ❑

Labor costs to maintain hardware ❑

Software Costs

Labor costs to scope, configure, and order software ❑

Purchase costs for operating systems software ❑

Purchase costs for infrastructure software such as communications, performance enhancement, or performance statistics ❑

Purchase costs for applications support software such as database management, graphical user interface, or ad hoc inquiry and reporting ❑

Labor costs to install and configure software ❑

Project Execution Costs

Project costs for travel and living ❑

Project costs for external consulting ❑

Project costs for training ❑

Project costs for supplies and materials ❑

Project Client Costs

Operating costs for staff attendance at training programs ❑

Operating costs for user participation on the client project team ❑

Operating costs for client involvement in the project ❑

(continues)

Exhibit 2.1. (Continued.)

Implementation Costs

 Operating costs for additional staff effort during implementation   ❑

 Operating costs for travel and living during implementation   ❑

System Operations Costs

 Operating costs for staff labor during the payback period   ❑

 Materials and supplies costs during the payback period   ❑

 Hardware and software maintenance contracts during the payback period   ❑

 Hardware leasing costs during the payback period   ❑

 Projected costs for hardware and software upgrades during the payback period   ❑

Define the scope of the project at a much greater level of detail than normal, and ensure that a solid scope change mechanism is in place. This should help overcome the difficulty of managing project scope without a clear statement of benefits.

The Client Refuses to Set Benefit Goals or Targets

If the client defines benefits but will not set targets, you will find it hard to implement the project in such a way that benefits can be realized.

Actions

Calculate the level of benefits that would be needed to justify the project. For example, if the client wants to reduce inventory levels, determine the level of reductions needed to recover the cost of the project.

If the level of benefits is reasonable, propose it to the client as a working set of benefits, to be reviewed and revised when the project is implemented. If it is not reasonable—for example, if the client will need to cut inventory levels by 85 percent—point this out. If the client still wants to proceed, recognize that you will be managing an unjustified project.

If your calculation of benefits levels is reasonable, consider deferring setting the benefit goals until you are planning for implementation on the expectation that as the client becomes more familiar with the project, goal setting will become easier.

The Project Is Being Done to Use Up Available Budget or to Make Work

In this case, the project is justified solely by its ability to spend somebody's budget; it has no inherent justification. However, this does not mean that it cannot deliver value to the organization.

Actions

In such projects, there is always an apparent justification. Few companies overtly execute projects without some excuse. Act as described earlier for the situation in which the purpose of the project is real but the client will not identify the benefits.

The Client Takes the Position That Justification Is a Business Issue Outside Your Mandate

The most obvious consequence is that you will not have a justification to work with on the project. However, there is a more serious issue: your role. In order to manage the project, you will need to be actively concerned with its business aspects, not just from the point of view of functionality but in terms of its context within the client organization. If you are to be blocked from anything beyond the narrow scope of the project, your ability to deliver real value will be seriously compromised.

Actions

Attempt to educate the client on your role. In particular, point out that your job is to deliver value to the organization and that that job is more than meeting a schedule. If possible, think of examples, such as the project in which you recommended a major shift in direction because of your understanding of the project context and created a more valuable product as a result.

Inform your client why you need to understand the justification. Describe its role in managing scope and in helping to reach day-to-day decisions.

If these attempts fail, escalate this as an issue to your management. Make it clear that this client's attitudes are hindering your ability to succeed.

* * * *

WHY BE CONCERNED WITH PROJECT JUSTIFICATION?

Some project managers argue that justifying projects is not their concern—that once a project has been approved, their job is simply to deliver results. However, delivering results means ensuring that the client enjoys the benefits used to justify the project. It also means being able to defend the project against cutbacks and to reevaluate the numbers when the scope or costs change.

Ensuring That Benefits Are Realized

Project planning includes the creation of implementation plans, which normally consist of training, parallel testing, handover, and phasing out of existing systems. However, to really deliver results, the implementation plan must also describe, in detail, how the client will realize the benefits described in the project justification. For example, if the project was justified by the ability to reduce inventory by 15 percent, how quickly will inventory be reduced? Which items will be cut back first? By how much? How will suppliers be involved? What is the role of the system in making decisions on reducing inventory? What steps are needed to ensure that customer service will not be jeopardized? The implementation plan must answer these and similar questions for all targets that were set when the project was justified. If you do not understand the justification for the project, you will not be able to plan how the client will realize the benefits.

Defending Against Cutbacks

Business conditions, including executives, change. Frequently, new executives, or those converted to the gospel of cost reduction, challenge a project in progress. If the original justification was well prepared, is reasonable, and, most important, actually justifies the project, it will be easy to defend. The project manager who protests that justification is someone else's responsibility will end up without any weapons to defend against cost cutting, and the project is unlikely to survive the exercise.

Reevaluating the Project

The costs, benefits, and scope of a project change: The costs usually go up, the benefits usually go down, and the scope usually grows. At some point, the costs may grow to exceed the benefits. One of your responsibilities is to identify this point and to inform the client that conditions no longer justify proceeding. Without a good justification, that task is impossible, and the project will devour resources, effort, and careers long after it should have been terminated.

Evaluating Scope Change Requests

When a project's justification is well defined, it can be applied to requests for changes of scope. For example:

During a sales analysis development project, users request a change to the screens that will cost $10,000. Should the change be made?

If the project was justified by increased revenue from better sales analysis, the question becomes "How, and by how much, will this screen change contribute to increased sales revenues?" If the answer is "More than $10,000," the scope change is justified. Otherwise, forget it. But if the justification was to produce a "state-of-the-art sales analysis system," who can say whether the changes to the screens will improve "state-of-the-art-ness"?

Establishing Client Attitudes

One reason that people are reluctant to set targets is the pain that comes with not achieving them. The more uncertain the target, the greater the potential for suffering. As a project manager, how can you protect yourself against the repercussions of not realizing a benefit?

It is critical to understand that your responsibility is not to deliver benefits but only to ensure that they have been defined and that the work you have produced can be used to achieve them. For example, if a project was justified by a targeted 15 percent decrease in inventory levels, it is your job to produce a system that others can use to cut stock. It is also your job, as part of implementation planning, to work with the responsible managers—in this case, the inventory manager—to plan how the benefits will be realized. However, it is not your job to actually make stocking decisions or to pull products from the shelves. That is the function of the inventory manager.

When you discuss benefits with your clients, you must make it clear that, while you will help them plan, realizing these benefits is up to them and that, unless they are willing to make you the manager of inventory (or human resources or marketing or operations or whatever area your project addresses), you cannot be held responsible for the results. Your role is two-fold: to ensure that a benefit exists and to produce a product that can be used to realize that benefit.

What If?

The Client Does Not Want to Expend Resources Preparing a Plan for Realizing Benefits

If the client does not plan how to realize benefits, they will not be realized and the project will be wasted.

Actions

Find out what the client's concerns are. Typically, they will be either financial ("I don't want to spend any money I don't have to"), organizational ("That's not your purview"), or schedule based ("We don't have time to fool around with side issues").

If the client's concerns are organizational, agree. Then ask who will be preparing the plan. You will now manage that person's deliverable.

If the client's concerns are financial or schedule based, prepare a set of arguments to establish that planning for benefits is not an irrelevancy but is central to the project. Review the list of people involved with the project and find one who is in a senior position and who has expressed a strong interest in the benefits. Approach that person with your arguments.

Consult with the steering committee and the executive sponsor (see the section "Who Are the Players?"), and present your arguments to them.

If none of these actions are effective, indicate to the client, preferably in writing, that the project cannot be depended on to provide the benefits used to justify it. If you are comfortable with taking a really strong position, recommend that the project be terminated, since it will not provide the required value.

The Project Evolves to the Point Where Benefits No Longer Outweigh Costs

If the project justification no longer applies because the costs have escalated or the benefits have evaporated, continuing with the project would be a further waste of the client's time and money, as well as diverting valuable staff resources into a losing effort.

Actions

Review the cost-benefit analysis to try to find some additional benefits or to increase the planned ones. This may sound like fudging the numbers, but new benefits usually arise during a project. However, you must be neutral in this exercise, or you will end up with insupportable numbers, which you will then be required to deliver.

If the revised numbers are favorable to the project, report them to the client and continue. If they are not, the project is no longer justified, and you must try to convince the client to end the project.

Revise the cost-benefit analysis to reflect the current position. Indicate the loss to the company if the project folds at this point and the potential loss if it is carried on to completion. Include any salvage value from the work to date that will reduce the current loss.

Determine where the project team would be assigned if the project were to fold, and try to place a value on this work. Here, you are trying to point out the positive side of ending the project.

Do not allow the client to take the position that the project has failed. Changing conditions have rendered it wise to back out before it eats up resources and careers and becomes a failure.

* * * * *

WHAT IS THE BACKGROUND TO THIS PROJECT?

Project managers are rarely involved at the very start of a project. By the time you appear on the scene, the project has usually acquired its own history and momentum. To understand it, you need to ask the following six questions:

1. What were the business conditions that prompted someone to propose the project in the first place?
2. How was the project presented to management, and how was it evaluated and approved?
3. What were the alternatives to the project that the client considered?
4. What were (and are) the arguments against the project?
5. What is the visibility of the project in the client company or department? How important is it seen to be?

6. What are the attitudes toward the project? Specifically:

- Is it welcomed as desirable, accepted as necessary, or condemned as wrongheaded?
- Is it regarded as easy, difficult, or impossible?
- Is it viewed with enthusiasm, resignation, or trepidation?

With the answers to these questions, you are equipped to become an advocate: to sell the project to the users and to create a positive expectation for it. You can now build an atmosphere that will make it easier to gain cooperation, to resolve issues, and to help the client achieve the expected benefits. Until these questions are answered, you are a passenger, unable to influence, much less dictate, the direction of the project.

Bad Attitudes

One of the consequences of asking about the background of the project is that you could find out things you would rather not know. For example, you may discover that few people support the project, that few think it will (or should) succeed, and that, for many, its failure would be widely regarded as a sign that all is right with the world. You have a problem.

First, you need to determine whether this attitude is deserved. Is this project truly a bad idea, or are you witnessing a power struggle between factions? From a neutral point of view—which may be difficult to maintain but is part of your job—in order for the project to be a bad idea, it must be either unjustified or infeasible. Nothing else qualifies, and any other opposition arises from internal strife.

If, upon examination, you conclude that the project is unjustified or unfeasible, then, as project manager, it is your responsibility to point out to the client that the detractors are correct and that the project should not or cannot be done. If the client insists on proceeding, then you are faced with managing either an unjustified project (see the preceding section, "Why Be Concerned with Project Justification?") or one that probably cannot succeed for technical reasons (see the section "Managing Risks" in chapter 5).

If, on the other hand, the project is both justified and feasible, then the opposition to it is organizational. You need to find out why.

People typically oppose a new system because:

- They see it as arising from another department's requirements without reference to theirs.

- They view it as being imposed on them.

- They will have to change long-standing, comfortable work habits.

- They suspect that it is a management stratagem to upset a labor relations balance.

- They suspect that it will not work and that its failure will be blamed on them.

- They recognize that developing and implementing it will require unwelcome extra effort from them.

- They suspect (and this is what frightens them most) that it will result in layoffs.

What can you do to overcome these and similar attitudes?

First, ask whether they are your concern. If the opposition to the project comes from people who are not members of either the project team or the client team, then dealing with these attitudes is an implementation issue that belongs to the client groups that will be rolling out the system. It is not your responsibility. This may seem evasive, but, unless you are the vice president of human resources, it is not your job to manage corporate relations. When you prepare the implementation plan, you must insist that these attitudes be recognized and that plans be developed to deal with them, but they cannot be allowed to intrude on the conduct of the project itself.

On the other hand, dealing with opposition is very much your responsibility if the people who oppose the project are part of it. An extreme case occurs when some of the people you rely on to make the project succeed will lose their jobs when it does. In such cases, resolving their negative attitudes is one of your biggest concerns.

How you deal with this problem is situational, but here are some suggestions:

- Evaluate whether the opposition is reasonable. For example, fears of layoffs are reasonable; anger at another department is not. (Keep in mind the difference between reasonable and justified attitudes. Negativity may be justified by past offenses, but it is not reasonable to withhold services because of them.)

- If you conclude that the opposition is unreasonable, make your opinion and your resolve to conduct a successful project clear to everyone. You may need to have heart-to-heart talks with a few of the team members, and, in extreme cases, you may need to replace those who are particularly vehement (see the section "Building the Team," in chapter 5). Your goal is to create a cohesive team despite the attitudes.

- If the opposition is reasonable, you need to do whatever you can to mitigate the problem that creates it. For example, if people will be laid off when the project is finished, ask the client to develop a transition plan to help them find new jobs. Your motive here is not compassion but recognition that unless the problem is resolved, your project will be plagued with low morale, passive noncooperation, and outright confrontation, and it will probably fail.

Of course, the major point is that unless you take the time to explore the project's background, you will be happily unaware of the poison that infects it—and unable to take any actions to create a successful project and a positive experience for all of its participants.

What If?

You Are Discouraged from "Wasting Time" on the Background

If you do not understand the background, you are vulnerable to project critics and you risk making serious misjudgments that not only endanger the project but compromise your ability to lead it.

Actions

Arrange to go for lunch—separately—with two or three people who have been involved from the start. Asking questions over lunch is not seen to be as obtrusive as an interview.

Pose questions that relate to specific incidents or people. For example, "Fred does not seem enthusiastic about this project," or "Why is the finance department not represented on the steering committee?"

If you encounter a background issue that could seriously hinder the project, raise it with the client in two contexts: as an issue that needs to be resolved and as an example of the problems that can occur when you are discouraged from doing your job.

You Get Conflicting Background Information

If the background information you get is not consistent—for example, Fred tells you that Mary is bitterly opposed to the project but George says that she is one of its strongest advocates—you do not have information, you have rumor. The risk is that you will make inappropriate, perhaps dangerous, decisions.

Actions

Treat the inconsistency as a valuable source of information. In the example just given, you have probably learned more about Fred's and George's attitude toward Mary than you have about her attitude toward the project.

Approach the object of the inconsistency—in this case, Mary—directly for clarification. Do not tell her what Fred or George reported, but ask a more general question, such as, "I understand that you have some concerns about this project."

You Find Out That Your Project Is the Object of a Power Struggle or Interdepartmental Rivalry

If two or more departments have conflicting opinions of your project's purpose, scope, or justification, you will find it extremely hard to manage, and no matter what you do, you will have opponents.

Actions

Identify the client department and managers. This may seem simple, but on many projects, the lines of responsibility are fuzzy.

For example, an operations director may insist that the project is the responsibility of operations, since that is the department that must implement it, while the finance director is claiming ownership because the finance department is paying for it.

Your job is to identify a single client: the manager who owns the project and who will be responsible for all decisions.

If project ownership is not clear, insist that the client organization pick a project owner. This demand will probably trigger internal machinations within the client organization, but as long as you have made your demands clear, you will probably end up with a project owner.

If the client organization does not select a clear project owner or tells you that it is your job to work things out between departments, pick one yourself and make it clear to the client organization that you must have a single client department. Identify which department you picked and why you picked it. If the client organization has named a client project manager or weighted the steering committee heavily toward one department, your choice will be clear.

In subsequent conversations, when members of another department attempt to get you to make certain decisions or take specific actions, simply say that you are willing to take the request to the client department but that you cannot comply without the client's approval.

* * * * *

WHO ARE THE PLAYERS?

"This would be a great project," goes a frequent lament, "if it weren't for the users." Or, "The politics of this project are murder."

Project staff yearn for the golden project where the users are compliant, technical recommendations rule, and "politics" does not exist. Like the Holy Grail or the Fountain of Youth, this is a myth. Given enough time, it may become equally enduring.

Politics vs. Sociology

There is a difference between politics and sociology. "Politics" refers to the sneaky, underhanded, double-dealing, two-faced, sycophantic, boot-licking, backstabbing behavior that the word usually implies. "Sociology" refers to the normal, honest, strongly held differences of opinion that emerge when more than one knowledgeable person is involved. Few projects have politics; all have sociology.

To view a conflict or unpleasantness as political is to ascribe malevolence to the people involved: The perpetrators are endangering the project for personal gain. But to interpret the same situation as sociological is to recognize that different people can reach different conclusions, yet share goals and concerns. Clearly, the second view is more likely to lead to discussion, clarification, negotiation, and resolution. Whenever anyone in a project utters the word *politics,* repeat the statement using *sociology* instead. There is no surer way to prevent hardening of attitudes.

However, politics, in its most vicious form, does exist. The second-best defense against it is to document everything, get signatures for all decisions, keep a daily diary of project events, log all phone calls you make and faxes you send (keep the fax logs), and, as a strategy, act like an attorney facing hostile opposition.

The best defense is to find another project.

Identifying the Players

To lead the participants in a project effectively, you must understand who they are and what their attitudes are toward the project. Specifically:

- Who are the project champions, those who have backed the project from the start and are enthusiastic about completing it? Why are they enthusiastic?

- Who are the project detractors, those who have fought against or opposed the project? Why are they opposed?

- Who are the project agnostics, those who have no strong convictions and can be swayed either way? What sways them?

- Who will appear to win if the project succeeds? Who will really win?
- Who will appear to lose if the project succeeds? Who will really lose?

The Executive Sponsor

The executive sponsor is a member of senior management who is committed to the project and who has enough clout to fill his or her primary role: saying to a panicking management committee or board of directors, "Get your hands off my project." The sponsor is not involved in the details and may even be invisible to the project team, but any project that does not have a sponsor is at risk.

The executive sponsor's second role occurs at the end of the project. When users stall, delay, and frustrate all attempts to implement the new system, the sponsor has the authority to ensure compliance, if not cooperation.

Find out who the executive sponsor is and provide brief, high-level status reports. He or she will appreciate the information and will be in a better position to fight for the project if necessary.

The Steering Committee

The project steering committee, which should consist of senior client management, is not a problem-solving forum or a place for a discussion of detailed issues. Its job is to enforce, from the client's point of view, the project terms of reference. The steering committee will also approve or deny requests for additional resources or changes to the scope or schedule.

A steering committee becomes a nuisance when it insists on dabbling in day-to-day issues. If it debates, for example, whether the identification code should be fifteen or sixteen digits long, it is no longer a steering committee, it is a user group. The problem is that the real user group will hesitate to make decisions because its members fear that they will be overridden by their bosses on the steering committee, and the project will grind to a halt.

To allow the steering committee to focus on its job, take control of the meetings, which should be monthly. Prepare the agenda, guide the discussions, and deflect any attempt to discuss details. (The latter can be done politely by saying, "Clearly, you have some concerns about this issue that I think we need to discuss in detail. When can we get together?" The phrase "discuss in detail" will be enough to send most of the other committee members mentally heading for the exits.)

This does not mean that steering committee members are dummies who have no special knowledge that would help the project. The reverse is undoubtedly true, and those who want to participate at a more detailed level should be allowed to do so, but keep the roles separate. No steering committee member, acting as a steering committee member, should be concerned with details.

The User Group

The user group is the set of people who will be responsible for the day-to-day details and decisions in the project. In the best user groups, one person has the authority to make decisions and the willingness to do so in the face of opposition. In the worst, "democracy" prevails and nobody is prepared to make a decision. Schedule plenty of time for meetings.

Regardless of the type of user group, when you need a decision, make sure to document the issues clearly and with alternatives. Distribute the documentation before the meeting, and ensure that nobody leaves the room until a decision is reached. (One project manager used to schedule such meetings for Fridays at 3:00 P.M. His track record in getting fast consensus was admirable.)

The Client Project Manager

The client project manager is a senior member of the client's user group and is the primary contact between you and the client organization. The client project manager should have the authority to approve deliverables or to resolve issues. This role on your project is critical. Ensure that it is filled, formally or otherwise.

What If?

The Client Does Not Appoint an Executive Sponsor or Appoints One Who Is Not Senior

The project will have nobody looking out for it at senior levels, which means that it will be vulnerable to cost cutting or changing priorities and will have a hard time competing with other projects for scarce resources.

Actions

Forestall this. When you request an executive sponsor at the start of the project, identify the seniority you require ("This person should be at least a vice president who wants to see the project succeed"). This makes it easier to object when the client proposes a middle manager.

When you do object, do not annoy the sponsor proposed by the client, or you will have real problems. Say something like, "Fred's good, but, as we discussed, I also need someone at the vice president level to be a project advocate. Who would you suggest?"

The Client Does Not Appoint a Steering Committee

Major decisions, particularly those that affect such matters as the budget, resources, or scope of the project, will be almost impossible to get. You will spend large amounts of time shuffling from manager to manager, hearing comments such as "Your recommendation sounds okay to me, but I don't have the authority to approve it by myself."

Actions

Identify a group of client representatives whom you think should be on the steering committee, then call a meeting to discuss a number of issues for which you need them all present.

After the meeting, state your intention to gather them together again when issues arise in the future. You are, of course, setting up an informal steering committee, which will never be called that but which will have the collective authority to make the decisions you need.

The Client Does Not Appoint a Client Project Manager

There will be no single person to whom you can report or with whom you can discuss issues. In addition, all client detailed work, such as arranging meetings, distributing deliverables for review, or navigating through the client organization, will fall on your shoulders.

Actions

Point out that this is a critical position and that if it is left unfilled, there will be significant risks and extra effort imposed on the project.

In your estimate, add time and costs for client project management. Inform the client that if you must accept these responsibilities, the costs and schedule will be affected. If you are external to the client organization, you can also point out that one of its people can do the job more efficiently than you.

The Steering Committee Insists on Overturning User Group Decisions

Steering committee meetings will be lengthy, frequent, and acrimonious because of the level of business detail, and the real user group will gradually withdraw from the project.

Actions

Take tighter control of the meeting agenda, which should be restricted to project status and terms-of-reference issues. Challenge any digressions into business details as being outside the scope of the meeting. Caution: This will not deter everyone.

You may be tempted to ask the more detail-oriented members of the steering committee to join the user group. Avoid this. First, they will probably decline because they are busy. Second, if they do accept, the dynamics of the user group will be upset by the presence of one or more of the bosses.

Assuming that you have clearly established how the project will be conducted (see the sections "Defining the Scope" and "Review and Approval," in chapter 3), the steering committee interference will be a departure from your approved structure. Approach the committee with a scope change request (see the section "Managing Scope Changes" in chapter 5) based on the additional effort needed to accommodate committee involvement. Take extra steps to involve the user group. Make sure they are copied on all memos that deal with details, and forward all steering committee decisions to them. If you should ever imply through your behavior or comments that they are extraneous to the project, they will voluntarily become so, and you will lose any enthusiasm for the project at the working level.

You Encounter Abusive or Surly Client Representatives

Not only will having to deal with these people make your life unpleasant, but the project will suffer because you will tend to avoid them, affecting the quality of any information or decisions for which they are responsible.

Actions

Recognize that you are not required to tolerate abusive behavior, even from senior clients.

If abusive attitudes are the norm for the client organization, you will not be able to find any relief. Whether you stay or go will be a personal decision, but if you decide to leave, make sure that everyone understands your reasons.

If the abuse is confined to one or two people, take strong action to stop it. For example, if, in a meeting, the person yells or slams things on the table, stand up, announce calmly that the meeting is over until people can behave reasonably, and leave. Rebook the meeting for the following week. If you are in a private or small-group conversation when the abuse occurs, inform the person that you are neither required nor willing to take abuse and that the discussion is over.

If the objectionable person apologizes, accept the apology. Anyone can have a bad day.

* * * * *

WHAT ARE THE CLIENT'S PRIORITIES?

Any reasonable client wants it all: on time, on budget, and fully functional. Nobody wants to start a project with the attitude that one of these will have to go, but there are times when meeting all of them is impossible, and it is prudent to understand in advance which can be sacrificed.

Some clients will say, "We must have this by September 30, regardless of what it takes." Some may say, "We're not fixated on the date, but we cannot spend one penny more than has been budgeted." Others may offer, "In a pinch, we can trim some of the functions." These are not invitations to ignore the budget, abandon the schedule, or trash the functionality; they are realistic statements of the client's priorities, and they must be respected.

Many clients recognize that system building is difficult and risky. In stating these priorities, they are not giving you permission to slip, they are giving you directions for managing.

If the client does not volunteer the priorities, make sure that you understand them by understanding the background and justification for the project. What are the consequences of missing the schedule? What happens if you exceed the budget? What is the impact if the system is not complete? If you understand these priorities, when the project runs into difficulty, you will be better able to recommend action that the client can accept.

One warning: Do not ask the client directly for these priorities. If you ask, in effect, "Which of these three can we discard if the going gets rough?" you will not imbue your client with confidence, and you risk hearing, "Absolutely none of them."

What If?

You Get Different Priorities from Different Client Groups

You will find it hard to set priorities within the project, even if you are able to meet the plan. Furthermore, this should be a danger signal to you that your project may become an object of contention within the client organization.

Actions

Regard this as an example of a conflict within the client organization over who has ownership of the project. See the section "What Is the Background to This Project?" earlier in this chapter.

Discuss the contradiction with the client project manager or individual members of the steering committee. You may get insights into the client organization that will help you manage the project.

If the day comes when you must report that, for example, the budget is in danger, discuss the problem privately with those who regard it as fixed. In general, avoid announcing this kind of problem in a meeting where people have not had the chance to assess it.

* * * * *

PROJECT INITIATION

Projects are expensive, which is why no organization should start one without first ensuring that it will provide value. Nevertheless, in many organizations, projects seem somehow to emerge. Nobody is sure how they got started, and nobody knows whether they are justified or even what effort they will require.

Often a project will appear when a senior executive asks a cooperative technical person to "have a look at this for me." The scope of the request then expands, drawing in other technical staff, until its demand for resources starts to interfere with other projects. The request has evolved into a surreptitious project, which is a problem for five reasons:

1. There is no evaluation to determine how much effort it will require, hence no ability to plan the deployment of resources.
2. There is no assessment to determine if the project supports or detracts from the organization's strategic direction.
3. There is no clear definition of scope, hence no mechanism to limit the effort.
4. There is no benefits analysis, hence no possibility of ensuring that the project will provide value to the organization.
5. The regular projects from which people are drawn will slip their schedules and exceed their budgets, increasing costs and delaying the realization of benefits.

The purpose of project initiation is to ensure that every project passes through an evaluation process designed to determine whether the project should be done, the approximate effort it will need, and what its priority is relative to the other projects. A project initiation process is described in *The Project Management Office Toolkit*.

As a project manager, it is not your responsibility to set up a project initiation process: that's the job of management or of a project management office. However, you do have two other responsibilities. The first is to ensure that any project you are asked to manage has gone through some form of evaluation to ensure three things:

1. That it supports the strategic direction of the organization
2. That it has a clear scope statement
3. That is has a clear benefits statement

During the initiation stage, the benefits statement is not a cost-benefit analysis, because you don't yet know what the costs are. It is a statement of the types of benefits the client expects that the project will provide.

Your second responsibility is to be vigilant for any attempts to pull your people off onto other assignments. If another project needs some effort from one or more members of your team, you will negotiate with that project's manager, balancing your desire to protect your resources with the overall interests of the organization (see the section "Negotiating for Resources," in chapter 5). However, the real problem that you will want to prevent is having your people pulled away to do some work on a "project" that does not officially exist.

Before you can take any action, you must first identify that there is a problem. In many organizations, senior executives routinely approach technical staff, upon whom they have come to rely, to do some work for them. You need to make it clear to your team that you must approve any such requests. Either the team member who is approached must refer the requester to you or, if that would create an uncomfortable situation, the team member must inform you of the request before he or she takes any action on it. If the project can afford the absence of the team member for a few days, you may decide to grant the request, but make sure that the requester knows that the approval is coming from you. If you cannot afford to lose the team member, even for one or two days, you will need to decline the request.

This is not a comfortable position. It can seem bureaucratic when you deny a request on the grounds that it has not gone through a formal initiation process. Perhaps more problematic is that doing so can be a career-limiting move. Before you take such a strong position, you need to be sure that you have the support of your direct management. If you don't, you have no backup and no defense against a senior manager's insistence that you comply.

Nevertheless, if you don't refuse the request, your project will be at risk when the team member is no longer available. Your strategy here is to recognize that if your project suffers, so does the organization and the benefits it expected. You need to meet with the manager who made the request and point out how important the team member is to your project and what will happen to its schedule and budget if he or she is pulled off, even for a few days. It is helpful if you can suggest an alternative, which may be the loan of a less critical team member for a limited period, the use of another staff member, or a suggestion that the request be deferred to a less critical time in the project. You may also consider informing the project's executive sponsor and asking for his or her assistance in protecting your team. Finally, if all of these actions fail, document the effect of the team member's absence, so that when you are asked why your project slipped, you have a formal response.

Exhibit 2.2 is a checklist that sums up this chapter, "Understanding the Project."

Exhibit 2.2. Checklist for Understanding the Project

Do you understand the project costs and benefits?	❑
Are the project justifications quantified?	❑
Does the client accept the project justifications as goals?	❑
Do you have a clear understanding of the project background?	❑
Can you classify each of the participants in terms of their support for or opposition to the project?	❑
Have you identified the executive sponsor?	❑
Is there a steering committee?	❑
If so, have you established that you will set the agenda for the meetings?	❑
Have you written down your understanding of the project justification, background, and people? (If not, do so, if only for your own reference.)	❑
Has the project been properly initiated?	❑

3

Defining the Project

Do I understand the project justification?
Do I understand the background to the project?
Do I understand the project politics?
Do I understand who the players are and the roles they will take?
Do I understand the client's priorities?

Have I defined the project deliverables?
Have I established the scope—both system and project?
Have I determined how deliverables will be reviewed and approved?
Have I defined the structure and organization of the client team?

Have I defined the risks and developed plans to mitigate them?
Have I documented the project assumptions and constraints?
Have I developed a quality plan?
Have I developed a list of detailed project activities?
Have I defined the dependencies between activities?
Have I built a project estimate of the work required?
Have I assigned resources and leveled them?
Have I completed the schedule, complete with milestones?
Have I aligned the schedule with the client's requirements?
Have I developed a project budget?
Have I planned for implementation?
Have I planned for completion?
Have I planned for communications?
Have I prepared an overall project plan?

Am I building an effective team?
Do I know where I stand against the schedule, estimate, and budget?
Am I managing risks?
Am I solving schedule problems?
Am I managing requests for scope changes?
Am I managing for quality?
Am I micromanaging when needed and not elsewhere?
Are my subcontractors delivering on their commitments?
Do I understand the expectations of the client, and can I meet them?
Am I conducting regular team meetings, and are they effective?
Do I report project status and outstanding issues regularly?
Am I taking the time to reflect privately on progress?
Do I and my team celebrate our successes?

Defining the Project

Many projects are managed on the explorer principle: "Let's get moving and see what happens." While this approach can be exciting, particularly at two in the morning before a milestone deliverable is due, it rarely produces what the client wants. Defining the project consists of finding out what that is. It may seem insultingly elementary to point out that in order to satisfy a client, you need to identify what will do that, but, too frequently, the client's needs finally become clear at implementation. That is too late.

You may wonder why so many projects do not define at the start exactly what will be produced, but a more useful question is what indicators will tell you that perhaps your project is not focusing on client needs. There are several.

1. There is a "done it before" attitude on the part of your team (including you). You may, therefore, be deluded into believing that because you understand the application (such as inventory), you know what the client needs and that there is little point in taking up valuable time asking silly questions.

2. When you and your team address problems, you focus on technical solutions instead of client needs. If you are to be client-focused, then all problems that you and your team discuss must be solved by considering what is best for the client, not by relying on technical ingenuity.

3. The project is rushed at the start. You have near-impossible deadlines to meet and the imminent inevitability of night and weekend work.

If this is the case, you are being pressured to "get on with it" and to produce something—anything—fast, and you will come to regard slowing down to talk to the client as a career-limiting move.

4. Your client or your management (or you) believe that the only valuable product from a computer-systems project is code, and that everything else is preamble—costly, time-consuming, and of limited value. If that is the case, any actions that delay the start of "real" work will be wasted and unwelcome.

If any of these conditions is true, then you have forces that are diverting you from laying the necessary groundwork. The counterforce to each of them is to insist that the requirements of the project be defined as clearly and unambiguously as possible.

There is another emerging threat to a clear definition of deliverables. Many projects are now structured around some form of iterative development in which prototypes are prepared, reviewed, and successively refined until the prototype evolves into the final system. In this approach to systems development, the prototype is often used to identify business rules and procedures, leading to a temptation to dismiss the need to define requirements because "they will become clear as we evolve the prototype." If you hear this argument, point out that iterative development is one way of reaching the desired end result, but that that result still needs to be defined. In fact, this approach to projects needs, if anything, an even clearer definition of the end goal.

To define a project, you must define, document, and gain client approval for two things: the deliverables and the scope. These are discussed later in this chapter.

However, defining a project is more than defining deliverables and scope. You also need to define how the project will be conducted. Specifically, you will need to establish:

- How you will manage requests for changes to the scope
- How the client will review and approve deliverables
- For development projects, what kind of approach the project will take

These are the subjects of chapter 3. A checklist at the end will help you ensure that you and the client agree on the important issues in the project.

* * * * *

DEFINING THE DELIVERABLES

On the face of it, defining deliverables should be simple. The client wants a recommendation on a software package, a set of models, a technology architecture, or an application system consisting of code and documentation. While these products might be complex to produce, defining them seems to be straightforward. Unfortunately, in the world of projects, straightforward usually leads off a cliff.

Problems arise from apparently innocuous statements such as "The new inventory system will facilitate processing of financial data by the general accounting system." This could mean that:

- The new system will provide a simple month-end report showing summary data to be manually entered into the accounting system, or

- The new system will create a month-end file of transactions to download into the accounting system, or

- The system will update accounting databases from inventory transactions in real time.

The efforts that correspond to each of these interpretations are vastly different. If you plan to produce a month-end report and the client insists on real-time database updates, you are in trouble. Before the project starts, you must understand not only what all such statements mean but also what the client thinks they mean.

A definition of project deliverables consists of a list, with a brief description, of everything tangible that the project will produce. Depending on the client's technical sophistication, the descriptions will vary in complexity. Hence, one client's deliverable may be described simply as a "data model of the inventory application, showing major data entities and their relationships," while another may require "logical data model of the inventory application normalized to Gane & Sarson third normal form." There is little point in showing the second description to the first client, since nobody will understand it, and if you show the first description to the second client, it will be regarded as simplistic.

A word of warning, especially if you are technically inclined: Do not build this list in seclusion. Discuss it with client representatives, and develop it with their active participation. Take the time to review each deliverable with the client, and if you detect any hesitations or areas where there is confusion, lack of clarity, or disagreement, make sure that you resolve whatever the issues are. Finally, get the client to sign off on the deliverables, which means that someone in authority signs his or her name agreeing to the deliverable list and descriptions.

Typical Deliverables

Exhibit 3.1 is a list of deliverables that a systems development project might be called upon to produce. Of course, if you are working with a development methodology, the list of deliverables is mandated. If not, the list in Exhibit 3.1 may be useful.

This list is not exhaustive, nor does it apply to all projects. It is provided here as a checklist to stimulate your thinking as to the deliverables your project will provide.

What If?

The Client Will Not Get Specific or Prefers to Leave the Details Until Later in the Project

You risk being surprised by new demands for deliverables or by increased complexity. In particular, you will not be able to establish a scope from which to identify scope changes.

Actions

Create your own list of deliverables with whatever level of detail you need, and document that your estimates of effort and the

Exhibit 3.1. Sample List of Deliverables

Planning Deliverables

Project plan, charter, or statement ❑

Statement of work ❑

Cost-benefit analysis ❑

List of deliverables ❑

Definition of scope ❑

Workplan ❑

Estimate ❑

Budget ❑

Schedule ❑

Project overview and approach ❑

Design Deliverables

Logical data models ❑

Logical process models ❑

Business rules ❑

Physical data models ❑

Physical process models ❑

Data dictionary ❑

Buy versus build analysis ❑

Acquisition Deliverables

Request for proposals ❑

Proposal evaluation procedures ❑

Hardware capacity plan ❑

Recommendations ❑

Maintenance plan ❑

Development Deliverables

Code ❑

Unit documentation ❑

Unit test plan ❑

Unit test results ❑

Integration test plan ❑

Integration test results ❑

System test plan ❑

(continues)

Exhibit 3.1. (Continued.)

    System test results ❏

    Application documentation ❏

Implementation Deliverables

    Implementation plan ❏

    Training plan ❏

    Training materials ❏

    Operating procedures ❏

    Cutover plan ❏

    Phaseout plan ❏

---

budget and schedule are based on that list. As the project proceeds, present the client with design documents, screen and report mock-ups, and business rules that reinforce your list of deliverables.

Treat any attempt to expand the deliverables, either in number or in content, as a change of the scope that you have defined.

The Client Demands Deliverables That the Project Size Does Not Warrant

You will spend a great deal of effort producing deliverables that have no effect on the project, and you risk the project's being bogged down by acrimony over irrelevant issues.

Actions

Estimate the additional cost of producing these deliverables and their effect on the budget.

Develop an alternative mechanism for providing what each such deliverable provides. For example, if the deliverable is a buy-versus-build analysis and there is no intention of buying a package, the client might be satisfied by a memo stating that you have considered the option of buying a package and rejected it for reasons presented in the memo.

Present your costs and alternatives to the client. If, after reviewing them, the client still insists on the deliverables, make sure that the budget and schedule reflect the extra effort.

* * * * *
DEFINING THE PROJECT OBJECTIVE

The project objective or goal is one or two sentences that describe what the project is intended to accomplish. An objective statement might be:

The Web Assessment Review Project will enable property holders to review their property assessments over the Internet.

This objective is clear: We are going to build a system that will post property assessment information on the Internet and allow homeowners and other interested parties to examine the assessments.

However, there are a vast number of details that this statement omits. For example:

- Will the project allow people other than property holders to review the assessments?

- Will there be special facilities for real estate agents or government departments?

- Will the facility require searchers to log on or to register before they can inquire?

- Will the Web site run on existing hardware, or will new servers be required?

In other words, an objective statement does not tell us what details are involved. Those will be identified in the scope statement, which will be built with reference to the project objective.

The purpose of an objective statement is to identify for all participants what the project will achieve, but a sound objective statement is more than a simple sentence—it must meet the following five criteria:

1. It is Stated in the positive.
2. It is Measurable.
3. It is Achievable.
4. It is Relevant.
5. It is Timely.

These criteria form the acronym "SMART."

Now let's examine the objective statement given above to see if it meets these criteria.

- It is Stated in the positive.
- It is not Measurable.
- It is not certain whether it is Achievable.
- It is not clear if it is Relevant.
- It is not Timely.

That is, it's not SMART.

If we apply the SMART criteria, we can modify the objective statement to the following:

The Web Assessment Review Project will enable our two million property holders to review their property assessments over the Internet, meeting our strategic Internet mandate. It will be complete by July 31, 2004.

Now let's examine it to see if it meets the criteria.

- It is Stated in the positive.
- It is Measurable.
- It is not certain whether it is Achievable, but we now have the information to assess that.
- It is Relevant.
- It is Timely.

That is, it's now a SMART objective.

As a project manager, your first step is to establish the project objective. Normally, this won't be a problem because the client knows the general purpose of the project. However, there are occasions in which the objective is anything but clear. For example, there may be a dispute among stakeholders as to what the project is to achieve, or the client may be ambivalent, trying to address two problems that are distantly related. In such cases, it is your job to lead the client in creating a clear project objective. Your primary tool is the set of SMART criteria.

*　*　*　*　*
DEFINING THE SCOPE

Scope changes are the most common source of project overruns. Clearly, they require firm management, but a scope *change* cannot be recognized until the scope *baseline* is established. If you do not define the scope at the start of the project, you will lose a lot of sleep because you will have no means to refuse apparently logical client requests for more work that will set your beleaguered project back even further.

It was a payroll project, and it was almost complete, when the client, reviewing a menu, asked, "How do I produce year-end taxation slips?"

Project manager: "Year-end taxation slips? They weren't part of the definition."

Client: "Of course, they were. Taxation slips are a standard requirement of all payroll systems."

Both were correct. The client had not specified taxation slips, and such slips are standard.

The problem, of course, is that not all details of the scope can be defined in advance, and some misunderstandings are inevitable. The more time you invest in clarifying the scope, the fewer problems you can expect as the project unfolds. Be prepared to spend time gaining agreement on scope before you expend effort on the project; otherwise, client expectations will solidify, and you may be stuck having to do more than you planned.

An Overview of Scope

To many project managers, "scope" is limited to a single statement of what the project will do. For example, "This project will develop an Internet-based order entry system that will allow customers to enter orders online." This is not a scope statement, it is a project objective and, as we have seen, not a complete one. A scope statement must specify, for example, what types of products the customers can order, whether the system will provide delivery schedules, whether it will allow customers to change their profiles, or to review their credit status, or to modify orders once placed. Furthermore, the scope statement must specify what activities are not in scope. If the system will not allow customers to review information such as stock levels or production schedules, that exclusion must be listed. A scope definition, in other words, specifies what the project will do as well as what it will not. However, scope is much more than the application boundaries of a system; it includes all the work that your project will be required to carry out. For example, the client may also expect you to develop changes to internal procedures, or to install new hardware to run the application, or to conduct stress testing, or to train users—all activities that are time-consuming, expensive, and destructive of carefully laid plans that are based solely on the limits of the application.

Exhibit 3.2 is a checklist of potential scope areas that your project may be required to undertake. For each of these activities, you should indicate whether they are in scope, out of scope, or not applicable. Note that this exercise is not intended to limit the scope; that's not your role. From your point of view, it does not matter whether an activity is in or out of scope, only that it has been defined as one or the other. (An obvious exception is if your company has bid on a fixed-price contract with a defined scope. However, even in this case, limiting the scope is a job for the account manager, not you.) Your interest here is solely to define the scope so that you can prepare a complete project plan.

In preparing a scope statement, remember that there are two types of scope: the scope of the product and the scope of the project. The scope of the product defines the work that the project will carry out, the scope of the project defines how that work will be executed.

The Scope of the Product

Defining the scope of the product means coming to a common understanding of its major boundaries and the business functions it encompasses.

Exhibit 3.2. Scope Definition Checklist

Application areas that are within the project scope
Application areas that are outside the project scope
Requirements of the project methodology
Implementation requirements
    Training users
    Populating databases
    Converting data from current sources
Providing a warranty period
Ongoing maintenance and support
    Setting up application maintenance procedures
    Training application maintenance staff
    Setting up database monitoring and maintenance procedures
Specialized or nonstandard testing requirements
    Testing the system under conditions of high volume
    Testing the system simulating a high transaction rate
    Testing the system simulating a high volume of users
Preparing interfaces to other systems
Developing changes to internal organizational processes or procedures
Developing changes to internal forms
Developing changes to external relationships
Equipment, software, or component acquisition
    Preparing purchase specifications
    Purchasing of hardware or software
    Installing hardware or software
    Maintaining hardware or software during the project
    Setting up hardware or software maintenance after the project
Moving, consolidating, or upgrading hardware or system software
Modifying LANs, WANs, or user desktops
Operations requirements
    Setting up operations procedures and schedules
    Setting up help-desk facilities and procedures
    Setting up systems maintenance and support procedures
    Setting up backup facilities and procedures including off-site backup
    Setting up capacity measuring and reporting facilities
    Setting up physical security procedures
    Setting up system security procedures
    Setting up disaster recovery facilities and procedures
    Setting up failover procedures

For example, an inventory control system may be defined to include manufacturing and finished goods inventory but to exclude fixed assets. More generally, the system may be defined to exclude (or include) bill of materials, purchasing, order entry, or any other functions that affect or are affected by inventory control.

The scope of any system becomes blurred because all business functions interact with one another. Purchasing interacts with inventory, which interacts with order entry, which interacts with sales, which interacts with . . ., and all these systems interact with general accounting. This interdependency makes project managers who want to be cooperative vulnerable to scope change requests, because it's hard to argue with a client who says of a purchasing system, "What good is it to capture vendor prices if I can't use that information to pay them?" The answer, of course, is that the system you are developing is purchasing, not accounts payable. If the client wants accounts payable, that's a scope change.

To help define the scope of the system, list and briefly describe the major inputs—forms, screens, and interfaces—and the major outputs—reports, calculations, interfaces, and inquiries. Note the word *major.* Until you are at the point of detailed specifications, nobody, not even the client, can exhaustively identify everything. However, by listing the major inputs and outputs, you and the client can reach an understanding of the general scope of the product. For example, if, while specifying an accounts receivable system, the client describes an inquiry showing a customer's purchasing history, then the scope of the project must include online access to a sales database. You can either include that access in the scope or question whether it should be part of the system. In either case, once the exercise is finished, both you and the client will have come to expect roughly the same thing.

The Scope of the Project

The scope of the project deals with how each deliverable is prepared and presented. For example, the deliverable item "program specifications" can vary in formality from some handwritten sentences on a sheet of paper to a fully elaborated program-structure diagram. Neither is inherently better, and both, being program specifications, fulfill the spirit of the deliverable. However, the two require vastly different levels of effort.

Be wary of statements that include the word *standards,* such as, "The system will produce documentation according to corporate standards." This could mean that all documents must conform to documentation standards specifying such things as fonts, headers and footers, or section numbering, but "corporate standards" could also refer to a development methodology that dictates what is to be produced and how it is to be approved. Some methodologies, if strictly followed, call for dozens of documents and demand that each be submitted to a multiphase review and approval process. Project managers who plan to produce only the obvious deliverables will see their plans shattered as the client requests documents they have never heard of.

The scope of the project is normally dictated by the client's development methodology and the rigidity with which it is applied. The methodology states what documents are to be prepared, the sequence of preparation, and the contents. Some methodologies include samples that show the level of detail expected in each deliverable. Be alert for differing opinions on standards. If your client is the accounting department, it may not care about development methodologies, but the information systems department may have some exacting requirements in this area. Do not rely on your client to understand the impact of or requirements for a methodology.

Methodologies are like rainwear: a nuisance to put on, but indispensable when the storms hit. The biggest problem with them is the way they are applied by systems departments. The best regard them as a toolkit stocked with techniques and procedures to be drawn on when required. There are two forms of the worst: One regards them as law to be followed rigidly, regardless of the application; the other regards them as a waste of shelf space and gatherer of dust.

To define the scope of the project, you must determine what methodology the client uses and how rigidly it is applied. If the client regards methodology as a waste of effort, you should still follow it to the extent that it contributes to the success of the project.

Scope and Indeterminate Projects

In some projects, the scope is indeterminate, either because the application area is new or because the client has not fully clarified the mandate of the project. For example, if the client has requested a system, "to help our outside sales force," but does not understand what technology can do, or even what kind of help the outside sales force needs, you will find it impossible to define an effective project. In cases such as this, since nobody can define the scope clearly, you are at risk of a runaway project. You have two options for approaching such a request.

First, you can recommend a "scoping project," a short project of a few weeks' duration that will define what the scope of the original project will be. In the scoping project, you or someone qualified to define business requirements meets with the client and may even conduct workshops with a few selected sales representatives. The purpose is to define what the problem is that the client wants to solve and what a solution would look like. The only deliverable from the scoping project is a scope statement that can be used to initiate the original project, which you can now approach with a solid scope.

Your second option for dealing with an indeterminate project is to attempt to define it in terms of work products. Defining scope by work products means basing the scope on measures such as function points, screens, interfaces, or reports. For example, you may stipulate that the project will not exceed 200 function points or that it will be limited to five data-entry and fifteen inquiry screens. This method of defining scope is not accurate, since a screen, for example, may be simple or extremely complex, but basing scope on work products does serve to delimit the work to some extent.

In extreme cases, the scope may be based on low-level technical work products such as the number of elements in the data dictionary, the number of entities in the data model, or even the number of programs or lines of code. Identifying scope in this manner is unsatisfying and, especially for the client, dangerous, since there is never a clean relationship between technical work products and business functionality. However, if the client cannot define the scope according to business rules, defining it according to this kind of measure is an alternative. In this case, the client is agreeing that if the magnitude of the project exceeds some predetermined threshold, there will be additional costs and extensions to the schedule.

Scope Change Mechanisms

Regardless of how conscientiously you define the scope, it will change, which means that you need a mechanism for managing it. Make sure that you and the client agree that when the scope changes, you will identify the impact on the cost and the schedule, and the client will either approve or reject the change. The degree of formality of the process will vary, but the central principle is constant: The scope does not change without authorization. If your organization does not have a scope change mechanism, here are some suggestions.

1. When you identify a change of scope, submit it to your technical people for estimates, and calculate the effect of the change on the project schedule and costs. (Identifying scope changes is a major problem in itself. See the section "Managing Scope Changes," in chapter 5, for ways to ensure that they do not creep in unobserved and unmanaged.)

2. Document the change and its impacts on a change request form. A sample form is shown in Exhibit 3.3.

3. Submit the change request form to the client. In particular, note that the form includes a "Date Required." This is the date by which a decision whether to proceed with the change must be made, because after this date, the change will be harder to accommodate and will have greater impact. For example, the change might affect a program that has not yet been designed. On the date required, the program design is scheduled to begin, and, once it is under way, the change will be more costly.

4. After this, the change becomes a matter of client approval. It may require negotiations or modifications of the change, but ultimately, the client must either approve or reject the change.

5. If the change is approved, redo the project plan incorporating the change.

What If?

The Client Is Unclear About the Scope of the System

Without a clear scope, your project will be vulnerable to new requirements, which the client will insist were always included.

Exhibit 3.3. Sample Change Request Form

Change Request Form

Project: _____ **Date:** _____

Manager: _____

Requested by: _____

Description of the Change:

Justification for the Change:

Impacts on the Project:

Impacts on the Schedule:

Impacts on the Costs:

Resolution: _____ Date Required: _____

Approved/Rejected: _____ Date: _____

Signed: _____

Actions

Determine whether the lack of clarity arises because of an unwillingness to be specific or because the nature of the project makes clarity impossible.

If the client is not willing to be specific, then prepare the estimate, budget, and schedule and present them to the client with a covering memo explaining that they are based on your understanding of the scope. The memo will state what you assume to be in and out of scope. If the client disagrees about the scope, you will be able to adjust your plans accordingly.

If the client cannot be specific because of the nature of the project, suggest that the estimates must be based on some agreed-upon measure such as function points, with some change mechanism triggered when the actual number of function points exceeds the estimate.

In your project plan, include a scope section in which you list the items that are in the scope and related items that are not. Ask the client to sign off on the plan.

The Client Department Does Not Want "All the Paperwork" That the Corporate Methodology Requires

Your project will be caught in a battle between the systems department and its requirement for adherence to its methodology and the client department and its desire for brevity and minimum overhead.

Actions

Recognize that the systems department will usually prevail, since systems are its responsibility. If the methodology requirement is reasonable, inform the client department that you cannot override the policy without good cause and that, in fact, you agree with it. If the methodology requirement is not reasonable for the size of the project, discuss the situation with the systems manager and attempt to get the requirement modified. However, if the systems department is adamant, you and your client will have no choice, and you should build your plan accordingly.

The Methodology Is Inappropriate for the Project

The methodology is probably inappropriate because:

- It is too cumbersome for the size of the project.
- It does not apply to your development approach.
- The methodology is new to the organization, and your project has not agreed to be a pilot.

In all of these cases, applying the methodology will extend the effort of your project beyond any benefit the methodology will confer.

Actions

Prepare two estimates, one with the methodology and one without, present them to the steering committee, and ask the committee to help you adopt a more appropriate methodology.

Failing that, request committee approval to charge the difference between the estimates to a nonproject account.

If the steering committee still does not agree, then, when you are running the project, ensure that you comply with the methodology, that you attempt, as much as possible, to extract value from its deliverables, and that you add necessary deliverables that the methodology does not include.

* * * * *
REVIEW AND APPROVAL

In the project manager's dreams, the client accepts all documents graciously and with appropriate humility and never imagines questioning the wisdom contained therein. In the real world, clients can be contradictory, inconsistent, and stubborn and have the temerity to insist that they are the experts in their application area. It is in that real world that clients get to review and approve everything you produce.

The review and approval process, more than any other aspect of a project, is the place where project sociology—and politics—arises. If you do not properly manage the process, it can cause your effort to double or triple over your estimates. It is crucial to define, at the start of the project, the procedure by which deliverables will be accepted.

In the worst case, a document is delivered to and reviewed by several members of the client staff and the commented copies are returned to the author who revises the document in accordance with the comments—a process that usually involves one or more meetings or phone calls and has ripple effects on other deliverables. In the meantime, those members of the client staff who are less than enthusiastic about the project have had time to erect more obstructions, so that the next iteration attracts a whole new set of comments, and the cycle continues.

It is best if review and approval takes place face to face. The author calls a walkthrough meeting and distributes the document, giving people enough time to read and digest it and to prepare comments. At the walkthrough, the participants acknowledge that all changes to the document must be agreed to and that when the changes are made, the document will be accepted. After the walkthrough, the author makes the changes and resubmits the document, and, assuming the revisions are as agreed, the process ends.

There will be exceptions that require further iterations. For example, the document may be inadequate and require extensive revisions, or there may be issues that the client cannot resolve on the spot and that need further work, but in the normal case, reviewers get one chance to correct a deliverable.

Whether reviews will be conducted in a walkthrough or by returning comments to the author, there are several principles that must be followed in setting up a workable review and approval process.

Forgo Perfection

Nothing is perfect. Anything can be improved. Every circle can be made rounder, and even if you think perfection has been achieved, there will be no shortage of dissenters and critics.

The purpose of a deliverable is to come "close enough." This does not sanction sloppiness, it recognizes the law of diminishing returns. Both project and client staff must acknowledge a threshold of acceptable quality.

Minimize the Number of Reviewers

As the number of reviewers increases:

- The number of comments increases arithmetically.
- The potential for acrimony increases geometrically.
- The probability that comments will contradict one another increases exponentially.

- The probability that any given sentence will confuse at least one reviewer approaches certainty.

Remember the Three Cs

The only acceptable comments are those that correct, complete, or clarify the deliverable. Comments are appropriate only where a business rule is incorrect, not fully elaborated, or not clearly stated. This principle excludes from comment the organization of the document or its grammar and spelling. Of course, reviewers will identify obvious errors, and conscientious authors will want to correct them, but approval of a document should not depend upon such trivia as whether *data* is singular or plural. (Comments on spelling are appropriate for visible system components such as screens, reports, or forms, where correct spelling is a reasonable expectation.)

The most contentious of the three Cs is clarity. A reviewer will often state that a section is not clear when others have no problem with it. For example, a reviewer may insist that "finished goods" be inserted before every occurrence of "inventory" even though the section heading and context of the document make it clear that the text refers to finished goods inventory. The best way to deal with clarity comments is to ask at the walkthrough, "Who else had problems with this?" If you see hands go up, change it; otherwise, leave it as is.

Limit the Scope of Comments

Reviewers should be restricted to one set of comments only. If the revised document must be submitted for a second review cycle, comments should be confined to that portion of the document that has changed. No new comments on previously reviewed material should be permitted, or the process will never end.

This principle has two consequences. First, it means that the author should identify revised text, either by redlining or by external references. Otherwise, the reviewers cannot know what is new and will be forced to re-review the entire document. Second, the author must refrain from making changes where there were no comments. Otherwise, text that has been closed to review will be reopened.

At times this restriction may seem onerous. What do you do, for example, if a user identifies a problem with previously approved material? You cannot ignore it, but if you accept the comment, you have opened the door to an unending cycle of reviews. Your protection is your reasonable assumption that the review team is conscientious, an expectation that you enforce with the change request procedure. If previously approved material, which is closed to revision, needs to be changed, a change request must be submitted. Two or three of these will ensure that even the most casual reviewers will take their responsibilities more seriously.

Review via Walkthroughs

The worst review and approval procedures are those in which written comments are returned to the author. Many reviewers lack tact and return comments that are often insulting, confusing, trivial, or cryptic. As a result, the author usually feels defensive and compelled to lash back at the reviewers.

The best approach is to conduct a face-to-face walkthrough. Reviewers will be able to place their comments in a context that the author will better understand, and most reviewers will self-censor their sillier reactions. In addition, a walkthrough allows general agreement on revisions, so there will be fewer follow-on comments.

Minimize Surprises

Never prepare a deliverable in isolation. In the first place, it will probably be wrong or inadequate. In the second place, it will come as a surprise to the reviewers. Surprises generate comments.

Ensure that deliverables are prepared in working groups or information sessions. Circulate drafts—clearly marked as such. Discuss tables of contents. Define approaches to the deliverable. In general, make sure that the contents, organization, and conclusions of the deliverable are well known to the reviewers before it is released. The idea should be to make a product as much the property of the client staff as it is of the developers, on the grounds that it is hard to criticize one's own work.

Qualify Reviewers

Reviewers must be the same people who participated in the preparation of the document. Absentee reviewers are intolerable and can, with little effort, destroy a project.

Foster Teamwork

Whether the review and approval process is marked by acrimony or by cooperation depends upon the attitudes of the project and client staff. If clients have the attitude that perfection is required and that the developers are underhanded technocrats who must be held in check, or if project staff have the attitude that clients are a group of bureaucratic jerks out to make themselves look good, then deliverable review will be unpleasant and con-frontative. To build teamwork, find a counterpart on the client side and build bridges so that the attitude is that each group trusts the competence of the other and accepts that both are attempting to create a quality product.

What If?

The Client Refuses to Accept a Limited Review and Approval Process

Important deliverables, particularly those on which project progress depends, such as design documents, will not be approved without excruciating effort that will polarize the project and client teams.

Actions

Determine why your client rejects a formal process and how the client is likely to deal with the deliverables you present. Some clients do not like a formal process simply because they do not like formality. They are generally prepared to approve deliverables that are reasonable, but they do not want to be restricted in their ability to make comments. Others are more strict in their demand for perfection and view your attempt to impose formality as an attempt to compromise that demand.

If you believe the client will be easygoing, accept the desire for informality, plan for minimal reviews, and be prepared, if you encounter problems during the project, to work with the client to get the approvals you need. If the deliverables are of good quality and you have read the client correctly, the lack of formality should not be an issue. If it becomes one, appeal to the steering committee.

If you believe the client will be difficult, you are faced with a no-win situation. This is an issue that is critical, and you cannot embark on a project with such a client without a clear agreement on review and approval. This issue is so important that it is reasonable to insist to your management that you will not continue with the project under these circumstances. If, for personal or career reasons, you are not willing to take so strong a stand, ensure that your management understands the problem, recognizes that the project will probably not meet its targets, and acknowledges that the time for review and approval of each deliverable will be at least as long as the time needed to prepare it.

The Client Ignores the Review and Approval Process and Insists on Additional Reviews

If this behavior continues, you do not have a review and approval process, and the consequence will be the same as if you had not worked to define one. The difference is that in this case, you have a procedure that has been accepted.

Actions

Assuming that the quality of the deliverables is reasonable, invoke the change request procedure for each review beyond those agreed to. These extended review cycles will incur additional costs and extend the schedule.

Inform the steering committee that the process is not being

followed and that there will be an impact on the budget and schedule.

When the client objects, point out that your estimates were based on an agreed-upon procedure for review and approval and that if that procedure is to be changed, your estimates will also change.

* * * * *
SYSTEMS DEVELOPMENT LIFE CYCLES

In the elusive search to build systems faster, cheaper, and more flexibly, organizations have cast about for better tools, workbenches, and methodologies. Much of this effort has been spent on defining new approaches to systems development, but as with any competitive field, there is a great deal of misinformation on the usage and merits of each.

As noted earlier (in the section "Some Comments on Project Life Cycles," in chapter 1), the use of any Systems Development Life Cycle (SDLC) approach is independent of project management. That is, project management principles apply to any development project regardless of which SDLC it uses; the choice of SDLC is a technical one. However, the project manager is responsible for ensuring that the project follows good development practices, however it is carried out.

This section reviews the principal SDLCs and describes the project management techniques that apply to each. We look at the waterfall life cycle, iterative development, spiral life cycle, rapid application development (RAD), and extreme programming. As you will note, there is considerable overlap among these approaches.

Clarifications on Terminology

Advocates of many of the SDLCs refer to their approaches as "methodologies." This is incorrect. A methodology is a specific set of processes to prepare a set of deliverables. It includes templates, checklists, and forms and may also dictate standards. Most methodologies are commercial products, available from consulting firms, usually with training and implementation assistance. The approaches that we consider here are SDLCs, not methodologies.

It is common in project management literature to read of the advantages of a preferred approach, such as RAD, over an SDLC. This is a confusion in that all approaches used to develop systems, including RAD, are SDLCs. An SDLC describes a set of processes to move a system from its initial concept through to its implementation. Whether those processes are highly structured or indistinguishable from random, they still constitute an SDLC, differing only in degree of formality. RAD is an SDLC, just as much as the often-maligned waterfall life cycle.

Many observers isolate some technical approach within an SDLC and offer it as a new SDLC. For example, some claim that joint applications design (JAD), now often called "joint application development," is an SDLC in its own right. However, JAD is a formal, workshop-based, structured approach to gathering user information such as requirements or, more recently, feedback on deliverables in progress. It should be obvious that any SDLC has to involve the users at all stages of a project, from gathering requirements to reviewing deliverables to training. JAD is an excellent way to do so, but whether it is used in a waterfall project, a RAD project, or any other type of development, it describes a process within an SDLC.

Similarly, some enthusiasts regard certain approaches to programming, such as object-oriented development as, if not a new SDLC, at least an enabler of a new SDLC. Again, this is a misconception. "OO," as its practitioners call it, is a valuable addition to the development toolbox, but it does not dictate which SDLC to use any more than does the choice of any other programming approach.

The Waterfall Life Cycle

This is the granddaddy of SDLCs. It was the first formal approach and, even today, is widely used in applications development. The waterfall life cycle defines a series of steps, each one of which must be complete before the next one can start. The steps are usually definition, design, development, and implementation. Some variations of the waterfall life cycle add a concept stage at the beginning, while others add maintenance to the end, but the principle is the same: You cannot start a stage until you have finished the preceding one, and once you have completed a stage, you cannot revert to a preceding one. It's like a series of waterfalls: You may be able to paddle down them, but you can never paddle back up.

The philosophy behind the waterfall life cycle is not debatable. Before you can start writing programs, you have to have a design. Before you can complete the design, you must have a set of requirements. This approach is common to all formal SDLCs, although, as we shall see, it is applied in different ways.

There are two major criticisms of the waterfall life cycle: that it is monolithic and that it is inflexible. Let's look at each one.

By "monolithic," critics of the waterfall life cycle mean that it handles a project as a single entity or phase. There is only one path from concept to implementation and, while this approach may be valid for smaller or well-defined projects, it does not work on large projects or those in which the scope is ill defined or changeable. There is merit in this argument. Any project manager who embarks on a project in which the client will not see results for two years is at high risk. Business conditions and user requirements can change substantially in that time, making backtracking inevitable. Faced with such a project, you should attempt to break it down into phases, each of which introduces a limited set of functionality. You then apply the SDLC to each phase independently.

Similarly, if the scope of your project is changeable, you should plan the project in smaller chunks, settling each area of scope as you go. Some of the other SDLCs are based on this approach, but, however you segment your project, you can still apply the waterfall life cycle to each phase.

The second major criticism of the waterfall life cycle is that it is inflexible, making it hard to go back and make changes to previous steps if you find that you've missed something or if business conditions have changed. There are two aspects to this complaint: that making changes to work that was previously completed is time-consuming and expensive and that the processes of the waterfall life cycle do not allow the team to revert to a previous stage.

There is no doubt that making revisions is expensive, but this is true regardless of the SDLC that the project uses. Any system, however developed, is built on a set of business rules and practices. If any of these change or is revealed to be incorrect, either during the project or afterward, the system will have to be changed accordingly. The complexity of those modifications depends not only upon the nature of the changes but also upon the flexibility of the system. An application built using flat files is more difficult to change than one that uses a relational database, and an application that is table driven is easier to change than one with hard-coded values. However, this type of problem is a reflection on the technology used in the project and the design of the system, not on the SDLC.

The criticism that the waterfall life cycle does not accommodate reversion to a previous stage is a reflection on the way the project is managed. A project manager who insists that once a stage is closed it cannot be re-opened is ignoring the reality of systems development. As a project manager, you have the obligation to ensure that, if some backtracking becomes necessary, you and your processes will not be an impediment.

As a project manager of a waterfall project, you are responsible for ensuring that the work of each stage is adequately completed before you allow the team to progress to the next stage. You are also responsible for establishing with the client that if it becomes necessary to revert to a previous stage, there are processes and costs involved. The tool that you use to handle these issues is signoff. Before you can declare a stage closed, you need to get two sets of signatures: one from the technical team that will receive the deliverable and will be required to apply it and one from the client that it reflects client needs.

If, later in the project, you discover that the deliverable is inadequate or incorrect, you can apply a scope change to cover the additional time and effort of recovering. As to who authorizes—and pays for—the change of scope, if the problem was that your team, in its eagerness to proceed, overlooked important aspects of the deliverable, you have an internal problem and your company or department will have to accept the costs of recovery. Since this is the worst case, you should ensure that all deliverables are subject to peer review and that, particularly for deliverables that complete a stage, professionals who are not part of your team review them and be allowed to comment. This may be cold comfort if your team and the reviewers both slipped up and missed important aspects of the deliverable, but at least you have done all you could to ensure a quality product.

On the other hand, if the problem with the deliverable is that the client missed important information, it is the client's responsibility to authorize the scope change. You do, after all, have the right to assume proper diligence on the client's part when the team is reviewing and commenting on deliverables.

Iterative Development

Iterative development is less an SDLC than a class of SDLCs. It is based on the idea that through a series of phases, each of which adds some functionality and each of which allows the client to refine the requirements, a team can deliver a final product that zeroes in on the client's needs, regardless of how vague they were at the start.

The danger with iterative development is that it is seen as a series of activities that, more or less through random trial and error, finally homes in on a finished product. If there is no clear project management in place, this is a likely description of the process, although not of the outcome. In the worst case, the iterations are regarded as some form of "best efforts" in which the team takes the position that "We'll do whatever we can within the limits we have." Such a project is doomed because each iteration is open-ended, with no clear goals or plan.

Any project based on an iterative prototyping SDLC needs three characteristics if it is to have any chance of success:

1. **An Overall Project Objective**. At the start of the project, this may be ill defined and not clearly scoped, but it is a general statement of where the project will end up.

2. **An Iteration Overview**. This is a plan that indicates how many iterations the project will pass through and, with decreasing degrees of certainty for more distant iterations, what areas of functionality each iteration will encompass.

3. **An Iteration Plan**. This is a detailed plan for the iteration. It treats each iteration as if it were a project in its own right. The iteration plan includes activities for:

   a. Producing a set of requirements or functional specifications for the iteration

   b. Producing a design specification for the iteration

   c. Producing and unit testing the code for the iteration

   d. Integrating and testing the code and moving it into a final form

You may note that each iteration follows the familiar waterfall life cycle of definition, design, execution, and implementation. As the project manager, your job is to ensure that each iteration is planned within the overall project objective and that each iteration is conducted in a disciplined manner, leading toward a final product.

As the manager of an iterative project, you have one other consideration: What will you do with the output of each iteration? There are two options: The output may be a refinement of some aspect of the requirements, used only to help develop a final set of specifications for the application, or the output may itself be a unit of functionality to be put into production at the end of the iteration.

The difference between these purposes is the difference between building some throw-away code and developing a production-ready system. If the product of each iteration will be used to develop specifications, its only value is in clarifying the client's requirements, so it needs only minimal testing; it does not need to conform to organizational standards; and, other than its input to the application's specifications, it does not require documentation. (In some cases, the product of an iteration may be used as a starting point for development, so the interests of efficiency dictate that it should conform to standards and carry some documentation; but the point is that it does not need to meet the level of readiness of a production system.)

On the other hand, if the output from an iteration will be handed over to the client as a operating unit of functionality, it must be treated as a new production application, fully documented, tested, subjected to quality measures, submitted for client approval, and handed off to groups such as production, support, and the help desk.

Your role as a project manager is to ensure that the development effort within each iteration corresponds to the purpose of the iteration—that technical perfectionism does not result in an over-refinement of a product that will be used only to develop specifications, or that a casual approach to iterative development does not lead to a slapdash product.

The remaining SDLCs in this section are all specific instances of iterative development.

The Spiral Life Cycle

The spiral life cycle is a class of SDLC that is iterative, passing through four major steps several times before it produces the final result. Exhibit 3.4 illustrates the process. The start of development is at the center of the spiral in the upper left quadrant. From that starting point, the project spirals

Exhibit 3.4. Spiral SDLC

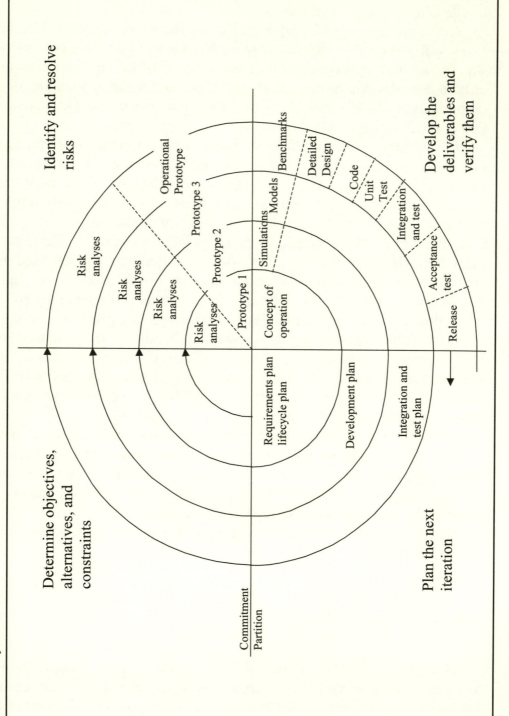

outward clockwise through four stages, each represented in the four quadrants:

1. **Determine objectives, alternatives, and constraints**. This stage establishes the goals of the specific iteration and gains the commitment of the client to proceed with the following stages.
2. **Identify and resolve risks**. Advocates of the spiral SDLC claim that one of its key features is a focus on risks. While there is no valid reason to ignore risks regardless of the methodology, the spiral SDLC formalizes risk analysis. In this stage, prototypes may be prepared.
3. **Develop the deliverables and verify them**. This stage builds the deliverables, which may be simulations, models, or benchmarks.
4. **Plan the next iteration**. This stage produces the plans for the products of the next iteration.

You will note that each iteration follows the waterfall life cycle of determining objectives (definition), risk resolution (design), development (development), and planning the next iteration (implementation). Advocates claim that the spiral SDLC is more appropriate to large projects or those in which the objectives are unclear. The iterations provide an increasingly detailed view of the scope and of the alternatives, until the final product is one that will be most likely to meet the client's requirements.

As a project manager of a spiral SDLC project, your responsibility is to ensure that all of the steps in the spiral are followed. In particular, each iteration must have clear objectives and each iteration must be planned, even if the overall objectives are still fuzzy. As we have noted, your job, when you are faced with any iterative development approach, is to ensure that each iteration is treated as an instance of a waterfall project with the stages clearly defined and managed.

Rapid Application Development (RAD)

RAD is less a specific SDLC than a philosophy of systems development within which different SDLCs may fit. RAD arose out of the perception that the waterfall life cycle was too inflexible, lengthy, and rigid to meet the fast-paced needs of modern business. One of the criticisms that RAD makes of the waterfall life cycle is that it does not sufficiently involve the end users, delivering results that are inappropriate. Hence RAD emphasizes end-user involvement. This criticism is valid: Many applications development projects were done in isolation from the users and the results "thrown over the transom" with the inevitable consequence that the project product was inappropriate and did not meet user needs. However, this weakness is not a necessary function of any particular SDLC, it is a result of poor project planning and execution. The value that RAD brings is that it focuses on user involvement throughout the development cycle with structured processes such as JAD sessions that can be used to define the requirements as well as to review and refine the product at intermediate stages during the development.

RAD also emphasizes the use of small teams using systems development tools such as object-oriented development, prototyping, and CASE (computer-aided software engineering) tools. However, as we noted earlier, the choice of development tool does not depend upon the SDLC, and, while these tools are valuable additions to any development project, they are able to fit in with any life cycle process.

Finally, RAD is also an iterative process, in which each iteration produces a prototype, the set of which refine the requirements, ultimately producing a valid and valuable product.

As the project manager of a RAD project, you will need to ensure that, as with all iterative projects, the work is planned within the context of an overall objective and that each iteration follows the waterfall life cycle.

Extreme Programming

Extreme programming is a recent entry into the SDLC field. It emphasizes a faster-paced, small-team, collaborative approach to building systems. Extreme programming includes such features as short, daily, stand-up meetings rather than weekly team meetings; pair programming, in which developers build code in pairs rather than individually; collective code ownership, in which code is owned and developed by the team; and user "stories," which are a more informal form of requirements. It also emphasizes testing, in which test plans are created at the start of development, rather than at the end, just prior to running them.

An extreme programming project is iterative within an overall release plan. At each iteration, the team reviews the user stories and, in conjunction with the users, decides which ones will be developed in the current iteration. Users are heavily involved in the development process, refining the stories, preparing acceptance test plans, and reviewing, testing, and accepting the deliverables. Each iteration, which may be as short as a few weeks, delivers a small release that the client can implement immediately.

The descriptions of extreme programming projects makes it seem as if the processes of collaboration, user involvement, and the fun of high energy combine to produce a final result that is unconstrained by conventional concepts of applications development, but the process, properly carried out, is anything but random. The overall release strategy is planned, each iteration is planned, and, within each iteration, the familiar stages of definition, through user stories; design, through test plans; development, through pair programming; and implementation, through user testing, are essential parts of the process.

As a project manager of an extreme programming project, you will need to absorb the vocabulary of the life cycle and the particular processes that it includes, but you will also need to ensure that the team follows the conventional steps of the waterfall life cycle, however they are labeled.

Summary

The field of applications development has produced numerous approaches to building systems better, faster, and cheaper. All of these approaches claim to have identified a failure of the preceding models, which the new one remedies. Yet, the formal exposition of all of these approaches has one thing in common: the underlying principles of the waterfall life cycle and their recognition that you can't build a system without a design and you can't design a system without a definition. Therefore, as a project manager, regardless of the life cycle preferred by your organization or team, you are responsible to impose the discipline of planning onto the project.

I contend that the failures of the waterfall life cycle that stimulated the development of iterative development, RAD, extreme programming, and other SDLCs are failures of project management, not of the SDLC itself. When critics of the waterfall life cycle argue that it does not consider risk, or that it excludes end users, or that it is monolithic, producing one product at the end of a tortuous single pass, or that it is inflexible, not allowing a reversion to a previous stage, these characteristics that they rightly attack are not intrinsic to the waterfall life cycle. Indeed, it is possible to plan a project in releases, manage risks, involve the users, and produce increments of code, all within the conventional waterfall life cycle. That projects have not done so is an indictment (or a lack) of project management. The solution is not to try to find some approach that automates or guarantees proper processes but to develop project managers who are able to apply sound principles of development to any project.

Checklist—Defining the Project

Exhibit 3.5 is a checklist to help ensure that you have considered all of the aspects of defining your project.

Exhibit 3.5. Checklist for Defining the Project

Is there a written list of all deliverables with a brief description?	❑
Have you reviewed the list of deliverables with the client?	❑
Have you agreed on the scope with the client?	❑
Have you reviewed, and do you understand, the client's methodology?	❑
Do you and the client agree on the extent to which the methodology will be followed?	❑
Do you have an approved, clearly stated review and approval process?	❑
Do all reviewers understand their roles and responsibilities?	❑
Do you understand the client team management style?	❑
Have you identified a de facto client team leader?	❑
Do you have a formal SDLC or life cycle approach?	❑

4

Planning the Project

Do I understand the project justification?
Do I understand the background to the project?
Do I understand the project politics?
Do I understand who the players are and the roles they will take?
Do I understand the client's priorities?

Have I defined the project deliverables?
Have I established the scope—both system and project?
Have I determined how deliverables will be reviewed and approved?
Have I defined the structure and organization of the client team?

Have I defined the risks and developed plans to mitigate them?
Have I documented the project assumptions and constraints?
Have I developed a quality plan?
Have I developed a list of detailed project activities?
Have I defined the dependencies between activities?
Have I built a project estimate of the work required?
Have I assigned resources and leveled them?
Have I completed the schedule, complete with milestones?
Have I aligned the schedule with the client's requirements?
Have I developed a project budget?
Have I planned for implementation?
Have I planned for completion?
Have I planned for communications?
Have I prepared an overall project plan?

Am I building an effective team?
Do I know where I stand against the schedule, estimate, and budget?
Am I managing risks?
Am I solving schedule problems?
Am I managing requests for scope changes?
Am I managing for quality?
Am I micromanaging when needed and not elsewhere?
Are my subcontractors delivering on their commitments?
Do I understand the expectations of the client, and can I meet them?
Am I conducting regular team meetings, and are they effective?
Do I report project status and outstanding issues regularly?
Am I taking the time to reflect privately on progress?
Do I and my team celebrate our successes?

Planning the Project

The dictum that "failing to plan is planning to fail" is better poetry than advice. While nobody plans to fail, simply creating a plan is no guarantee of success. Planning divorced from the reality of the project is worse than no planning because it gives the illusion of control. A less lyrical, but more accurate statement is "Poor planning guarantees failure."

Planning a project consists of the following fifteen activities:

1. Defining project risks and identifying actions to mitigate them
2. Listing the project assumptions and constraints
3. Identifying how quality will be managed
4. Constructing a list of activities and cost components
5. Establishing dependencies between activities
6. Estimating effort and costs
7. Preparing a schedule and milestones
8. Assigning and leveling project resources
9. Aligning the budget and schedule to client requirements
10. Preparing the project budget
11. Managing project paperwork
12. Planning for implementation
13. Planning for completion
14. Planning for communications
15. Writing the project plan

This chapter deals with each of these separately.

The culmination of the planning process is the project plan, a document that describes the project and how you intend to execute it. The final section in this chapter presents a sample table of contents for the project plan.

* * * * *

DEFINING AND MANAGING RISK

A risk is a potential problem, a situation that, if it materializes, will adversely affect the project. Risks that materialize are no longer risks, they are problems.

All projects have risks, and all risks are ultimately handled. Some disappear, some develop into problems that demand attention, and a few escalate into crises that destroy projects and careers. The goal of risk management is to ensure that risks never fall into the third category.

There are five steps to managing risks: identify them, categorize them, mitigate them, plan for them, and manage them.

Identifying Project Risks

Although all projects are different, the same risks tend to recur, but no list is exhaustive, and in identifying the risks for a project, you must continually ask, "What can possibly go wrong?"

If there is one risk that is universally the most dangerous for all projects, it is the following:

Corporate management views the project manager's risk analysis as alarmist and will not take the risks seriously until they materialize.

The only way to mitigate this risk is to document all other risks, identify the actions you take, and keep management informed, especially as the risk becomes more probable. It is only by stressing your risk analysis, by making explicit recommendations, and by insisting that management understand the risks that you can avoid having to say, "See, I told you so."

Common Project Risks

Exhibit 4.1 lists common risks that most projects encounter. They form a starting point for developing a catalog of risks. However, the list is not

Exhibit 4.1. Sample List of Project Risks

Staff Risks

Key staff will not be available when needed.

Key skill sets will not be available when needed.

Staff will be lost during the project.

Equipment Risks

Required equipment will not be delivered on time.

Access to hardware will be restricted.

Equipment will fail.

Client Risks

Client resources will not be made available as required.

Client staff will not reach decisions in a timely manner.

Deliverables will not be reviewed according to the schedule.

Knowledgeable client staff will be replaced by those less qualified.

Scope Risks

Requirements for additional effort will surface.

Changes of scope will be deemed to be included in the project.

Scope changes will be introduced without the knowledge of project management.

Technology Risks

The technology will have technical or performance limitations that endanger the project.

Technology components will not be easily integrated.

The technology is new and poorly understood.

Delivery Risks

System response time will not be adequate.

System capacity requirements will exceed available capacity.

The system will fail to meet functional requirements.

Physical Risks

The office will be damaged by fire, flood, or other catastrophe.

A computer virus will infect the development system.

A team member will steal confidential material and make it available to competitors of the client.

exhaustive; most project managers will find several more risks that they can add, and project experience will tend to increase this number. When you are assessing the risks for your projects, always refer to a list such as this. Otherwise, you run the project management risk that not all project risks are identified.

Categorizing Risks

There are numerous statistical methods for defining degree of risk, but the simplest categorization, and the most effective, is to describe risks as extreme, high, medium, low, or minimal.

The degree of risk depends upon two characteristics: the probability that the risk will occur and the impact on the project if it does. Probability and impact are both categorized as high, medium, or low, and their relationship, as illustrated in Exhibit 4.2 indicates the degree of risk.

Consider two risks: that a team member will resign during the project and that a fire will consume the office, destroying the installation and all the work that has been done. Both risks are of medium degree. In the first case, although the probability is high, the impact is low: You assume that the team member will give adequate notice and can be easily replaced. The second risk has a high—in fact, potentially devastating—impact, but the probability is low and the risk is easily mitigated by ensuring proper off-site backup. You categorize risks so that you can identify those that are the most dangerous and therefore require the most attention. It is the extreme and high risks that need your attention first.

Mitigating Risks

Since the riskiness of a risk is a function of its probability and impact, you mitigate it by reducing its probability, its impact, or both. Since every

Exhibit 4.2. Categorization of Degree of Risk

	Impact		
Probability	*High*	*Medium*	*Low*
High	Extreme	High	Medium
Medium	High	Medium	Low
Low	Medium	Low	Minimal

project is unique, so are the mitigating actions. However, some principles apply across projects and risks.

- **Remove excuses**. When the project depends on someone (such as a supplier, client, or line manager) to provide something (such as staff, equipment, or material) in accordance with a schedule, ensure that the provider knows the schedule, knows what is expected, and understands the consequences of a slippage. For major providers, such as the client, make up a schedule giving the exact dates when the project will require client resources. If you are not able to give an exact date now, give a date by which you will be able to.

  You remove excuses by providing visibility into the project, an active process in which providers are forced to understand what is expected of them. For example, if you have ordered a piece of equipment with a two-month lead time to be delivered by a specified date, just putting a required date on the purchase order is not enough. Four weeks before delivery, call the sales representative to verify the schedule. Three weeks prior, call to clarify, for example, the power requirements. At two weeks, call to clear up a technical question. One week ahead of time, call to establish shipping procedures. With each call, of course, you will ask if there are any problems that could delay delivery, and you will emphasize how critical timely delivery is. After this series of calls, the supplier has no excuses to fall back on. There is no guarantee, of course, that the equipment will actually be delivered on time, but by actively reminding the supplier of the schedule, you have reduced the probability of a late delivery.

- **Demand visibility**. When the project depends on someone delivering something and there is a process that the provider must follow before delivery, you must understand at least the milestones of the process. For example, if a piece of equipment must be manufactured, identify the checkpoints in the manufacturing process, have the sales representative attach dates to each checkpoint, and call on those dates to ensure that the milestones have been met and there are no delays.

  If the process is repetitive, such as client review and approval of project documents, understand the process. What happens to a document when it is received? Who reviews it? How are individual reviews reconciled? Is there a final authority for approval? Who? What is the priority of the project for the reviewers? With this understanding, you will be able to suggest changes in the process that will speed things up if there are delays.

- **Help people communicate**. When there is a surprise, the project manager is frequently the last to know, even though the informal communications network (or "rumor mill") among team members and users contains various tidbits and snippets of information that provide inklings of problems to come. Helping people to communicate increases the probability that useful information will find its way to you. See the section "Building the Team," in chapter 5, for more about communication.

  The communications network can provide advance warning that an employee is dissatisfied and looking elsewhere, that the performance of a system may be slower than required, that software components may not integrate smoothly, or that covert scope changes are being smuggled into the system. In other words, the rumor mill is a prime source of information about emerging risks.

  The key rule to using the rumor mill is "Don't shoot the messenger." No matter how painful the information, thank the deliverer; otherwise, like the jilted spouse, you will be the last to know.

- **Prepare contingency plans**. If the technology does not perform adequately, what can be done to improve it? If a critical team member is lost to the project, how will those skills be replaced? If the building burns down, how does the project recover? Contingency plans describe what you will do when the worst happens.

  Contingency plans must be capable of being put into action, either now or when they are needed, and they must be capable of being handled within the budget, schedule, and functionality of the project. If this is not the case, they are not contingency plans; they are wishes with nothing to anchor them but the fervent hope that they will never have to be exercised.

Planning for Risks

There are two aspects of risk planning that will affect your project plan: mitigating activities and contingency plans.

Mitigating activities are those that arise from the mitigation of project risks. For example, if you identify a risk that you could lose your database analyst, Mary, one mitigation might be to assign Fred, who is also on your team, to spend some time with Mary learning the trade and becoming, in effect, an understudy. However, if you do not include in your project plan the activities for Fred to shadow Mary, or to meet periodically with her, or to take some courses in database technology, nothing will happen, and, when the risk materializes and you lose Mary, you will have no fallback. Your risk mitigation must produce a set of activities that becomes part of your project plan; otherwise it is wasted.

Contingency plans are the steps you will follow when a risk materializes. For example, if you do lose Mary, what will you do? Your contingency plan for that risk will include steps such as "Assign Fred as database analyst," "Request a C++ programmer to replace Fred," "Assign Fred's tasks to the new programmer," "Review the impact of Mary's loss on the schedule of the project," and "Modify the project plan accordingly." By preparing such plans in advance, you will have a set of actions to follow when the risk materializes, actions that you defined when you were cool and collected, instead of upset and angry, which you may well be when Mary is pulled off the project for something else.

Managing Risks

Risk management is both a planning and a managing activity. It is not enough to set down some risks at the start of the project and then ignore them. You must manage them. Managing risks means continually reevaluating the risks that have been defined and identifying new ones. There are three main mechanisms for managing risks: project team meetings, project status reports, and project manager reflection.

The biggest problem with risks is that they tend to get lost in the day-to-day hubbub of a project; since they are only potential problems, they are lower in priority than real ones. Therefore, to manage risks, you must ensure that they are an overt part of the project team's, and your, consciousness.

All team members must be aware of the risks that have been identified and awake to situations that affect them. To keep risks visible, devote part of each team meeting to a "risk review" (see the section "Team Meetings," in chapter 5) in which the risks are addressed one by one and team members are instructed to comment on anything that affects each risk. The purpose of the risk review is not to take action, it is to identify what risks, if any, have changed. The risk review also uncovers new risks as team members become attuned to dangerous situations.

Your project status report (see the section "Reporting Status," in chapter 5) should include a section entitled "Risk Review," in which you report on risks that have become more, or less, probable or serious. By regularly reporting risks, you are also able to prepare management for unpleasant news so that it does not come as a surprise.

Project manager reflection (see the section "Reflection," in chapter 5) is thinking time apart from the daily activities of the project. Devote part of that thinking time to reviewing existing risks and identifying new ones.

Prepare a risk management worksheet, similar to the one in Exhibit 4.3. The sample worksheet contains a short name of the risk to be used in status reports or risk reviews, a longer description, and a table to track how the risk has changed. When a risk has been eliminated, enter "Resolved" under "Comments." The risk management worksheet keeps the risks visible.

Exhibit 4.3. Risk Management Worksheet

Risk Management Worksheet

Project: _____   Date: _____

Short Name of the Risk:

Description of the Risk:

Date	Comments	Prob.	Impact	Degree
____	_____	____	____	____
____	_____	____	____	____
____	_____	____	____	____
____	_____	____	____	____
____	_____	____	____	____
____	_____	____	____	____
____	_____	____	____	____

What If?

Others Claim That You Have Overstated the Risks

You may be faced with complacency on the part of the client or an unwillingness to plan for problems. This becomes serious when the client refuses to expend resources to mitigate a risk that you see as high or extreme.

Actions

Seek other, less expensive mitigation procedures that you can use to reduce the risk to some extent.

Document your reasons for categorizing the risks as you did. State the probability, and describe the impact in graphic terms. Present your analysis to the steering committee, and request the resources you need to mitigate the risk.

If you are not given the resources you requested, alert your management to the danger, and ask if it can apply leverage to the client.

Plan the actions you will take if the risk materializes.

Others Claim That You Have Understated the Risks

You could be faced with a large number of high or extreme risks, all of which require effort and action. You could also be led into mitigation procedures that are excessive, expensive, and time-consuming.

Actions

If the risk assessments of others suggests that the project faces a large number of high or extreme risks, ask the complainants whether they really believe the project is that risky and, if so, whether it should be undertaken. Most people will back down and acknowledge that things are not as risky as they have made out.

Honor the risk assessment by others who are knowledgeable, but do not be intimidated into abandoning your own view of the risk. You will encounter people who will claim, usually loudly, that a risk is "unacceptable" and cannot be mitigated except by the most extreme safeguards. If your experience and that of others on your team tells you that this opinion is alarmist, respect the risk, but prepare your plans based on a more reasonable assessment.

* * * * *
PROJECT ASSUMPTIONS AND CONSTRAINTS

When projects have problems, the cause is frequently an assumption that turned out to be invalid or a constraint that was never identified. By documenting the assumptions and constraints, you can spot danger areas that may require some work.

Assumptions and constraints are frequently the reverse of one another. For example, if a project needs a network administrator and one is available half of the time, you may *assume* that the resource is available half time, while being under the *constraint* that it is not available more.

Assumptions

In general, the things you assume to be true will assist the project. If your assumptions are invalid, the project will suffer, and, conversely, if there are assumptions you do not identify, the project will usually benefit. For example, if you assume that the client mainframe will be available twenty-four hours a day, the project will suffer if the client restricts the team to a normal eight-hour day. On the other hand, if you have assumed a normal workday and overtime becomes necessary, the project will benefit when the client offers twenty-four-hour access.

Assumptions, therefore, positively affect a plan by reducing effort and ensuring resources. You usually assume, for example, that hardware and people will be available when you need them, that statistics used in planning are accurate, that critical components will be delivered on time, and that key people on both the project and client teams will perform adequately.

Exhibit 4.4 lists typical types of assumptions. For any given project, the specific assumptions will vary, but this list provides a starting point. Several

Exhibit 4.4. Sample List of Project Assumptions

Resource Assumptions

Project staff resources will be available when and as they are needed.

Required computer resources will be available when and as they are needed.

Required client resources will be available when and as they are needed.

At least n percent of the project staff will have experience with the development environment.

The client will provide staff capable of adequately describing in detail the functional requirements of the system.

Delivery Assumptions

Deliverables submitted for approval will be returned within n working days.

Equipment order lead times will be [specify].

Environmental Assumptions

No industrial action will be taken that will affect the project.

Issues will be resolved in a timely manner.

The project organization [describe it] will be put in place.

The methodology [name it] will be used in the project.

Client internal processes (such as purchasing) will be completed in a timely manner.

Systems development components will be capable of being integrated.

Budgetary Assumptions

The statistics used in preparing the estimates [list them] are accurate within n percent.

No travel and living expenses will be required *or* Travel and living expenses will be limited to those described.

No outside consulting will be required *or* Outside consulting will be limited to n days at $\$n$ per day.

Functionality Assumptions

The scope of the project is limited to [describe it].

---

of the assumptions refer to project planning components such as project organization. It is sufficient to refer to a chart or table in which you have described the component.

Constraints

Constraints are limits or boundaries within which you must work. If your constraints prove not to exist, the project will probably benefit, whereas constraints that you fail to identify will cause the project to suffer. For example, if your plans include the constraint that a key analyst will be available half time, the project will benefit if the constraint turns out not to exist. Conversely, if you did not identify that constraint, the project will suffer when it surfaces.

Constraints, therefore, negatively affect a plan by limiting resources and increasing work. Your constraints usually include limitations on availability of hardware or people, the need to consider effects on other application systems, or requirements to conform to a methodology.

Exhibit 4.5 lists some areas in which you need to look for potential constraints.

Why Identify Assumptions and Constraints?

Not all assumptions and constraints need to be stated. For example, it would be gratuitous to state the assumption that the estimates will be met. What else would you assume? Similarly, you would not want to offend the client by stating the assumption your bills will be paid on time. Nevertheless, most assumptions and constraints need to be made explicit for two reasons. First, your client, your management, and you need to understand the basis on which you are planning. For example, if you have assumed that deliverables will be reviewed and returned within five working days, it is valuable, if frustrating, to hear your client say, "We can't guarantee fewer than ten days." Documenting the assumption allows it to be challenged. Similarly, documenting constraints allows the client or management to remove them if possible.

The second reason to identify assumptions and constraints is to help

Exhibit 4.5. Sample List of Project Constraints

Resource Constraints

    Key staff resources will be available only on a part-time basis.

    Computer resources will be available on a limited basis.

    Key client resources will be available on a restricted basis.

Delivery Constraints

    Deliverables submitted for approval will require at least *n* working days for review.

    Equipment order lead times cannot be specified with accuracy.

Environmental Constraints

    The development environment is new, and no development staff are familiar with it.

    An overtime ban is in effect that restricts all work to normal working hours.

    Key decision makers are based out of town and are difficult to contact when issues arise.

    The project does not have a client project manager (or executive sponsor, or steering committee).

    Client internal processes (such as purchasing) are inefficient and unpredictable.

    The methodology [name it] is new and not familiar to the development team.

    The systems development environment is new, and the components have not yet been successfully integrated.

    The project depends upon the successful and timely completion of associated projects.

Budgetary Constraints

    Statistics used in preparing the estimates are unreliable.

    Travel and living expenses cannot be accurately estimated.

    Outside consulting requirements cannot be accurately estimated.

Functionality Constraints

    The scope of the project is unclear.

    The project depends upon receiving data from other, external applications.

    The project has relationships to other projects in progress and will depend on their status.

---

you when you need to negotiate with the client during the project. If you have explicitly assumed that deliverables would be reviewed in five days and none have come back in fewer than ten, you have a case for extending the schedule and increasing the costs, but if the assumption was unstated, you have no defense when your client says, "We never committed to a five-day turnaround."

By making your assumptions and constraints explicit, you allow them to be challenged, and you establish a more realistic basis on which the project will run.

What If?

Somebody Challenges Your Assumptions

Normally, you welcome a challenge to your assumptions. You need to find out as quickly as possible whether they are correct so that you can revise your plan appropriately. However, in some cases, you may not trust the challenge. For example, suppose the client says, "Of course we'll provide whatever user people you need. You don't need to state that as an assumption." However, your experience tells you that you will have trouble getting commitments from client staff because of their workloads. In such a case, if you drop the assumption, you will have no recourse when the project slips because client staff are unavailable.

Actions

Unless you are convinced that the assumption need not be stated, leave it in. You can do this by saying, "I'm sure there's no problem, but I like to document all the assumptions I made when I prepared the estimates." Then move on to another subject. If the client insists that the assumption be removed, do so, but revise your estimates as if it were not valid.

Somebody Challenges Your Constraints

As with assumptions, you want to hear these challenges, particularly those concerning constraints, because removing constraints will make your job easier. However, if you discover during the project that the constraint actually exists, your project will suffer.

Actions

Ask the client for a commitment that the constraint does not exist. For example, if you have stated the constraint that online access will be limited to normal working hours and the client says that you can have access twenty-four hours a day, you can ask the client to inform the system manager so that any account set-ups can be completed properly.

Turn the constraint into an assumption. In the example, your assumption would be that online access is available twenty-four hours per day. If the client does not object to the assumption, it is now part of your plan.

* * * * *

PLANNING FOR QUALITY

Here is a question: Which is of higher quality, an expensive luxury sedan or a cheap economy car? How does a finely tooled Swiss timepiece with a gold wristband compare with an all-plastic digital watch? If you chose the luxury sedan and the Swiss watch, you will have problems managing quality on your projects because you are confusing quality with grade.

Quality is an increasingly important part of project management. Some authorities claim that it is at least as important as the traditional three measures of project success—budget, schedule, and scope—but quality is one of the most misunderstood characteristics of a product because the commonplace usage of the word is vastly different from the professional use.

If you ask people what *quality* means, you will get a list of adjectives such as *excellent, first-class, expensive,* and *distinctive.* Accordingly, the luxury car and the Swiss watch clearly are of higher quality than the compact car and the digital watch. In the professional sense, however, *quality* means "conformance to specifications." If a product meets the requirements defined for it, it is a quality product. Otherwise, it is not. Therefore, a compact car that provides cheap, reliable transportation is a quality vehicle, and a luxury car that is always being serviced is not. As far as the watches are concerned, the one that keeps better time is of superior quality, regardless of its cost. It is true that the luxury car and the Swiss watch have a higher grade than their low-cost counterparts, but their quality depends solely on the degree to which each meets its requirements.

Conformance to specifications for information systems projects has two aspects: (1) the product arising from the project must conform to the requirements or specifications that were stated for it—normally handled by managing scope and customer expectations, (2) errors should be kept to a minimum. It is this second aspect that quality management is intended to address. Briefly stated:

The purpose of quality management in information systems projects is to minimize errors.

The most familiar computer systems errors are programming bugs, but there are many others. Exhibit 4.6 lists some of the more common errors that can occur, along with their cost consequences to the project. Costs incurred reflect either increased labor or additional expenses. In this exhibit, the cost consequences represent the additional effort beyond what would be expected if there were no errors. For example, one of the cost consequences of programming bugs is unit-test and debugging time. True, all programs require effort for unit testing, but the presence of programming bugs increases that effort.

Exhibit 4.6 illustrates one of the key principles of quality management: *Errors are expensive.* Not only do they incur the additional costs listed, the slippages they cause will delay the realization of benefits from the project.

Eliminating or minimizing these and other errors requires a quality plan. To help you build that plan, take note of some principles that have arisen from the quality movement that are also applicable to systems projects.

Quality Must Be Measurable

The management adage "You can't manage what you can't measure" is not quite true. For example, you can take steps to reduce programming bugs without having a measurement system in place. However, unless you can measure the number of bugs that occur after you intervene and compare that count to a baseline, you will never know the extent to which your efforts have worked. To tell you how successful you were, you need to know two things: the baseline error rate and the error rate after your intervention.

Exhibit 4.6. Common Sources of Error

Error	Cost Consequences
Programming bugs	• Unit test and debugging time • Debugging and rework during integration • Maintenance after release of the system
Data file format or layout errors	• Debugging and rework during integration
User documentation errors	• Assisting users • Rewriting documentation
Systems documentation errors	• Maintenance after release of the system • Support by maintenance programmers • Rewriting documentation
Errors in requirements specifications	• Identifying requirements errors during systems acceptance • Revising the system
Errors in report layouts, calculations, sequencing, or totaling	• Identifying requirements errors • Revising reports
Errors in online inquiry requests and responses	• Revising online request screens and responses
Errors in screening for security access and authorization	• Revising security and authorization facilities
Communications protocol conversion errors	• Resolving protocol problems • Purchase of additional communications software or hardware
Incompatibility among hardware components	• Resolving hardware integration problems • Purchase of additional hardware
Incompatibility among network components or between the network and the host computer	• Resolving network problems • Purchase of additional communications hardware
Incompatibility between the operating system and the infrastructure software	• Resolving software integration problems • Purchase of additional software
Incompatibility between the systems software infrastructure and the application	• Resolving software integration problems • Purchase of additional software • Revising the application
Inadequate response time under stress or high volume	• Purchase of equipment to upgrade computer or communications components • Analyzing operational requirements
Inadequate or improper systems capacity for the application	• Purchase of equipment to upgrade computer or communications components • Analyzing operational requirements

Exhibit 4.7 lists a set of cost consequences for different types of error. Each of these cost consequences, such as number of programming bugs, can be measured. However, in order to determine whether your quality efforts are successful, you need a baseline for each measurement. It is not enough to know that a system contained seventeen bugs; whether that is good or bad depends upon the size of the system and the severity of the bugs. While seventeen bugs in a small system may be unacceptable, the same number of bugs in a large complex system could be praiseworthy. Your measurement system, therefore, needs to include a baseline error rate. Exhibit 4.7 suggests measurements that could apply to each of the cost consequences listed in Exhibit 4.6. Your goal in managing quality is to reduce the value of each of these measurements.

The measurements in Exhibit 4.7 are expressed as averages that apply across projects within an organization. Ideally, each measure includes not only an average but also a high and a low score. A sound quality goal is to beat the low score and to lower the average. Obviously, if your organization does not record these statistics, you cannot compare your project with others. Nevertheless, you can still generate the measures from your project for future use, and you can still manage for quality. When you succeed, you may not be able to compare your measures to a baseline, but you can expect observers and participants to comment on how smoothly the project went and how few errors it generated.

Quality Is Planned In

The traditional approach to quality centers on inspection. In manufacturing, this means randomly sampling products after they are produced and establishing a reject rate. In computer systems, it means conducting some tests to catch the major bugs, then releasing the system to the users and waiting for the phone to ring. In effect, users serve as unpaid quality control inspectors.

A set of requirements is handed over to a team member, who produces and submits a deliverable. Any errors are identified after the deliverable is put to use. For example, an analyst might prepare programming specifications, which are then distributed to programmers, who, in turn, write programs based on them. Any errors in the specifications are not identified until integration testing—and frequently not until after implementation.

Exhibit 4.7. Measurements for Cost Consequences

Cost Consequence	Measurement
Unit test and debugging time	• Average debug time per simple, average, and complex program
Debugging and rework during integration	• Average number of revisions required per program • Average number of hours spent on integration as a percentage of development time
Maintenance after release of the system	• Average debugging maintenance hours during the first year as a percentage of development hours
Assisting users	• Average number of hours responding to user complaints per hundred function points or as a percentage of development hours
Rewriting documentation	• Average number of hours spent in rewriting as a percentage of original document preparation time
Maintenance time from faulty documentation	• Average number of hours spent by maintenance staff in resolving documentation errors
Identifying requirements errors during systems acceptance	• Average number of hours spent in identifying requirements errors as a percentage of original effort to define requirements
Revising the system	• Average number of hours spent in revisions arising from faulty requirements as a percentage of total development hours
Revising the reports or online screens	• Average number of hours spent in revising reports or screens as a percentage of development hours to produce them
Revising the security and authorization facilities	• Average number of hours spent in revising security and authorization procedures as a percentage of development hours
Purchase of additional software or hardware	• Average purchase cost of additional unplanned hardware or software as a percentage of total project hardware and software purchase costs
Resolving hardware, software, or network integration problems	• Average labor cost spent in resolving hardware or software integration problems as a percentage of hardware or software purchase costs
Analyzing operational requirements	• Average purchase cost to upgrade hardware or software components as a percentage of total project hardware and software purchase costs

The modern quality management approach centers on the idea that quality arises from adequate planning and from proper processes invoked while a product is being produced. Hence, quality is part of a team member's daily activities. To illustrate, the analyst in the previous example would be subject to quality controls on his or her work to ensure that the specifications were error-free before they were handed over to the programmer. One immediate result of this approach to quality is that team members adopt the mind-set that the quality of their deliverables is their own responsibility. The alternative attitude—that it is someone else's job to find and fix errors—cannot help but lead to degraded results.

The primary tools used in the modern type of quality management in information systems projects are *peer review* and *version control.*

Peer Review

Peer review, as the term implies, means that a team member's technical peers review the product before it is released. This review is normally carried out in a walkthrough, which is a technical meeting called for the sole purpose of reviewing a deliverable. The reviewers should be concerned with the following aspects of the deliverable:

1. Does it meet organizational standards for layout, composition, structure, and functionality? An example of the latter is ensuring that a computer program meets standards for error handling in case of a fatal program error.

2. Does it meet operational requirements in such areas as operator messages or security?

3. Does it conform to communications or network standards?

4. Does it meet functional requirements?

The last aspect is the most complex. It requires reviewers to understand the requirements and to translate them into the approach used by the team member. It also requires them to dig deeply into the deliverable to ensure that it is adequate.

Peer reviews should include people from the project as well as from affected departments, such as operations, security, network support, and quality assurance. This mix recognizes that the quality of the deliverable affects not only the project but the entire information systems community.

In preparing your project plan, you will need to make sure that you include time for peer reviews of all deliverables. These include systems design, program design, program code, implementation plans, test plans, architecture recommendations, functional specifications, capacity plans, and any other deliverable—including your project plan. You must also make clear to your team that no deliverable will be considered complete until it has been reviewed and the comments from the review incorporated into it.

A peer review produces its own deliverable. The walkthrough review worksheet, a sample of which is given in Exhibit 4.8, lists the participants in the review and itemizes the changes that the reviewers and the author agree to. It also gives the team member's estimate for the due date of each revision and an indicator that the change has been made.

Version Control

There are few things as frustrating for a committed team member as spending a sunny weekend working on a deliverable, only to find out on Monday that he or she has been working from an obsolete set of requirements. In any project where team members rely on deliverables that other team members produce, you will need to ensure that a mechanism exists that:

- Identifies different versions of deliverables
- Describes the differences between versions
- Allows any team member to find the current version

The management of versions and of changes to deliverables is the function of version control.

On a large project, version control is handled by a project librarian, who provides a set of procedures for updating versions and a facility for identifying the latest one. On smaller projects, you will have to design a means for keeping track of versions. One simple approach is to require that a copy of all deliverables be placed in a central file (paper or electronic) and that the file include, for each deliverable, a version control sheet (see Exhibit 4.9). One feature of the sample is that it contains an indication that the current

Exhibit 4.8. Walkthrough Review Worksheet

Walkthrough Review Worksheet	

Walkthrough Review Worksheet

Project: _____   Page _____ of _____

Deliverable: _____   Date: _____

Author: _____

Reviewers _____   _____

_____   _____

_____   _____

Actions   **Due Date**   **Done**

_____   _____   _____

_____   _____   _____

_____   _____   _____

_____   _____   _____

_____   _____   _____

_____   _____   _____

_____   _____   _____

_____   _____   _____

_____   _____   _____

_____   _____   _____

_____   _____   _____

_____   _____   _____

_____   _____   _____

Exhibit 4.9. Version Control Sheet

Version Control Sheet

Deliverable: _____ **Page** _____ **of** _____

Version	Date	Initials	Description of change
_____	_____	_____	_____
_____	_____	_____	_____
_____	_____	_____	_____
_____	_____	_____	_____
_____	_____	_____	_____
_____	_____	_____	_____
_____	_____	_____	_____
_____	_____	_____	_____
_____	_____	_____	_____
_____	_____	_____	_____
_____	_____	_____	_____
_____	_____	_____	_____
_____	_____	_____	_____
_____	_____	_____	_____

When you are modifying a deliverable, initial the next line and leave the date blank.
When you have finished your revisions, enter the version number, date, and a description.

version is being revised. This will allow anyone who needs the deliverable to consult with the author before taking any actions that depend on it. A word of caution: *Do not rely on version information embedded within the deliverable.* There is no way for team members to tell whether the version they are holding in their hands is the latest one unless version information exists apart from the deliverable itself.

Summary

Quality management is normally separated into quality assurance and quality control. The role of quality assurance (QA) is to ensure that procedures are in place that will lead to the development of a quality product. Quality control (QC) is the day-to-day management of those procedures throughout the project. Both are necessary to ensure that the project produces a quality product—one that conforms to its requirements and is error-free.

What If?

The Client Manages Quality by Testing Instead of Reviewing

Testing is a form of inspection. It looks for errors after the fact. If the client already has a quality control function with defined procedures in place and those procedures do not involve peer review, you will find it hard to manage the quality of your project.

Actions

Attempt to convince the client of the importance of peer reviews. In particular, focus on the reduced time, effort, and costs of rework when deliverables are properly reviewed.

If the client does not concur, increase the time in your plan for integration and testing activities.

During the project, encourage your team members to conduct informal reviews of one another's work. Keep track of major errors that were discovered during these reviews, estimate what their effect on the project would have been if they had not been detected, and, during project closeout, report to the client the savings that resulted from reviews. You are acting as a proselytizer for quality planning.

There Are No Baseline Measurements of Quality

If the client has no measurements of error rates, you cannot determine how successful you were at managing quality in terms of other client projects.

Actions

It is likely that if the client organization has no measurements at all, the quality of its projects is low, because a concern for quality necessitates measurement. Look for areas where the client has problems. Typically, these will be integration, systems testing, and acceptance.

When you prepare your work plan, allow for peer reviews and a minimum time for integration.

When the client objects that your integration schedule is too short, lengthen it to what the client deems to be acceptable.

At project closeout, point out to the client the benefits of your approach to quality. These should include reduced time for integration and systems testing, easier acceptance, and a general sense that there were fewer problems in the project.

Team Members Object to the Concept of Peer Reviews

If team members do not concur with peer reviews or oppose them outright, reviews will not be effective. You will lose the benefits of reviews, as well as any time team members spend in the pretense that they are conducting a review.

Actions

Determine the cause of the opposition. It will probably be based on either a concern for workloads or a fear that reviews are a stratagem for management intervention.

If the concern is workloads, show your team that your work plan includes time for reviews and that, without them, even though the level of effort during development would be lower, the effort for integration and re-work will be substantially higher.

If the concern is management intervention, make it clear to your team that nobody from management will attend reviews and that review results will not be used as input to employee performance evaluations.

Finally, point out that a reduced error rate will reflect favorably on the entire team. Insist that reviews be carried out and that you expect the full cooperation and involvement of the entire team.

* * * * *

DEFINING PROJECT ACTIVITIES

Planning is the act of determining what needs to be done when. The simplest plan is "We will have the project finished by August 31." Unfortunately, unless the project starts after August 15, such a "plan" is doomed because, until the completion date, there is no way to tell whether the project is on track.

The purpose of planning is to permit you to run the project—to take whatever actions are needed to ensure that it will complete on time and within budget. Planning has no other purpose or intrinsic value. Once the project is complete, the plan's job is done. Other than for project review or to guide future planning, it may be discarded.

To track progress, the project must be broken down into small, manageable activities. The piecemeal approach is simply to begin listing activities and hope that the ones you miss don't sink you. There is an alternative, a systematic approach known as *hierarchical decomposition*.

Decomposition is the process of breaking down an activity into smaller chunks. *Hierarchical* means that the decomposition proceeds top-down by defining the major components of the project, then breaking each component into smaller pieces. The process continues through successively lower levels until the activities are "small enough." With some practice, this top-down approach ensures that all activities will be identified. The result is the work breakdown structure (WBS).

The Work Breakdown Structure (WBS)

A WBS is a list of all project activities, arranged hierarchically in levels. It also includes costs, such as equipment purchases, travel, materials, or training course fees. Hence, the lowest level of the WBS consists of activities and costs. The activities are used to prepare estimates, assign resources, and track progress. They also include charges for the team members, which, with the costs, constitute the project budget. Exhibit 4.10 gives a WBS for a typical project that involves development and some hardware and software acquisition.

Numbering a Work Breakdown Structure

Since a WBS is hierarchical, its elements can be numbered in levels, as illustrated in Exhibit 4.10. For example, number 10.20.15 is an element at the third level.

One of the major uses for WBS numbers is time reporting. Team members will complete time sheets, charging their time to specific activities identified by WBS number. The number will also be used to identify activities in the schedule, as well as costs in the budget. Once the project has started to gather statistics by activity, the activities cannot easily be renumbered, so it is wise to use a number scheme that allows new activities or costs to be inserted.

Do not number the WBS until it is relatively stable and will not need to be renumbered. That is, number it when corporate management and senior technical staff have reviewed it and you are satisfied that there will be few changes. Otherwise, you will have to undergo the frustration of manually renumbering the activities and ensuring that they are consistent wherever they have been used.

Components of a Work Breakdown Structure

At the lowest level, a WBS consists of three types of components: work activities, distributed activities, and costs.

Work activities are those that contribute to a clearly defined deliverable,

Exhibit 4.10. Sample Work Breakdown Structure

1.0	**Management and support**
1.5	Project management
1.10	Configuration management
1.15	Quality control
1.20	Scope control
1.25	Internal walkthroughs and reviews
1.30	Secretarial and clerical support
1.35	Materials and supplies
1.40	Project reviews and status meetings
1.45	Travel and living costs
1.50	Miscellaneous costs
1.55	Contingency
5.0	**Hardware selection and acquisition**
5.5	Hardware selection
5.5.5	Define requirements
5.5.10	Identify qualified vendors
5.5.15	Prepare and issue request for quotation
5.5.20	Evaluation
5.5.20.5	Evaluate written quotations
5.5.20.10	Conduct demos and presentations
5.5.20.15	Check references
5.5.20.20	Negotiate terms and prices
5.5.25	Make final hardware selection
5.10	Hardware acquisition
5.10.5	Purchase and expedite delivery
5.10.10	Install hardware and system software
5.10.15	Conduct acceptance tests
5.10.20	Train the project team
5.10.25	Conduct ongoing maintenance and support
10.0	**Systems development**
10.5	Requirements specifications
10.5.5	Conduct information-gathering sessions
10.5.10	Prepare logical data model
10.5.15	Prepare logical process model
10.10	Physical design
10.10.5	Prepare physical data model
10.10.10	Prepare physical process model
10.15	Subsystem 1
10.15.5	Prepare detailed design
10.15.10	Program and unit test

10.15.15	Document
10.20	Subsystem 2
10.20.5	Prepare detailed design
10.20.10	File management subsystem
10.20.10.5	Code and unit test
10.20.10.10	Document
10.20.15	Inquiry and reporting subsystem
10.20.15.5	Code and unit test
10.20.15.10	Document
15.0	**Integration**
15.5	Conduct system integration
15.10	Conduct system test
15.15	Prepare user documentation
20.0	**Client**
20.5	Conduct milestone reviews
20.10	Review and approve deliverables
20.15	Conduct user training
20.20	Acceptance testing
20.20.5	Prepare user acceptance tests
20.20.10	Conduct user acceptance tests
20.20.15	Prepare revisions from acceptance tests
20.25	Hand over to client
25.0	**Implementation**
25.5	Plan for implementation
25.10	Provide support for implementation
25.15	Conduct post-implementation review

such as a report, a specification, or program code. An activity that does not actually produce a deliverable is still a work activity if its output will be used by other activities that do produce deliverables.

Distributed activities are those that do not directly produce deliverables but are required of project team members throughout the project. Examples are project team meetings and internal walkthroughs and reviews. They are called "distributed" because effort spent on them is distributed over the entire project.

A special type of distributed activity is overhead, such as project management, quality control, or support services. This is normally associated with a small group of people, such as the project manager or quality control manager.

Cost components are costs that are not directly incurred by work activities. Examples are materials, hardware or software purchasing costs, and travel and living expenses. Staff costs for doing the work are associated directly with the activities that incur them. Hence, the purchase of a testing tool for $10,000 is a cost component, whereas the effort to evaluate testing tools is a work activity. If that work activity requires forty hours by one $50-per-hour analyst, it will cost the project $2,000, which is separate from the $10,000 purchase price.

Some work may be treated as either a work activity or a distributed activity. For example, since a code walkthrough contributes to the code deliverable, it may be treated as a work activity. On the other hand, it is easier to treat walkthroughs as a distributed activity than to plan individual walkthroughs for each deliverable. Whether walkthroughs are treated as work activities or as a single distributed activity will depend upon your preferences, the methodology, and the client. However, where you have a choice, keep things simple. Use a distributed activity for walkthroughs and reviews.

Preparing a Work Breakdown Structure

The first step in preparing a project WBS is to identify the major sets of activities. Consider a typical systems development project that also requires selection of hardware or software. Exhibit 4.11 gives one possible list of major activities.

These major activities correspond to the highest-level activities on the WBS given in Exhibit 4.10.

Once the major activities have been defined, break each one down further. For example, activities to select and acquire hardware or software can

Exhibit 4.11. Typical Major Activity Groups

- Activities that provide management, coordination, and control
- Activities to select and acquire hardware or software
- Activities to build and unit test the system
- Activities to integrate and systems test the system
- Activities that involve the users
- Activities to implement the system

---

be broken down into selection activities and acquisition activities, and each of these can be further broken down into lower-level activities or costs.

Activity Independence

To the extent possible, activities should be independent of one another. That is, each activity should be done with as little knowledge of the other activities as possible. For example, common areas between programs should be designed separately from the program, rather than as part of them. Designing them separately means that programmers can work independently without the need to constantly consult others. If any programmer needs changes to the common area, the requirement will be given to the person responsible for maintaining that area. That person will make the changes and inform any other programmers who are affected.

Designing activities to be independent has three main advantages:

1. **Staff can be more readily transferred among activities.** If some people finish their activities in advance while others fall behind, those who finish first can be reassigned to more critical activities.

2. **It is more feasible to add staff if the schedule slips.** If activities are independent and can be done with a minimum of knowledge about other activities, it is easier to add new staff than if activities are tightly interwoven.

3. **The need for communication across activities is reduced.** That results in less confusion, fewer opportunities for misunderstandings, and a smoother project.

When Activities Are Small Enough

One problem with any decomposition is knowing when to stop. Obviously, activities can be broken into levels of detail so fine that each hour of each team member's day for the duration of the project is planned. Just as obviously, such a plan will be obsolete by the end of the first day.

However, if knowing when to stop is difficult, setting criteria for stopping is even trickier. For example:

- Some authorities have suggested that activities should not exceed some given duration, such as two weeks, and that all longer activities should be further decomposed. But if a single activity, such as coding a complex program, will take one person five weeks, there is no merit in arbitrarily cutting it into smaller chunks.

- Some have suggested that an activity should produce a deliverable and that once all deliverables are covered, the decomposition is complete. But this criterion raises the question of what a deliverable is. Those that are contractual requirements may be too extensive—for example, "program code to execute the inventory system"—to be easily managed. Good project managers break such deliverables into smaller internal products, thus shifting the question of when to stop decomposing activities to one of when to stop decomposing deliverables.

- Some have proposed that an activity should be conducted by one person only and that activities requiring more than one person should be further decomposed. But activities such as integration or systems testing typically require the participation of several team members, and the plan must reflect those requirements.

These difficulties illustrate the fact that planning is a process that requires judgment; there are no fixed rules. In deciding whether to further decompose an activity, your sole consideration must be whether the activity is large, complex, or unwieldy enough to require further breakdown. In other words, an activity is "small enough" when you are satisfied that it is manageable.

However, some may argue, there are activities that consist of a series of smaller steps. For example, installing a new computer requires loading the operating system, communication software, performance monitors, security software, compilers, database engines, and other components. Should you not list each one to be sure that nothing gets missed? Yes, you should, but not as separate activities; if you list them separately, your WBS will become unmanageable and it will be impossible to record time accurately against such minuscule pieces of work. The best way to handle these tasks is to use the notes facility of your project management software. This allows you to attach free-form notes to any activity on the plan. To handle tasks associated with installing a new computer, create an activity called "Install software components." Then, in the notes section for the activity, list each of the components. In this way, when you are tracking progress, you can review the list to make sure everything was done, but the actual number of activities against which your people will record their time will be vastly reduced.

Decomposition is subjective. Not only will it depend on the project manager, but the same project manager will decompose differently depending on the experience of members of the project team and their track record of timely delivery.

Occasionally, your judgment may be overridden by methodology or standards. In such cases, the methodology imposes additional work on the project. You must factor it into the schedule and budget.

Project Phases

Frequently, you cannot complete a WBS because you do not know how the bulk of the project will be carried out. For example, if the project includes a build-versus-buy analysis, you cannot describe the implementation activities because you do not know whether you will be developing a new system or implementing a package. Or, you cannot plan construction activities because you do not yet understand the complexities of the project. In such cases, you do not know how you will handle the project, and all you can say is, "We need to do some analysis before we will know how to proceed. That analysis will be complete by. . . ." In other words, you separate the project into phases.

The first phase is usually analysis, in which you assess build versus buy, develop requirements, define scope, or conduct any activities that will allow you to identify clearly your approach and activities for the main project. In such cases, you can build a detailed WBS for the analysis phase and a skeleton for the rest of the project. One of the deliverables from the analysis will be a detailed project plan.

Documenting the Activities

Once the WBS is complete, describe the activities. Exhibit 4.12 gives a sample description.

Exhibit 4.12. Sample Activity Description

Activity Description

Project: Project name   Page 1 of 1

Activity: 5.5.20.5 Evaluate Written Proposals

Description: Evaluate written proposals received from vendors in response to the RFP.

Inputs: • Requirements definition (5.5.5)
                    • Request for proposal (5.5.15)
                    • Written proposals from vendors

Effort: • Review vendor proposals
                    • Reject proposals that do not meet mandatory requirements
                    • Weight proposals for degree of compliance to optional requirements
                    • Prepare recommendations for short list

Resources: • Project manager (20%)
                    • Hardware analyst (80%)

Outputs: • Evaluation results consisting of:
                        Short list of qualified vendors
                        or
                        Rejection of all proposals
                    • Letters to vendors informing them of evaluation results

---

The activity description gives an overview of the activity for those who will be carrying it out. However, its most important function is to help you ensure that no activities have been missed. It does this by requiring that you document the inputs and outputs for each activity.

All activities have inputs, which are usually documents, forms, standards, or code. All inputs must be either external to the project or provided by an activity within it. Similarly, all activities have outputs, usually documents or code. All outputs must be project deliverables or inputs to other activities.

Hence, documenting the activities with their inputs and outputs allows you to determine that all inputs are accounted for, either by external sources or by other project activities, and that all outputs have a destination, either as project deliverables or as inputs to other activities.

Once you have established the source for all inputs and the destination for all outputs and you have determined that no activity has a mystery input or a hanging output, you can be confident that you have not missed any activities.

What If?

One of Your Analysts Provides You with an Activity Breakdown That Is Too Fine

Novice estimators and project managers confuse quantity of activities with quality of planning. It is not uncommon to see activities with durations measured in hours. Such a plan cannot be followed because the actual sequence of activities will vary once the project starts, and technical staff will typically group small activities into a larger package. When you review status, you will hear reports such as, "We haven't done the bandwidth analysis yet because it makes more sense to include it as part of the network design which we'll start next week." Your problem is that, although the report makes sense, you now have a late activity (bandwidth analysis). Even worse, given a number of these, you can never tell with any confidence if the project schedule is at risk.

Actions

Redo the WBS, creating larger work activities.

Thank the analyst for the level of detail, and make sure that you include it as a note on the larger activity. For example, if you created an activity called "network design," attach a note to it that includes "bandwidth analysis." In that way, when you are reviewing progress on network design, you can verify that the bandwidth analysis was completed.

You Receive Conflicting Information on the Steps to Complete a Major Activity

When you are not sure about how to complete a major activity, you will need to rely on technical advice, but if two or more members of the technical staff give you conflicting advice, you will not be able to develop a WBS that is accurate. The result is that you may build a plan that will not reflect how the project will actually be carried out.

Actions

Bring the technical people together, and ask them to develop a plan for completing the major activity. Outline your understanding of their different approaches, and tell them that you need an agreement.

If they fail to reach agreement, seek the advice of a third party to help you decide which approach to use.

Assess the arguments of your technical staff, pick the approach that makes the most sense and that best fits your experience, and impose that approach on the project.

* * * * *

ESTABLISHING DEPENDENCIES

You can't put on the roof until the walls are built. In other words, putting on the roof depends upon having built the walls. Planning requires more than a list of activities, it means knowing the order in which the activities must be carried out. That order is dictated by the dependencies.

A dependency is a relationship between two activities in which one activity cannot start or end until the other has started or ended. Dependencies exist only between work activities; they do not apply to distributed or overhead activities or to cost components.

A dependency applies to just two activities; there are no three-way or four-way dependencies. However, any given activity may participate in more than one dependency. Where one activity is dependent upon another, the dependent activity is called the *successor* and the activity upon which the successor depends is called the *predecessor*. That is, the successor depends upon—or more properly, has a dependency on—the predecessor.

Note that "successor" and "predecessor" describe a dependency relationship, not an order in which activities are carried out. While a successor usually follows its predecessor, they are frequently concurrent, and the successor may actually come first. Do not describe dependencies ambiguously. The statement "There is a dependency between design and coding" does not indicate whether design is dependent upon coding or vice versa. Clear statements of dependency are "Coding is dependent upon design," or "Coding has a dependency upon design." In both these cases, design is the predecessor and coding is the successor.

There are four types of dependency between activities: finish-start, finish-finish, start-start, and start-finish. However, we will ignore start-finish dependencies, which are rare; most project managers use only the first three types. There are also two time components: lag and lead.

Finish-Start Dependencies

Finish-start (F-S) dependencies are the most common. The predecessor must finish before the successor can start. With F-S dependencies, the successor always follows the predecessor (unless there is a lead time, as described later).

As an example, detailed design (the predecessor) must finish before program coding (the successor) can start. Hence, program coding has a finish-start dependency upon detailed design.

Finish-Finish Dependencies

With a finish-finish (F-F) dependency, the predecessor must finish before the successor finishes. With F-F dependencies, the predecessor need not precede the successor, but it must finish first.

As an example, systems documentation (the successor) must reflect program coding (the predecessor); hence, although it can start any time that coding is in progress, it cannot finish until coding finishes. Hence, systems documentation has a finish-finish dependency on program coding.

Start-Start Dependencies

In a start-start (S-S) dependency, the predecessor must start before the successor can start. With S-S dependencies, the successor and predecessor usually overlap.

An example is information gathering and the preparation of the data model. The information gathering (the predecessor) must start before data modeling (the successor) can start. Hence, data modeling has a start-start dependency upon information gathering.

Exhibit 4.13 illustrates the three types of dependency and the relationships between predecessors and successors. The arrow entitled "permissible" indicates when, in relation to the predecessor, the successor may be carried out. For example, the permissible arrow for a finish-start relationship indicates that the successor can start ("S") any time after the predecessor finishes, but not before.

Lag and Lead Times

Not all dependencies are immediate; you may have finished pouring the foundation, but you can't start building the walls until the concrete has set. A lag time is the duration between the start or finish of a predecessor and the start or finish of the successor. Conversely, a lead time is an overlap between dependencies.

Lag and lead times are not optional slippages, they are demanded by the nature of the activities. For example, installation of equipment has a finish-start dependency upon the issue of a purchase order, but installation

Exhibit 4.13. *Types of Activity Dependency*

Finish-Start	Predecessor	S--------F
	Successor	S--------F
	Permissible	S-->
Finish-Finish	Predecessor	S--------F
	Successor	S-----F
	Permissible	F-->
Start-Start	Predecessor	S--------F
	Successor	S------F
	Permissible	S-->

(the successor) cannot start until the equipment is actually delivered. Delivery lags the issuing of the purchase order (the predecessor) by the time that the vendor needs to receive the purchase order, process it, and physically deliver the equipment. Thus, installation has a finish-start lag dependency on the issue of the purchase order.

An example of a lead time is program coding, which is finish-start dependent upon completion of programming standards. You may decide to prepare a draft set of standards, then begin coding before the standards have been approved. If the final approvals and revisions will take two weeks, you will be able to overlap coding and standards by that amount, giving coding (the successor) a finish-start lead dependency on programming standards (the predecessor).

Lead and lag times, combined with the four types of dependency, become complex, and some will probably never occur. Exhibit 4.14 is a summary of the dependency types and time components. The table assumes that lag and lead times are stated as n days.

Defining Dependencies

To define dependencies, examine the work activities, and, for each one, ask the following questions:

1. What work activities must finish before this one can start?
2. What work activities must finish before this one can finish?
3. What work activities must start before this one can start?
4. What work activities must start before this one can finish?
5. For each dependency, what lag or lead times do the activities impose?

Exhibit 4.14. *Dependency Lag and Lead Times*

Type	Lag Time	Lead Time
F-S	Successor cannot start for n days after predecessor finishes.	Successor can start up to n days before predecessor finishes.
F-F	Successor cannot finish for n days after predecessor finishes.	Successor can finish up to n days before predecessor finishes.
S-S	Successor cannot start for n days after predecessor starts.	Successor can start up to n days before predecessor starts.

One important principle is that dependencies are based on activities, not resources. For example, coding is dependent upon design because coding cannot start until design is complete, not because the same person will do both. When you are defining dependencies, *assume that you have unlimited resources*. You will get to play with people availability later.

Dependencies complicate project plans. Indeed, one time-honored way of compressing a schedule is to remove some dependencies, increasing the overlap among activities. As a general rule, ensure that dependencies are real: that is, activity B absolutely cannot start until activity A is finished. If B "should not" start until A is finished, or if it is a "good idea" to finish A before starting B, there is no dependency. A dependency may be physical (development cannot start until workstations are installed) or methodological (coding cannot start until design has been approved), but it must always be unyielding—at least at the time of planning.

Frequently, activities are dependent but there is an intervening dependency. For example, consider a project with the following dependencies:

- Systems integration is dependent upon completion of program development and unit testing.
- Programming is dependent upon installation of hardware.
- Systems integration is dependent upon installation of hardware.

In this case, do not create a dependency between hardware installation and systems integration: the dependency already exists via a path through programming. In your plan, create dependencies only when there are no intervening activities; otherwise your plan will become unwieldy and cumbersome, particularly when you need to make changes.

On the other hand, consider the following example:

- Systems testing is dependent upon hardware installation.
- There are no intervening activities.
- Hardware installation is scheduled to complete three months before systems testing will start.

In this example, the tendency is not to enter the dependency because it is irrelevant: The predecessor will finish long before the successor starts. However, this is a mistake. If you do not enter the dependency and hardware installation slips by four months, you risk that you will not notice the impact on your project until it is too late. By entering the dependencies, you will always be aware of the results of any significant changes in the schedule.

Precedence Diagramming

A precedence diagram is a picture of the dependency relationships. Some project managers feel that precedence diagrams are an essential planning tool, while others regard them as a waste of time. As a visual presentation of the dependencies, they are useful in conducting reviews or identifying erroneous or invalid dependencies, and they certainly make impressive wall displays of project complexity.

Volumes have been written about types of precedence diagramming. Career positions have been staked out on the basis of such esoterica as whether the activity should be on an arrow or a node. Fortunately, the advent of project management software, which imposes a particular type of precedence diagram, has made such debates irrelevant, and precedence diagrams, in whatever format the software allows, can now be created with a few keystrokes.

What If?

Your Dependencies Are Challenged

Dependencies are the core of the schedule. Without them, everything could be done at once, and no project would be longer than the longest activity. If your dependencies are not correct, your schedule will be inaccurate. If there are too many dependencies, the schedule will be longer than necessary. If there are too few, the schedule will be impossible to meet.

Actions

Review the challenge, and, if it makes sense, alter your dependencies accordingly. Otherwise, leave the schedule as is.

If the dependency that is being challenged is methodological, ask the challenger to commit to relieving the dependency. For example, if you are told, "We don't need to wait for approval of the design before we start coding," and the methodology says that you do, ask the challenger for a commitment allowing a deviation from the methodology for this project. If you do not receive one, stick with your original plan.

＊　＊　＊　＊

ESTIMATING THE PROJECT

When you are preparing an estimate, understand this: *The estimate is not the budget*. The estimate tells management, including you, how much *effort* will be needed to complete the project. The budget tells you how much the project will *cost*. Estimates deal with effort expressed in periods such as workdays. Budgets deal in dollars.

Do an estimate bottom-up. That is, estimate effort at the lowest level of the WBS, making sure to include both work and distributed activities. You do not need to estimate higher level activities; their effort is simply the sum of the efforts of their lower level activities.

An estimate of effort has three components:

1. The job classification of the person or people needed to do the work
2. The percentage of time required for each job classification
3. The total work effort, in hours or days, required by the activity

A complete estimate, therefore, tells management how much time the project will need from each type of resource.

Estimating is not concerned with the allocation or availability of staff. These are handled as part of resource leveling.

Resource Classifications

Activities are carried out by individuals, but planning usually starts with classifications such as technology architect, systems analyst, or programmer analyst. To complete an estimate, you need to know what types of skills each activity needs and what staff classifications have those skills. You will ultimately have to put names to each activity, but, for now, you are concerned with letting your management know how many of which type of staff you need.

Distributed activities sometimes involve one person (project management) or a number of people—up to and including the entire project team (reviews).

Percent Commitment

Some people will be required full-time on an activity, while others will be needed less. Usually, more junior staff are full-time on activities such as program coding, while senior staff are split among several different activities, part-time on each.

Percent commitment is not the same as percent availability. The former refers to the requirements of the activity; the latter refers to the availability of the person to your project. An example of an activity that does not need 100 percent commitment is network support. This activity may only require 10 percent of a network analyst's time.

Period vs. Effort

The work required of an activity may be estimated either as a *period* or as an *effort* and is expressed as a *duration*.

- If you estimate an activity as a *period*, you are estimating an elapsed time such as four weeks. A four-week activity will take four weeks, regardless of the number of people assigned to it.

- If you estimate an activity as an *effort*, you are estimating a work period such as four workweeks. A four-workweek activity will take one person four weeks, two people two weeks, or one person half-time eight weeks.

- The *duration* is the actual length of time the activity will take, regardless of how it is estimated. If you have estimated activities as periods, the duration equals the period. If you have estimated as effort, it equals the effort divided by the number of people times the percent commitment.

The type of estimate affects the schedule. If you estimate activities as periods, then adding or removing people will not change the duration; a three-week activity always takes three weeks. If you estimate as effort, the schedule will be affected whenever people are added to or removed from activities. The duration of a six-workweek activity will be halved if the resources are doubled. (These calculations are strictly arithmetic. They do not allow for reductions in efficiency when staff are added.)

Principles for Estimating

Your estimates will improve if you respect these principles:

- Base the estimates on the performance of average staff. Do not assume that the superstars will be available. (If they are, make it clear that they are expected to outperform the estimate.)
- Ignore any external schedule constraints. That means part-time availability or project deadlines. These will be factored in later but must not affect the estimate.
- Ensure that all estimates are completed by those who will—or are qualified to—do the work. In the first place, the estimates will be more accurate. In the second place, doing the estimate implies a commitment. It is reasonable to say to a team member, "You said this would take three weeks, so three weeks is what you've got."
- Have the estimates reviewed by knowledgeable people. In particular, ask them to watch for overestimates by staff who have decided to build in massive safety factors.

Exhibit 4.15 is an estimate for the sample project stated in workdays.

Sticker Shock

The first time you complete an estimate for your project, you may feel as if you have been multiplying durations rather than adding them; the total

Exhibit 4.15. Estimate for a Sample Project Stated in Workdays

ID	Task Name										Duration	Start	Finish
3	Define requirements										5 days	28 Jan	03 Feb
	ID	Resource Name	Units	Work	Delay	Start	Finish	Ovt. Work	Baseline Work	Act. Work	Rem. Work		
	1	Tech. Architect	100%	40 hrs	0 days	28 Jan	03 Feb	0 hrs	0 hrs	0 hrs	40 hrs		
4	Identify qualified vendors										2 days	04 Feb	05 Feb
	ID	Resource Name	Units	Work	Delay	Start	Finish	Ovt. Work	Baseline Work	Act. Work	Rem. Work		
	1	Tech. Architect	50%	8 hrs	0 days	04 Feb	05 Feb	0 hrs	0 hrs	0 hrs	8 hrs		
5	Prepare and Issue RFQ										5 days	06 Feb	12 Feb
	ID	Resource Name	Units	Work	Delay	Start	Finish	Ovt. Work	Baseline Work	Act. Work	Rem. Work		
	1	Tech. Architect	100%	40 hrs	0 days	06 Feb	12 Feb	0 hrs	0 hrs	0 hrs	40 hrs		
6	RFQ issued										0 days	12 Feb	12 Feb
8	Evaluate written quotations										5 days	12 Mar	18 Mar
	ID	Resource Name	Units	Work	Delay	Start	Finish	Ovt. Work	Baseline Work	Act. Work	Rem. Work		
	1	Tech. Architect	100%	40 hrs	0 days	12 Mar	18 Mar	0 hrs	0 hrs	0 hrs	40 hrs		
9	Conduct demos and presentations										10 days	19 Mar	01 Apr
	ID	Resource Name	Units	Work	Delay	Start	Finish	Ovt. Work	Baseline Work	Act. Work	Rem. Work		
	1	Tech. Architect	100%	80 hrs	0 days	19 Mar	01 Apr	0 hrs	0 hrs	0 hrs	80 hrs		
10	Check references										2 days	02 Apr	05 Apr
	ID	Resource Name	Units	Work	Delay	Start	Finish	Ovt. Work	Baseline Work	Act. Work	Rem. Work		
	1	Tech. Architect	50%	8 hrs	0 days	02 Apr	05 Apr	0 hrs	0 hrs	0 hrs	8 hrs		
11	Negotiate terms and prices										2 days	06 Apr	07 Apr
	ID	Resource Name	Units	Work	Delay	Start	Finish	Ovt. Work	Baseline Work	Act. Work	Rem. Work		
	1	Tech. Architect	100%	16 hrs	0 days	06 Apr	07 Apr	0 hrs	0 hrs	0 hrs	16 hrs		
12	Make final hardware selection										1 day	08 Apr	08 Apr
	ID	Resource Name	Units	Work	Delay	Start	Finish	Ovt. Work	Baseline Work	Act. Work	Rem. Work		
	1	Tech. Architect	100%	8 hrs	0 days	08 Apr	08 Apr	0 hrs	0 hrs	0 hrs	8 hrs		
13	Hardware selected										0 days	08 Apr	08 Apr
15	Purchase and expedite delivery										1 day	09 Apr	09 Apr
	ID	Resource Name	Units	Work	Delay	Start	Finish	Ovt. Work	Baseline Work	Act. Work	Rem. Work		
	1	Tech. Architect	100%	8 hrs	0 days	09 Apr	09 Apr	0 hrs	0 hrs	0 hrs	8 hrs		
16	Install hardware and system software										3 days	10 May	12 May
	ID	Resource Name	Units	Work	Delay	Start	Finish	Ovt. Work	Baseline Work	Act. Work	Rem. Work		
	1	Tech. Architect	100%	24 hrs	0 days	10 May	12 May	0 hrs	0 hrs	0 hrs	24 hrs		
17	Conduct acceptance tests										1 day	13 May	13 May
	ID	Resource Name	Units	Work	Delay	Start	Finish	Ovt. Work	Baseline Work	Act. Work	Rem. Work		
	1	Tech. Architect	100%	8 hrs	0 days	13 May	13 May	0 hrs	0 hrs	0 hrs	8 hrs		
18	Train the project team										2 days	14 May	17 May
	ID	Resource Name	Units	Work	Delay	Start	Finish	Ovt. Work	Baseline Work	Act. Work	Rem. Work		
	1	Tech. Architect	100%	16 hrs	0 days	14 May	17 May	0 hrs	0 hrs	0 hrs	16 hrs		
19	System ready for development										0 days	17 May	17 May
20	Conduct ongoing maintenance										1 day	18 May	18 May
	ID	Resource Name	Units	Work	Delay	Start	Finish	Ovt. Work	Baseline Work	Act. Work	Rem. Work		
	1	Tech. Architect	100%	8 hrs	0 days	18 May	18 May	0 hrs	0 hrs	0 hrs	8 hrs		

effort will seem ridiculously high. In an attempt to get the estimates down to a reasonable level, many estimators return to the WBS and begin to estimate activities at higher levels. For example, if the activities to complete a software evaluation add up to two work-months, there is a temptation to look at the entire set of evaluation activities and say, "This can't be any more than one month" and to discard the original estimate. That way lies trouble.

If your estimates are greater than you expected, you can use higher-level activities as a kind of sanity check, but any estimates you change must be at the lowest level and the changes for each activity must be reasonable. If, after you review your low-level estimates, they do not change much, then your higher-level gut feeling is probably wrong. While the sum of lower-level estimates is generally greater than an estimate taken at a higher level, lower-level estimates also tend to be more accurate. (The exception to this occurs when there are a large number of small activities in the WBS. Because of rounding, this tends to increase the overall estimates. Therefore, be sure that the activities at the lowest levels of your WBS are reasonable in terms of effort.)

Contingency

A contingency is an allowance for problems. It is better to state it overtly as an activity on the WBS than to covertly bury it in each work activity. If it is overt, you can make explicit decisions to use some of it and to direct it to problem areas. If it is hidden, not only can it not be formally used, but the estimates for individual work activities are overstated by the amount of the contingency. The inevitable consequence is that the work will expand to occupy the inflated time period, the contingency will be used up, the project will take longer than it should, and, when problems arise, there will be no contingency left to deal with them.

Why, then, is contingency ever buried? The reason is that management tends to regard it as potential profit rather than as a legitimate project cost and becomes annoyed when project managers try to use it. Project managers who have been burned when they try to apply contingency will bury it and attempt to track it covertly—which never works.

It is commonplace to estimate contingency as a percentage of the project estimate—"Let's add 10 percent of the workdays as a contingency"—but the contingency varies with different project activities and should be estimated at the topmost level of the WBS. For example, the contingency for management and support might be 5 percent, while that for integration may be 20 percent. The project contingency is the total for each section of the WBS. (However, contingency may be applied anywhere on the project. It is not reserved for activities in the same proportions as it was calculated.)

Danger Areas in Estimating

It is a cliché, supported by endless project overruns, that information systems people are poor estimators. Yet the reality is not so simple. In fact, most people are fairly accurate at estimating activities they have done before. Estimates for coding, documentation, training, and even analysis tend to be close to actual numbers. Where estimates fall apart is on activities that are new or those that vary substantially from project to project.

There are several danger areas in estimating:

- **Integration**. Integration of code can be as simple as an act of assembling tested pieces that fit together nicely or as complex as completely redeveloping code that appears to have been written in isolation from the rest of the project. Unfortunately, most estimates assume that integration will be closer to assembly than to redevelopment.

  The keys to a smooth integration are adequate, detailed work during the definition and design phases and a mechanism to ensure that whenever anyone decides, for example, to add just one more element to the data dictionary, details of the change are distributed to the project team. If the project does not have these features, either add them or quadruple the integration estimate.

- **New Technology**. If the project uses a new technology such as a language, operating system, database, or tool kit, ensure that the estimate includes ample time for familiarization. A new technology is one which no member of the project team has ever used, either by itself *or in combination with other project technologies.*

  A technology is new even if it has a different brand name. It is tempting, for example, to assume that, since Fred has worked with a relational database and the project uses one, no new technology is involved, even though the project's database is different from the one Fred used. Wrong. While Fred may adapt to the new database faster than someone who has no experience, he will still need time to learn the subtle differences.

  There are two problems with a new technology: use and integration. Use is the ease with which the project team learns and masters the technology. It is measured by the time spent in rework and is mitigated by ample training at the start of the project. Integration is the problem of making a new technology work with other technical components of the project. It is all too common to hear statements such as, "We've discovered that version 1.2 of the operating system, which we're using, does not support version 4.0 of the communications manager. It does support version 3.2, but that version does not have the asynch protocol support, which we can do without if we switch to version. . . ." The problem increases exponentially with the number of new components. When integrating new technologies, find or buy expertise. It is cheaper to fly an expert in from across the country for a week than to tie up an entire project team for a month or more trying to figure out how to get one component to talk to another.

- **External Dependencies**. Externally, the project will depend on the performance of the client and suppliers. The problem is that you have no direct control over either one. See the sections "Managing Subcontractors" and "Managing Client Expectations," in chapter 5, for some techniques for influencing external groups.

    Of the external activities, the most critical are those that are repetitive, such as client review and approval of deliverables. If you underestimate delivery from a supplier by a week, the most the project will suffer is one week's delay, but if you underestimate the review and approval cycle by just one day, twenty deliverables will cost you a month.

    It is therefore critical to get estimates of repetitive activities right. Naturally, client input is important, but, if possible, find out from people who worked on other projects for the client what the bottlenecks and delays were. Then make sure the estimates reflect that history.

- **Methodologies**. A new methodology is a danger, as is a decision to apply an existing one more stringently than before. The problem is that a methodology dictates a set of deliverables and, without experience, it is difficult to estimate the work needed for each one.

    If you are faced with a new methodology, make sure you know what deliverables it demands and that you understand their scope. If possible, meet with someone who has worked with the methodology, get examples of deliverables, and ensure that you and the client expect the same level of detail.

Confidence Ranges

When you first prepare an estimate, how accurate do you expect it to be? Do you believe, when you complete an estimate of 1,250 workdays, that the project will take precisely (or even closely) that amount of effort? If so, give yourself two stars: a gold one for confidence and a lead one for discernment. The fact is that the further you are from the actual work, the less accurate your estimates will be. During the initiation stage, when the project is first being planned, your estimates could be out by as much as 100 percent. When you complete the requirements stage, they could be out by 50 percent, and when you have finished design, the margin of error might drop to 10 percent. Therefore, whenever you prepare an estimate, be aware of the gap between now and the time that the activities you are estimating will be carried out, and hedge your estimate with a confidence range.

A confidence range is a range of estimates within which you feel comfortable that the project will complete. For example, during the initiation stage, when there are still a lot of uncertainties, you should not feel comfortable stating that the project will take 1,250 workdays of effort. Typically, the estimates of a project in initiation could be out by as much as 100 percent, meaning that the actual range could vary from zero to 2,500 workdays. Clearly, the zero end of the range is silly, but the project might complete in as few as 1,000 workdays with some luck. You could therefore express the estimate as 1,000 to 2,500 workdays or, in percentage terms, "1,250 workdays + 100% − 20%." At the completion of requirements definition, your estimates might be expressed as "1,250 workdays + 50% − 10%," and, after design is finished, as, "1,250 workdays + 10%."

Of course, the actual percentage ranges will vary depending upon your degree of familiarity with the application, the firmness of the requirements, and the riskiness of the project itself. By providing confidence estimates, you are making management aware of the uncertainty that surrounds the project and you are preparing them for the higher number if things don't work out as well as you had hoped.

One word of caution: A confidence range is not intended to absorb large changes of scope. It is there because the entire project has uncertainties. It is not padding that the client can use to add more features. As you become aware of new elements of scope, you will redo the estimates, and, unless your comfort in those estimates has increased, you will use the same confidence ranges. So, for example, if, during project initiation, the client requests that the project must include additional functionality that you estimate will take 250 workdays, your revised estimate will be "1,500 workdays + 100% − 20%," a range of 1,200 to 3,000 workdays.

Presenting the Estimate

The estimate is expressed as a workday (or workweek or work-month) requirement by classification. For example, a project needs 150 project manager workdays, 300 systems analyst workdays, 750 developer workdays, 50 quality assurance workdays, and 50 clerical support workdays. This type of estimate allows management to recognize the extent of the project and the resource commitments that will be needed.

The estimate is also the first thorough check against the approximations that have accompanied the project thus far. An estimate of 1,000 workdays will come as a shock to managers who have been thinking in terms of 200. Therefore, before you present an estimate, be aware of what they expect, and make your presentation accordingly.

What If?

Your Estimators Present You with Estimates That You Think Are Too Low

If your estimates are low, your project will overrun its schedule and budget, and you and your team will become frustrated in trying to meet an impossible set of targets.

Actions

Clarify in your own mind why you think the estimates are low. This could be because of your experience on similar projects or because you know that this particular estimator is always optimistic.

Present your concerns to the estimator and ask for a commitment to complete the work within the estimated time.

If the estimator declines to change the estimates but fails to convince you that they are achievable, prepare your project plan using your higher estimates. However, if during the project you can assign the work to the estimator, use the lower estimates that you were given. If the team member meets the lower schedule, you will have come in under budget. If not, your schedule will accommodate the "slippage," and you will have some background to better judge future estimates.

Your Estimators Present You with Estimates That You Think Are Too High

If your estimates are high, you run the risk that management will reject your project plan. In particular, if there is a fixed budget for the project, you will come under pressure to trim the estimates.

Actions

Clarify in your own mind why you think the estimates are high. One common reason is that some estimators opt for a conservative approach.

Explain to the estimator why you believe the estimates are too high, and ask for a detailed review.

If the estimator is not willing to reduce the estimates but cannot convince you that they are reasonable, seek a second opinion and accept the results.

Your Management Rejects Your Estimates as Too High

If you believe that your estimates are valid (and if you don't you should not be presenting them), then, by asking you to reduce them, your managers are asking you to create an estimate that is not achievable. The problem is that you will then be expected to deliver according to that plan.

Actions

This is not an area for compromise. If your judgment, and that of your technical staff, says that the project will take 1,000 work-days, it is your responsibility to defend that estimate.

If your management insists that the project be done with less effort, you have just two choices: Refuse to adjust your plan, or accept the reduced effort with the caveat that the estimates are not yours and have been imposed on you.

Your Management Rejects Your Estimates as Too Low

In very few cases will management insist that you increase your estimates. However, those cases are critical. For example, if your company is bidding on a job, your low estimate may win it, but if your estimates are so low that your company loses money, the blame will be laid on you alone.

Actions

Review your estimates. Get a second opinion. Be as sure as you can that the estimates are valid.

If your management insists on increasing the estimates, do not resist strenuously. But if, at the end of the project, you come in under budget and ahead of schedule, you can point out the accuracy of your original estimates.

*   *   *   *   *

PREPARING THE SCHEDULE

One of the things project managers are supposed to do is to meet the schedule—which, of course, implies having a schedule to meet. The schedule is one of the two major parts of the project plan (the budget being the other), and, complex as it is, it is a by-product of the work that has already been done. Putting together a schedule requires a list of activities and their dependencies and durations. With these pieces and at least one fixed date, the schedule follows automatically.

This point bears repeating: A schedule is a consequence of planning; it is not a primary. Some project management tools allow the user to move activities around, in effect creating their schedules directly. While this facility can have some limited use (see the section "Resource Leveling," in this chapter), you should change schedules only by changing the activities: either their durations or dependencies. The activities determine the schedule, not the other way around.

Producing the schedule is a three-stage process. First, create the initial schedule based solely on the activities and their durations and dependencies. Second, assign resources to each activity. This will probably cause some problems, with some people being double-booked or worse. See the section "Resource Leveling" for ways to smooth out the schedule. Finally, you need to align the schedule to the client's expectations and requirements (see the section "Aligning the Schedule," in this chapter). All three steps are necessary to create a final schedule with which you can run the project.

Scheduling is an automatic function of project management software: Enter the activities and the software will produce your schedule instantly. However, before you can understand it and begin to adjust it, there are some scheduling concepts that you will need. This section is concerned with those concepts: the *critical path* and *slack time*, the project *milestones*, and the *Gantt chart*, a chart that displays the activities.

Critical Path and Slack Time

Assume that there are two programs to be written. Program A requires four weeks and program B, three. Both can start at the same time, and integration will begin when both are finished.

Exhibit 4.16 shows a schedule for coding and integrating the two programs. Each character, dot, dash, or equal sign, represents one day.

From Exhibit 4.16 two things are apparent. First, the coding of program B can slide within the four-week period. It can start as early as September

Exhibit 4.16. Illustration of a Simple Schedule

	Sept.	Oct.
	1....8...15...22...29....6...13	
Code program A	--------------------	
Code program B	...----------------..	
Integration		----------

1 or as late as September 8 without affecting the overall schedule. Since there are five days within which the coding of program B can slide, the activity is said to have five days' *slack time*. Second, if the project is to finish by October 13, program A must start on September 1. It cannot slip without affecting integration and therefore has zero slack time.

Activities with zero slack time are called *critical* because they cannot slip without affecting the overall project schedule. Critical activities that follow one another from the start to the end of the project form the project's *critical path*. Exhibit 4.17 is the simple schedule with special symbols to indicate critical activities.

Every project has a critical path. Clearly, critical activities require the most attention since the project schedule does not allow them to slip. Unfortunately, the critical path is fluid. As the project progresses, activities that were on the critical path may develop slack time, and other, noncritical activities can lose theirs. Exhibit 4.18 illustrates what can happen. Here, the coding of program B started on September 8 but slipped by a week. It therefore became critical, and the coding of program A, which started on time, acquired five days' slack. Situations such as this are commonplace, requiring the project manager to constantly review the critical path as activities are completed or rescheduled. In this example, the slippage in program B has caused the entire project to slip by one week.

Exhibit 4.17. Critical Path and Slack Time

	Sept.	Oct.
	1....8...15...22...29....6...13	
Code program A	====================	
Code program B	...----------------..	
Integration		==========

Legend:	=====	Activity on critical path
	-----	Activity not on critical path
	.....	Slack time

Exhibit 4.18. Critical Path and Slack Time Adjusted

	Sept.		Oct.	
	1....8...15...22...29....6...13...20			
Code program A	`-------------------.....`			
Code program B	`.....====================`			
Integration			`===========`	

Legend: `=====` Activity on critical path
         `-----` Activity not on critical path
         `.....` Slack time

Milestones

A milestone is a specific date in the project when some clearly defined work will have been done. Many project plans have just two milestones, start and end, which means that the project manager will not know how the project is doing until it should have finished.

The purpose of milestones is to identify problems of two types: schedule slippages and functional deviations. A late milestone indicates a schedule slippage; a functional deviation occurs when the client says, "That's not what I wanted." Milestones provide a formal mechanism for the project manager to become aware of both kinds of problem in time to fix them.

Milestones come in two flavors: external and internal. External milestones involve the client and some form of approval, whereas internal milestones are restricted to the project team. There is usually an external milestone for each deliverable or set of deliverables. Internal milestones mark such points as the completion of a program or the planning for a workshop, where the outputs will not be formally delivered to the client. To ensure that you can judge when milestones have been met, they must require the delivery, in final form, of some concrete project output. Note the stipulation "in final form." A milestone that requires, for example, that a document be 50 percent complete is useless; nobody can judge percentage completion.

Milestones involve handovers: from the project to the client, from team members to other team members, or from one activity to the next. A milestone is met when whatever is being handed over is ready. No further time will be spent on it. A conditional handover, "This is about 95 percent done, but you can start on it now," does not count. The milestone is met only

Exhibit 4.19. Sample Schedule with Milestones

	Sept.	Oct.
	1....8...15...22...29....6...13	
Design finishes	M	
Code program A	====================	
Code program B	...-------------..	
Coding finishes	M	
Integration	=========	
Integration finishes	M	

Legend:	=====	Activity on critical path
	-----	Activity not on critical path
	.....	Slack time
	M	Milestone

when the item is 100 percent complete. If you are using a time recording system in which team members enter their time against specific activities, "complete" means that the activity will be closed and no more time can be booked against it. (It may be argued that program code delivered to an integration team is not complete since integration and system test will identify changes that need to be made, but those changes are properly part of integration. When the WBS activity "Code and unit test" is finished, the activity is complete, even if other activities will modify the results.)

Milestones should be liberally distributed throughout the project. A good rule of thumb is to plan at least one external and one internal milestone per month. The more frequent they are, the earlier you will become aware of problems. Exhibit 4.19 shows the sample project schedule with milestones attached. If you are using project management software, you enter a milestone as an activity with zero duration.

The Gantt Chart

A Gantt chart is a graph of activities against time. It is the most effective way to present a project's plan and its progress. Exhibits 4.16–4.19 are examples of simple Gantt charts.

In its basic form, a Gantt chart consists of a line for each activity that runs along a date scale. The line's start and end points specify when the activity will be done. By varying the symbols, a Gantt chart can indicate:

- Milestones
- Slack time
- Activities on the critical path

Once the project has started, the Gantt chart can also show:

- Activities that have started and their actual start dates
- Activities that have finished and their actual completion dates
- Revised milestone and activity dates
- Revised slack time and critical path
- Actual performance compared to the original plan

Exhibit 4.20 presents a Gantt chart for part of the sample project whose WBS is given in Exhibit 4.10. The Gantt chart shows the hardware selection and acquisition activities from that project.

The Role of Project Management Software

It can be argued that the most important feature of project management software is its ability to produce a schedule. Simply enter the activity data and the Gantt chart automatically appears. In fact, many packages allow you to build the schedule graphically.

Software packages differ in their power and also in their ease of use. For example, most packages schedule noncritical activities to start as soon as they can, thus planning for the slack time to follow the activity. Many packages allow you to specify that the activity should start as late as it can, so that the slack time precedes the activity, but this involves extra work and limits the ability of the software to adjust the schedule as things change.

Some of the more powerful packages even allow you to define the profile of work within an activity. For example, assume that you have a five-day activity that will be done over ten days. You can specify that two days of the activity will be done on the first two days, nothing will be done on the next three; the next four will be half-days, followed by one full day. If you are a perfectionist, this type of facility is as dangerous as an addictive drug. Avoid this level of planning. You do not have the time, and whatever you plan will not be reflected in how the work is really carried out.

Exhibit 4.20. Sample Gantt Chart

ID	Task Name	Duration
1	Hardware selection and acquisition	80 days
2	Hardware selection	52 days
3	Define requirements	5 days
4	Identify qualified vendors	2 days
5	Prepare and issue RFQ	5 days
6	RFQ issued	0 days
7	Evaluation	19 days
8	Evaluate written quotations	5 days
9	Conduct demos and presentations	10 days
10	Check references	2 days
11	Negotiate terms and prices	2 days
12	Make final hardware selection	1 day
13	Hardware selected	0 days
14	Hardware acquisition	28 days
15	Purchase and expedite delivery	1 day
16	Install hardware and system software	3 days
17	Conduct acceptance tests	1 day
18	Train the project team	2 days
19	System ready for development	0 days
20	Conduct ongoing maintenance	1 day

Legend:
- Task
- Split
- Progress
- Milestone
- Summary
- Rolled Up Task
- Rolled Up Split
- Rolled Up Milestone
- Rolled Up Progress
- External Tasks
- Project Summary

Project: Information Systems Project M
Date: 04 Oct

With feature-rich software tools, it is tempting to fine-tune the work products. This is defensible in such areas as sales presentations or user manuals, but project plans are never followed precisely; the best you can hope for is to hit the milestones. The more detailed your plan, the less likely it is that it will be followed. If you say to a team member, "Here's a two-week activity. I expect it to be done in two weeks," your expectation is clear, and it is up to the person to plan and execute the task. But if you say, "Here's a two-week activity and a profile of the number of hours I expect you to work on it each day," not only have you usurped the person's professional right to plan the work, you have also guaranteed that your plan will not be followed.

When you plan, resist any urge to finely hone how the activities will be done. Use your meticulousness to make sure that you have the activities identified and properly defined.

What If?

Your Client Insists on Having Fewer External Milestones

You will be tempted to comply. After all, external milestones are at best nuisances and at worst disasters. However, their purpose is to reassure both the client and you that the project is on track. Without the discipline of having to meet them, you run the risk that the project will slip and that you will deviate functionally from the plan.

Actions

Determine why the client is opposed to milestones. Most clients welcome them as a chance to keep current on the state of the project. The most common objection is the demands that milestones make on client staff.

Try to negotiate some form of review or checkpoint for each of your milestones. Even if the review is cursory, it is better than having no contact with the client.

> Manage the project as if the milestones were in place, and appoint yourself as the client representative.

* * * * *

RESOURCE LEVELING

Resource leveling is one of the trickiest and most frustrating parts of project planning. The first attempt to assign people usually gives bizarre results: Fred works 4 hours one week and 104 the next, while Mary works double time on alternate weeks only. A credible project plan is one that approximates what people will really do: Work about 40 hours a week consistently while they are on the project. Resource leveling is the process of smoothing out people's planned workloads to a realistic level. One word of caution: Most project management software packages include a facility for resource leveling. Avoid it. It will eliminate overbooking of resources, but at a cost of massive underbooking and a schedule that extends far into the future. Resource leveling requires judgment—a characteristic not common in automated systems.

There are three steps in leveling resources:

1. Assign specific people to activities.
2. Determine percent availabilities for each person.
3. Smooth the resource requirements.

Assign Specific People

Even on the most massive of projects, each activity is done by individuals rather than by skill classifications. Since you need to know who will do what, you must assign people to activities.

In many cases, you have no choice. If you have just one technology architect, that's the person who is assigned wherever the technology architect is needed. In other cases, such as programmers, you have some flexibility.

When you are planning a project, you do not always know who will be on the team, so you will have to define and assign generic individuals such as programmer 1 and programmer 2. However, you should consider what specific skills these people will need. For example, if the project uses a relational database, you may want a programmer experienced in embedded Structure Query Language (SQL) to handle the more complex data access programs. Or, if the project presents a Graphical User Interface (GUI) to the user, you will want to assign user interface programs to a programmer familiar with the GUI language. In other words, your generic individuals would become SQL programmer, GUI programmer, and so on. This avoids the problem where you have assigned programmer 2 to work on an interface in C++ and Fred, who becomes programmer 2, is not even sure how to pronounce it.

Where you have a choice of people to assign to an activity, there are two schools of thought. One says to assign the most experienced person to maximize your chances of success. The other says to assign an inexperienced person in order to expand the company's base of skills. Both are legitimate, but as a project manager, your primary interest is the project, and you want to get the best person for the job. If the company requires you to treat part of the project as a training exercise, then build time for training and mastery of skills into the schedule, request funds from the training budget to help defray the costs, and document how much of the project estimate is devoted to learning.

Determine Percent Availabilities

While many people on the project will be available full-time, some, particularly those with specialized skills like network management, will be available on a more limited basis. Make sure that management and all team members clearly understand the percent availabilities on which your plan is based.

Full-time does not mean 100 percent. With corporate commitments such as staff meetings, performance reviews, committees, and training, as well as personal time off for illness or compassionate leave, most people will be unavailable, on average, for at least half a day a week. This means that full-time is no more than 90 percent. For a margin of safety, most observers recommend scheduling people at 80 percent maximum availability.

On the other hand, where a project is short and timing is critical, team members may be asked to work overtime and to excuse themselves from their corporate commitments. In such cases, availability may be as much as 150 percent. However, except in extreme cases, do not plan for a project to require overtime, otherwise you will have no fallback if the project slips.

Smooth Resource Requirements

The goal of smoothing resources is to plan activities so that all members of the project team are busy to the extent of their availability while they are on the project. Ideally, there will be no idle time where someone has nothing to do, and no overtime where someone else has to work sixty hours a week. In reality, the ideal balance is impossible to achieve, and actual resource smoothing becomes dynamic as the project progresses.

However, any plan that shows large amounts of idle time or overtime is flawed in that it is not capable of being followed. Furthermore, as the following example illustrates, idle time is a threat to the estimates.

Mary is assigned to a set of activities totaling 500 hours (12.5 weeks). According to the schedule, the activities are spread over fifteen weeks. For three weeks, Mary is scheduled only half time, and for one week, she is not scheduled at all. In other words, she has two and a half weeks of idle time, which represent an overrun of 20 percent over the actual 12.5-week estimate.

In this example, if Mary's time can be absorbed by another project, there is no overrun. In practice, Mary will be there, charging time to your project, for all fifteen weeks.

To smooth resources use a mix of the following tools:

- **Use slack time**. If the same person is assigned to overlapping activities where there is slack time, slide one or more of the activities within the slack time to reduce the amount of overlap.

- **Reassign people**. If one person is idle and another is overworked, and they have about the same skills, reassign them.

- **Alter percent commitments**. If a person is split among several activities, reduce the percent of time required for each. For example, if a senior analyst is assigned 40 percent to each of three activities, change the percent assignments to 33 percent. This may seem like cheating, but if a person is needed only part-time, it is reasonable to adjust the requirement to the availability. Never, however, drop the availability below whatever you think is needed.

One way to smooth resources is to extend the length of an activity while reducing the percent commitment. For example, if a person is committed 40 percent to a two-week activity (four days), extend the activity to three weeks (assuming you don't interfere with the critical path) and reduce the commitment to 27 percent. The same effort, four days, is needed in both cases, but the person has additional time available for other overlapping activities.

- **Decompose activities**. Sometimes an activity can be decomposed into two or more subactivities, which can then be distributed to two or more people.
- **Tolerate short-term imbalances**. If a person is assigned to two or more activities and is relatively idle one week, overworked for two, then idle the next, you may decide to leave the schedule as is and let the person smooth out the workload when it happens.
- **Request additional resources**. Sometimes one or two extra short-term people at the right time can make an impossible balancing act realistic.
- **Schedule overtime**. Scheduling overtime is not the same as tolerating short-term imbalances. With the latter, you assume that the person will adjust the workload to balance between idle time and overtime. With scheduled overtime, in contrast, there is no idle time.

Avoid scheduled overtime except in critical situations for a short term. Starting a project with overtime built in is a good way to demotivate a team. It also deprives you of a tool to help you recover when activities slip.

What If?

You Need a Specific Resource for More Time Than Is Available

If, for example, you need a network analyst for 75 percent of the time during a four-week phase of the project, and you can have one for only two days a week (40 percent), you will not be able to complete the work within the schedule.

Actions

Determine whether you have someone else on the team who can work with the network analyst and take up some of the work.

Review your plan to find out whether you can extend the work of the network analyst, either earlier or later in the project.

If none of these works out, revise the plan showing the effect of a 40 percent availability and escalate it to management.

You Need Resources That Have Been Promised But Are Committed to a Project That Is Running Late

If the other project slips and retains the people you need, your project will also slip.

Actions

Identify alternative people who may be available.

Negotiate with the other project manager to determine whether you can get at least some of the time of the people you need.

Determine whether you can modify your project plan to defer the need for these people.

Identify a date by which you absolutely must have the resources if you are to meet the project schedule, and make sure management is aware of the problem.

You Cannot Get the Resources You Need

Without adequate resources, your project will not meet its schedule.

Actions

Identify projected dates by which you expect resources to be available.

Redo your project plan with the availabilities you have been given. In particular, note the effect on the schedule.

Present the plan to your managers. You are, in effect, escalating the resource issue to them.

* * * * *

ALIGNING THE SCHEDULE

Congratulations. The schedule is now complete, the resources are fully balanced, and you are ready to proceed—except that the project will end in March and the client wants it in January. You are now faced with the job of aligning the schedule to the client's requirements.

Why is aligning the schedule a separate step? Why not simply take the client's requirements into account during the initial planning? The reason is that those requirements will influence your plans and will hinder your ability to develop a true picture of what the project really needs. When you prepare the schedule independent of what the client wants, the alterations you will have to make become visible. Then, when you chop estimates or alter dependencies or reassign resources, you will be acutely aware of the effects.

If you have built an honest schedule, as opposed to one with a lot of fat built in because you knew you would have some aligning to do, you will not have much flexibility. Nevertheless, there are some things you can do.

Absolute vs. Desirable Dates

Some required dates are absolute. For example, if you are building an election system that must be ready by election day, you have no choice: The project must be finished when the client specifies.

On the other hand, some dates are merely desirable. If the client wants the system in January, "in time for the start of the fiscal year," the date is flexible: If the system is not available until March, it could simply mean that the client will have to enter two months' history.

There are two problems: determining whether a date is absolute or desirable and, if it is merely desirable, convincing the client of this. The best approach is to ask yourself, "What would happen if this date is not met?" If the answer is something like, "We'd have to do a lot of work to catch up," then catching up is possible and the date is desirable rather than absolute. But if the answer is closer to "We'd miss out on a major business opportunity and lose a $10 million investment," then the date is absolute and cannot slip.

Segment into Releases

You may find that although the client's date is absolute, the entire project does not need to be finished at the same time. For example, although the online processing must be done by January, the client may not need management reporting from the database until March.

You need to plan how to present this approach to your client. If it appears that you are proposing to enter production with an incomplete system, be prepared for some strong objections; nobody wants to risk a company on something that is not finished. Instead, talk about *release development,* a process in which a system is developed and implemented in self-contained chunks. In the examples given, release 1 consists of the online processing, and release 2 provides the management reporting facility. Release 1 is not unfinished; it is a complete release of a system to which subsequent releases will add further functionality.

You can use the concept of release development to align the schedule by defining release 1 to include whatever is required by the absolute date. Anything the client agrees can be deferred goes into release 2 (or release 3). If you can complete release 1 by the required date, you have successfully aligned the project to your client's requirements.

Reduce Functionality

If the date is absolute and you cannot segment the system into releases, it may be possible to compress the schedule by reducing functionality. This is another type of release development in which release 1 contains all the components of the complete system scaled down to a lower level of functionality. Subsequent releases will enhance the system to the functional levels that were originally planned.

This approach is different from the segmentation described earlier. Consider a project that is to deliver a system with components A, B, C, and D. Release segmentation might deliver A and B in release 1, with C and D in subsequent releases. Reduced functionality will deliver all four components in release 1, but each will be less comprehensive than was originally intended.

To reduce functionality, step through all the deliverables with the client and identify sections or pieces that are not absolutely necessary. It is vital that you enroll the client in this process. First, the client must understand why the system is being cut back. Second, only the client can identify functionality that can be deferred.

Additional Staff

Another approach to aligning the schedule is to assign additional staff. This depends upon the availability of other people, as well as the nature of the project and the extent to which the activities are independent of one another.

Adding people is more realistic if you have planned to do so than if the requirement appears after the project has started. At the planning stage, you can add time for increased communication and the distributed and overhead activities.

Subcontracting

One way to spread the work over more people is to subcontract part of the project to another company that specializes in systems development. This method is especially valid if your company is not one in which extra effort is the norm. The productivity of focused companies can be as much as 100 percent greater than that of their larger, more structured counterparts. In a tight project, they can sometimes provide the boost that the project needs. This approach can be expensive, but meeting the schedule may be worth it for the client.

Corporate Permission to Flout Regulations

Another approach is to get your company's permission to ignore office standards, conventions, paperwork, or any other corporate demands in a focused attempt to get the job done. If, for example, bringing the team physically together would help but the company policy is for individuals to work at their assigned desks, request space dedicated to the project and bring the team together. If Fred is more productive working from 2:00 P.M. to midnight wearing jeans and a T-shirt with a beer logo, give him your blessing and block any attempt by the company's clothing police to intervene. If team members are active on the company's social committee, ask that they be excused for the duration.

This approach calls for a team commitment. You are saying to your team, "We've been asked to get this critical job done, and I will ax whatever gets in the way. If you will commit to this tight schedule, I will commit to insulate you from whatever company policies or standards slow you down."

Warning: If you do not get full team commitment and complete company cooperation, this approach will not work, and you should abandon the attempt. Otherwise, you will be fighting two continual battles: one with your management (which did not think you meant *that*), and one with your team (which thought you did).

If All Else Fails

If you cannot change the date, defer functionality, cut components, assign more people, subcontract, or ignore company procedures, then, assuming your schedule is accurate, the job cannot be done.

One of your responsibilities as project manager is to ensure that project goals are achievable. If you are convinced that you cannot meet the schedule, you have just two choices: Decline the project or accept it. If you decline the project, make sure your management understands that your reasons are for its good. It is a disservice to mislead management into believing you can meet the schedule when you know you cannot.

If you decide to accept the project, make sure that your management understands the magnitude of the task and the likelihood of failure. Above all, make sure that you understand—and are willing to accept—what will happen if you fail. Then tackle the job with all the creativity, talent, energy, and commitment you can muster.

* * * * *

PREPARING THE PROJECT BUDGET

Of the big three conventional measures of project success—budget, schedule, and scope—the budget is, in many ways, the most important. It is the budget that determines whether a project is worthwhile—the cost side of the cost-benefit analysis. It is also frequently the most sensitive aspect of project progress. Dollars are, after all, the universal corporate standard of measure.

It follows, then, that the budget should receive a degree of attention at least equal to that given to the schedule.

A project budget consists of four kinds of cost items: staff charges, expenses, capital costs, and general office overhead. If the client will make periodic payments, the budget may also include a cash flow analysis. Exhibit 4.21 gives the budget for part of the sample project.

Except for general office overhead, all cost items are contained within the WBS. Staff charges are the charge rates for team members multiplied by the time spent on each activity. They are derived from work, distributed, and overhead activities. Expenses and capital costs have their own WBS items and normally include travel and living, materials and supplies, and acquisition costs.

General corporate overhead may or may not be part of the budget, depending upon company policy. If it is included in the budget, it is usually calculated using a formula based on a percentage of staff charges.

Assembling the budget, therefore, should involve little more than adding up some numbers from the WBS and, where required, adding in the general corporate overhead. In other words, the budget should be automatically generated from the WBS and presented in a report that can be produced by project management software. Of course, as anyone who has ever presented a budget can attest, it's not that simple.

The problem is that, just as the client had an expectation of the schedule, management has an expectation of the budget. (A note on terminology: I assume that the schedule is the primary concern of the *client,* whereas the

Exhibit 4.21. Sample Project Budget

ID	Task Name	Fixed Cost	Total Cost	Baseline	Variance	Actual	Remaining
3	Define requirements	$0.00	$4,600.00	$0.00	$4,600.00	$0.00	$4,600.00
4	Identify qualified vendors	$0.00	$920.00	$0.00	$920.00	$0.00	$920.00
5	Prepare and issue RFQ	$0.00	$4,600.00	$0.00	$4,600.00	$0.00	$4,600.00
6	RFQ issued	$0.00	$0.00	$0.00	$0.00	$0.00	$0.00
8	Evaluate written quotations	$0.00	$4,600.00	$0.00	$4,600.00	$0.00	$4,600.00
9	Conduct demos and presentations	$0.00	$9,200.00	$0.00	$9,200.00	$0.00	$9,200.00
10	Check references	$0.00	$920.00	$0.00	$920.00	$0.00	$920.00
11	Negotiate terms and prices	$0.00	$1,840.00	$0.00	$1,840.00	$0.00	$1,840.00
12	Make final hardware selection	$0.00	$920.00	$0.00	$920.00	$0.00	$920.00
13	Hardware selected	$0.00	$0.00	$0.00	$0.00	$0.00	$0.00
15	Purchase and expedite delivery	$225,000.00	$225,920.00	$0.00	$225,920.00	$0.00	$225,920.00
16	Install hardware and system software	$5,000.00	$7,760.00	$0.00	$7,760.00	$0.00	$7,760.00
17	Conduct acceptance tests	$0.00	$920.00	$0.00	$920.00	$0.00	$920.00
18	Train the project team	$0.00	$1,840.00	$0.00	$1,840.00	$0.00	$1,840.00
19	System ready for development	$0.00	$0.00	$0.00	$0.00	$0.00	$0.00
20	Conduct ongoing maintenance and support	$0.00	$920.00	$0.00	$920.00	$0.00	$920.00
		$230,000.00	$264,960.00	$0.00	$264,960.00	$0.00	$264,960.00

budget is the primary concern of *management*. Obviously, this is not always true, but I need to differentiate between groups with a different focus, and this terminology is as good as any. Management may, of course, refer to the management of the systems organization executing the project or to a separate group within the client organization.)

When the budget is presented, it is usually met with the objection that it is too high and that it must be reduced. The estimators are required to "go back to the table," "sharpen their pencils," and produce the kind of numbers management expected.

As you may have observed, cutting the budget is akin to aligning the schedule, and the comments that applied in that section apply here. Just as you had to resist the pressure to arbitrarily cut estimates to meet the schedule, you must show the same resolve with regard to the budget. Assuming that you have an honest estimate, it is your responsibility not to yield to the pressures to change it.

Nevertheless, there are means to cut each of the components of the budget: staff charges, expenses, capital costs, and even general corporate overhead.

Staff Charges

Staff charges are hours times rates. While "sharpening your pencil" implies reducing hours, staff charges can also be lowered by cutting rates.

While rates in many companies are sacrosanct, they are also arbitrary. They may be tied to salaries, job classifications, seniority, or other factors, but they are always the product of company policy. Hours, on the other hand, arise from the work to be done. If the choice is between changing hours and changing rates, change rates first.

Not all companies will allow you to change rates, but where the option exists, a slight reduction in rates can have a marked effect on the budget.

Another approach to reducing rates is to base them on lower-cost people. If Mary, a senior analyst, has to do work that could be done by a more junior person because no junior people are available, it is reasonable to object that the rate should be that of a junior person and not Mary's, because the project should not have to bear the higher cost imposed by external factors.

At times, you may actually be able to use lower-cost people. If Fred costs $50 an hour and Joan $30, and Joan takes three weeks to do what Fred can do in two, it is less expensive to use Joan (of course, the schedule will be affected). In any case, charging at the rate of the lowest-cost people is one way to cut a budget.

Expenses

Expenses are the extraordinary costs of the project, such as travel or special supplies. They do not include everyday items such as stationery or photocopier charges because life is too short to spend it accounting for pieces of paper or photocopy toner. These items should be covered under general office overhead.

Expenses such as travel can be reduced if you insist that the project pay only for expenses that are necessary to get the job done. If the project requires that you or members of your team travel, those expenses are legitimate charges against the budget. However, if management or sales staff travel in order to cement relationships or develop new business, their expenses should be covered by their own departments.

Consulting services and training can be major expense items that can sometimes be trimmed by finding lower-cost alternatives. Some of these services may even be available in-house, and the rates will be far lower than outside organizations will charge.

Other expenses tend to be trivial compared to the overall budget. Do not waste time trying to trim something that would not have a significant effect if it were eliminated entirely.

Capital Costs

If capital items such as hardware are to be acquired and then turned over to the client after the project, the costs will be handled either as a flow-through or as a profit item. In either case, such capital costs should not affect the budget, since the client will pay for the items, whatever they cost.

However, if you need to purchase equipment for the project, such as workstations for the project team, the budget is affected. There are two approaches for acquiring such items: purchase and amortization.

With purchase, the project buys the equipment outright and turns it over to the systems organization after the project. With amortization, the systems organization buys the equipment and charges the project for its use on the basis of some payment schedule.

If you need to acquire equipment, calculate the lowest cost to the project. For example, if you need ten $4,000 workstations, it will cost you $40,000 to buy them (plus taxes and maintenance contracts; do not forget them). If the company buys the workstations and agrees to amortize them over three years, your one-year project should be charged just over $13,000, a savings of about $27,000.

An old and honorable approach to reducing capital costs is to negotiate the best price. Many companies have standard suppliers and do not bother to challenge their prices, but if you can find another vendor who is prepared to offer suitable equipment for less, you can insist that the lower-cost equipment be purchased or that the project be charged the lower amount and not be penalized by the company's poor purchasing procedures.

General Corporate Overhead

General corporate overhead is normally applied as a standard formula, not subject to change or negotiation. However, you may be able to argue that some of the expenses or even capital items in the budget should be financed from other company funds rather than having to be paid for by the project. For example, if the company has a policy of continuously upgrading equipment (and, more important, a fund to do so), you may propose that the policy be applied to your project's workstations, which the company will own when the project ends. If the company has a research and development fund and your project uses new technology, you may request that training and familiarization be covered by the fund.

Contingency

Just as there is contingency in the schedule, so there must be in the budget. The schedule contingency, stated in workdays, implies a budget contingency of the number of workdays times a rate. The rate should be the average rate for the project, which is calculated as the total staff charges divided by the total staff hours (or days).

However, the budget should also include a contingency for other costs. Some emergency travel may be required. Another workstation may be needed. Consulting services may be required. More training may be needed. All of these should be allowed for by the contingency.

Like schedule contingency, budget contingency should be overt, rather than hidden in the various expense and cost items.

Cash Flow Analysis

Many systems development organizations, particularly those with external clients, want projects to be self-financing. In other words, at any point in the project, the cash in must always equal or exceed the cash out.

On projects run by such companies, progress payments based on milestone deliverables are usually required from the client. If you are asked to set up the payment amounts and the milestones, use a spreadsheet showing the accumulated expenses by month, the milestone payments, and the surplus. You are attempting to build a schedule of milestone payments that will ensure that the cash received to date always exceeds the costs to date. Since you have no flexibility with regard to the costs—they are consequences of the plan—you will have to adjust milestone payments so that they are frequent enough and large enough to cover the ongoing costs.

Complete self-financing is not always possible. It depends on the company's ability to negotiate payments from the client. The cash flow analysis will tell the company where additional financing will be required.

Cost vs. Effort

In many organizations that conduct internal projects, staff costs are not charged back to the client department, leading their project managers to conclude that the budget is unimportant because the staff costs are zero. Such project managers make the mistake of confusing effort and cost.

The budget is expressed in dollars because money is the common denominator that ties together all of its components, but the most important aspect of the budget from a project management point of view is not the staff dollars but the staff time—the effort. Each activity requires a certain amount of effort, expressed in work-hours or workdays or some similar measure. Whether you convert that effort to dollars at some rate and charge it back to the client or leave it as a duration for your internal use, your job is to track the effort on each activity because:

- When the time spent exceeds the estimates, it is likely that the schedule will slip.

- A consistent excess of time spent over the estimate is an indicator either that the project estimates are too low, that the team members are adding extra work beyond the project's scope, or that the team's expertise is below what was assumed.

- Variances between estimates and time actually spent can be used to generate more accurate estimates on future projects.

The point is that it is a mistake to assume that, just because the effort of your team is not converted to dollars, you are at liberty to ignore the effort estimates of your plan.

✳ ✳ ✳ ✳ ✳

PAPERWORK

Projects generate paper. Even the smallest projects seem to be awash in memos, reports, and meeting minutes in volumes out of proportion to the importance of the project. It is said that the largest of modern military cargo aircraft cannot carry the paper that was generated by the projects that created them.

There are two types of project documents: those that you need in order to manage the project and the vastly more voluminous technical data. You should keep the latter in a library accessible to all project staff. If the project is large enough, you will need a project librarian to help maintain the library and to ensure that the right versions of material are available.

The Project Binder

A critical tool to help you organize the management parts of the paper-work is the project binder: a three-ring binder, usually large, with tab dividers for sections such as memos, meeting minutes, issues, and project planning. The project binder serves three main purposes. First, it provides a single repository for the important project management material. When you are late for a project meeting, you do not need to search your desk for the relevant documents. You simply grab the project binder as you sweep through your office. When you arrive at your meeting, turn to the "Meetings" section of the binder and pull out the minutes of the previous meeting—which, of course, you scrupulously placed there as soon as they were distributed.

Second, there will come a time in any project when somebody will question your memory of an event, such as a commitment, a meeting, or a decision. It is satisfying to flip open your binder, search deliberately through the appropriate section, then say, "At a monthly status meeting on August 17 held at the headquarters building, all participants agreed that. . . ." Having all necessary material organized in a single place makes it easy to keep project participants honest.

Third, the project material provides you with a current snapshot of what is happening in the project. Once weekly, during your reflection meeting (see the section "Reflection," in chapter 5), scan the memos and meeting minutes of the past month to ensure that you have not overlooked some aspect of the project. Because all this documentation is together, you do not have to go through the demotivating process of looking for it or run the risk of not finding it.

The sections of the binder will vary depending on the project, but these four will always be present.

1. "Project Plan" will contain your project plan and the current version of the issues log.

2. "Memos" will contain all important memos, either from you or to you.

3. "Meetings" will contain all meeting minutes and agendas.

4. "Status Reports" will contain all project status reports, including those to various levels of the client organization.

The documents in each section should generally be in date order, with the most recent at the front. However, there will be exceptions. For example, you may want to group all documents that relate to project benefits in one place. This may include memos, working papers, specification sheets, or anything else that is relevant to that subject. For convenience, paper clip the pages together for quick reference. This may violate the strict organization of the binder, but you are organizing a living entity, not a permanent library.

If the binder is to be effective, one rule is paramount:

Add new material to the binder religiously. Do not even think about keeping some material in another place.

Disobey this rule, and your binder will be useless. Adhere to it, and you will always have the material you need immediately at hand.

* * * * *

PLANNING FOR IMPLEMENTATION

One of the places where many projects stumble is implementation. In part, this is because implementation is not a technical activity; it is primarily administrative and therefore of little interest to the technical staff who will willingly provide you with the details of the project work but are unconcerned with what happens after the technical effort is finished. As part of project planning, you need to identify all of the implementation activities.

The set of implementation activities will vary depending upon the nature of the project, but in general, they fall into five categories: training, support handoffs, client handoff, benefits, and retirements. In some projects, data conversion is also included as part of implementation, but that is a technical activity and should be included in the other technical activities of your plan.

Training

Training is easy to remember if the project is to implement a new application and the users need to be trained on how to use it. It is less obvious for projects that have little end-user impact, such as a server consolidation or an upgrade of an application to a new database. Nevertheless, unless the project leaves absolutely no traces in the user community, some level of training will be required.

For example, consider a project in which several servers are consolidated into one or two. Since there is no change in applications functionality, such a project is normally considered to be transparent to the users. However, the server name usually appears on the users' screens, and when the servers are consolidated, that name will change. The effect may seem slight, but if the users are not expecting it, they will inundate server support with trouble calls. They may even stop working for fear of creating problems until their concerns are resolved. In this case, training is easy: Simply send out three e-mail messages. The first one will go out a week before the cutover, informing the users of the change and its effect on their screens; the second one will be sent the day before the cutover, reminding them of the implementation; and the third will go out the morning after the cutover, letting them know that things went smoothly and that they can continue with their work uninterrupted.

Another aspect of training is to consider who needs it. Obviously, any application end users will be included, but you also need to consider other groups, such as application maintenance, operations, the help desk, and any of the support groups that are affected.

Handoffs

A handoff is the physical act of providing a recipient group with the information and tools it needs to receive the project product and to undertake its role in the life of that product. One obvious type of handoff is to the client, but we discuss that later under "Client Handoff." Here, the groups we consider are applications support, operations, database support, server support, network support, and the help desk.

Not all projects involve these groups, but for those that do, proper planning for the handoff is crucial. Many projects have been derailed when a recipient group refused to accept the product because its processes for handover had not been followed. Accordingly, during planning, you need to meet with representatives of each of these groups to present the details of your project and to clarify what they need before they will accept its product. Exhibit 4.22 is a list of each of the recipient groups, with the normal requirements of each. Most such groups have a process for receiving a handoff. It is your responsibility as the project manager to find out, during planning, what those procedures are, to ensure that each group is properly informed and involved during the project, and to ensure that its procedures

Exhibit 4.22. Handoff Groups and Requirements

Recipient Group	Requirements
Applications support	• Familiarity with the application, its architecture, its design, and the code of each program unit • Knowledge of the user community
Operations	• Knowledge of any batch operations requirements, including the schedule, the processes, and failure recovery procedures • Knowledge of the backup cycle and processes • Knowledge of failover requirements • Knowledge of business continuity and disaster recovery requirements
Database support	• Knowledge of the database schema and physical structure • Knowledge of the maintenance window • Setup of database monitoring tools
Server support	• Knowledge of the technology architecture • Knowledge of failover requirements • Knowledge of business continuity and disaster recovery requirements • Knowledge of the maintenance window • Set up of capacity-measurement tools and analysis processes • Setup of system-monitoring tools and processes
Network support	• Knowledge of the network requirements • Set up of network-monitoring tools and processes
Help desk	• Knowledge of the support groups that are involved and the contacts within each group • Knowledge of how to resolve common minor problems • Knowledge of the major potential problems • Knowledge of the escalation paths • Setup of automated alerts

are followed at the end. You may even invite representatives of the relevant groups to your status meetings or include them on the distribution list of your status reports.

Client Handoff

Client handoff is the handoff of the project's product to the client. The client can be a manager of a department who is receiving a new or enhanced application, an infrastructure manager who is receiving a modification to an infrastructure, or a product manager who is receiving a new or enhanced product for marketing.

In all cases, you need to clarify with the client what steps are involved in the handoff. In the simplest of cases, it can be little more than a memo and a set of files. In more complex cases, it could involve a set of phased implementations in different sites, including training, infrastructure readiness, software installation, and rollout for each site. For a product, the client handoff may involve providing documentation for marketing materials, reviewing packaging and distribution procedures, or training sales staff in the features of the product.

As with other types of handoff, you need to prepare for this one during the planning stage. During the project, you will need to keep the recipient informed of progress and ensure that you understand the complete set of steps the client needs for a successful handoff.

Benefits

Your implementation planning should include a set of activities that the organization will take to realize the benefits from the project. You identify these activities by meeting with client representatives. It must be emphasized that it is not your job to realize benefits, only to deliver a product that the client will use to generate them.

In some cases, this planning is easy. If your project produced a product for marketing, the sales manager will not need prompting on how to generate the revenue the company expected. Similarly, on a server consolidation project that was justified by reduced maintenance costs on the retired servers, realizing the benefits is a simple matter of canceling maintenance contracts—keeping in mind any requirements for advance notice.

However, for projects in which the benefits are reduced internal costs, such as staff cutbacks or reduced inventory levels, the planning will be more complex and will need to focus on the steps to reduce costs and the schedule for doing so. It is here that you can provide value by helping the client prepare a plan that will allow the organization to realize the project benefits overtly, rather than by chance.

Retirements

As part of implementation, you may need to retire existing components. Software retirement involves uninstalling existing software, deleting files, and cleaning up directories. You can identify the steps that are needed for software cleanup by asking applications maintenance for its input and assigning it the responsibility for software retirement. If the software is a package, don't forget to cancel any maintenance contracts.

Hardware retirement involves getting rid of existing hardware. You need to ensure that all disks are cleaned and reformatted, or even destroyed, so that no confidential company information finds its way into unauthorized hands. Your operations group may be able to let you know the steps for physical retirement, or, if you are replacing old servers with new, the vendor may have a disposal service.

The point is that you need to plan how you will get rid of existing components, otherwise you risk having extra unplanned work at the time when you thought the project was finished.

* * * * *

PLANNING FOR COMPLETION

One of the hurdles of project management is project completion and, in particular, gaining client signoff. It's hard to see why this should be the case. After all, once the project team has done whatever is within its scope, the project should be finished. Nevertheless, project completion is one of those frustrating steps that somehow never seems to end.

One of the problems arises from the paradox that the more successful a project manager is in establishing good client relations, the harder it can be to get agreement that the project is over. After all, the client has come to regard the project manager as a valuable resource who is now about to depart, creating a type of separation anxiety. Conversely, if the project did not go well, the client can also be reluctant to sign off for fear of being left with an inferior or untrustworthy product.

Another barrier to gaining signoff occurs when the client makes demands that are difficult to counter and impossible to meet. For example, how does a conscientious project manager respond to a client who insists that a new system be bug-free before it is accepted? On the surface, this seems reasonable; who would want to accept a buggy system? However, unless the client is willing to spend vastly more than normal on the kinds of systems engineering that characterizes "life-and-death" systems, such as those that deliver radiation to cancer patients, a custom system without bugs is unrealistic.

The key to smooth signoff is to establish completion criteria and to agree that once they have been met, the project is over. A project's completion criteria are the conditions that, once satisfied, mark the conclusion of the project. They consist of such items as completion of training, delivery of systems and documentation, or handover to support groups. For applications development projects, there is one other important completion criterion: the user acceptance test, defined later.

One caution: Some clients may propose a criterion such as "The general manager will be satisfied with the system." Reject this: There is no objective way to satisfy someone. If the client persists, ask, "What would satisfy him?" and keep digging until you have a testable set of criteria.

Completion criteria should be defined at the start of the project. Specific criteria vary depending upon the type of project, but Exhibit 4.23 provides some suggestions for completion criteria for different projects.

You should document the completion criteria, either in a memo or on a form such as that given in Exhibit 4.24. However you choose to document them, it is essential to get the client to sign off, agreeing with them. Exhibit 4.24 includes signature blocks for two sets of approvals, one at the start of the project approving the criteria and one at the end agreeing that the criteria have been satisfied.

User Acceptance Testing

For applications development projects, one key completion criterion is the user acceptance test.

Exhibit 4.23. Suggested Project Completion Criteria

Type of Project	Completion Criteria
Applications development	• Successful completion of acceptance tests
	• Completion of user training
	• Rollout of the application
	• Date comparison
	• Retirement of current system
	• Handover to support groups
Systems integration	• Completion of warranty period
	• Setup of applications maintenance procedures
	• Setup of help desk procedures
	• Setup of production procedures
	• Handover to production
Infrastructure	• Completion of installation of hardware
	• Completion of installation of systems software
	• Successful completion of system testing
	• Completion of desktop modifications
	• Setup of system support procedures
	• Setup of help desk procedures
Analyses (e.g., requirements specifications, strategic planning)	• Delivery of the final report, reviewed and approved
	• Delivery of a presentation on findings, observations, and recommendations

A user acceptance test is a set of tests, defined in detail, that the client develops and executes once the project team has completed all of its testing. The client and the project manager have agreed, as part of the initial project plan, that once the application has passed the acceptance test, the client will sign off that the project is complete.

Some points need to be made about user acceptance tests.

- **The client prepares them**. It is up to the client to define what functions are part of acceptance testing. If the client asks you to have someone on your team prepare acceptance tests, you must decline. Your role as a project manager is to ensure that the acceptance test is prepared, but the person responsible for that activity is the client.

Exhibit 4.24. Sample Completion Criteria Form

Completion Criteria Form

Project: _____ Date: _____

Project Manager: _____

Following are the completion criteria for this project. Once these criteria have been satisfied, the project will be considered complete.

User-defined acceptance tests have been successfully completed.   ____
The application users have been trained.   ____
The application has been accepted by applications maintenance.   ____
Help desk procedures have been set up.   ____
Production procedures have been set up.   ____
The application has been accepted by production.   ____
The warranty period has been completed.   ____

At project start:

These completion criteria are agreed to.

Signed: _____
        Client

        _____
        Project Manager

At project completion:

These completion criteria have been satisfied.

Signed: _____
        Client

        _____
        Project Manager

- **They are subject to project manager approval**. You have the obligation to review the acceptance test, or to have someone on your team review it, to ensure that some of the tests do not exceed the scope of the project.

- **They must be detailed**. The acceptance test must specify exactly what functions are to be tested and how. For example, a plan may specify, "Add a customer, including name, mailing address, telephone number, and account number," or "Change customer data including name, mailing address, telephone number, and account number." When test plans include such sweeping instructions as "Verify the customer management processes," there are two problems. First, the test is too vague and open to interpretations that can exceed the scope of the project. Second, if the tests are conducted minimally, the client may not be satisfied that the system was properly tested, and may be unwilling to sign off. If you find that a user acceptance test is too vague or general, suggest that the client engage the services of an experienced test-script writer.

- **They must fall within the project scope**. If an acceptance-test plan includes a test of a function that is outside the project's scope, you will have to deal with client dissatisfaction when the test fails or is not conducted. It is your responsibility to ensure that the plan is within scope.

- **They must be made available to the project team no later than the end of design.** If an acceptance test is not completed until the end of the project, you run the risk that it will include tests that are out of scope and you will now become embroiled in a debate over what should be tested. By insisting that the plan be completed early in the project, you avoid this potential conflict, and you have an additional verification of the client's view of the project scope.

- **The client executes them**. It is the responsibility of the client to provide staff to execute the acceptance test plan and to document the results. You will want to have your team standing by as observers, but the client will actually carry out the tests so that there can be no dispute about the outcomes. Of course, you will have privately carried them out as part of systems testing before you deliver the application to the client for acceptance testing.

What If?

The Client Does Not Agree to Prepare an Acceptance Test Plan

You will find it extremely difficult to get project signoff. You need to determine why the client is reluctant.

Actions

If the client is reluctant because of concerns about how to prepare a test plan, offer to show the client some samples of acceptance test plans for similar projects or to provide some guidance to the client's resources in preparing the plan.

If the client is reluctant because there are not sufficient resources, you can offer to refer the client to an experienced test-script writer, either internal or external. If the client is reluctant because he or she does not want to be locked in to an acceptance process, this is a symptom that the client is not comfortable with the defined scope and does not want to be committed to specifics. You may need to involve your management to negotiate with the client.

* * * * *

COMMUNICATIONS

It has been said that it is impossible to overcommunicate. While this proposition may be doubtful, most projects suffer from inadequate rather than overabundant communications. It is a cliché that good communications are important for the success of a project, but for the project manager, they are also critical to the client's assessment of how the project was conducted. Many project managers have been criticized by clients when their projects were unqualified successes—the project completed on plan and produced a valuable product for the client—but the clients were dissatisfied because they felt that they were ignored, bypassed, or treated as little more than nuisances.

Furthermore, many projects stumble at implementation because the client staff who are being called upon to use the product are resistant to change or are concerned by rumors they have heard about problems.

Finally, some projects falter during handover when recipients, such as operations, the help desk, or product support, are not ready for the product or offer up last-minute objections.

As the project manager, it is your responsibility to address all of these problems by communicating from the project to the various project stakeholders.

In many projects, communications from the project manager to the client are limited to status reports and perhaps status meetings. These are valuable, but they address only a few of the people who have an interest in the project. In planning for communications, you need to determine who the stakeholders are and how you can best communicate with them. In general, stakeholders fall into eight categories: client project management, client team, project team, users, client management, your management, recipient groups, and external stakeholders.

- **Client project management** consists of client staff who are directly involved in the management and direction of the project itself, and include people such as the client project manager, the client sponsor, the client approver, and members of the steering committee.

- **The client team** consists of client staff who are directly involved in the project and who provide details on business and technical requirements.

- **The project team** is your team.

- **Users** are members of the client staff who are not directly involved in the project but who will be affected by the project product once it is implemented. They may be affected by having to use the product, by receiving output, such as reports, from it, or even by being subject to layoffs or transfers.

- **Client management** consists of the executives of the client organization. They are not directly involved in the project but have an interest in its success.

- **Your management** consists of everyone in your organization or department who is superior to you in the hierarchy.

- **Recipient groups** are those that will receive the product and be responsible for its operation and support. They include production, the help desk, support and maintenance groups, and operations.

- **External stakeholders** are customers, suppliers, or users of the client organization's products who will be affected by the project. They are not part of the client organization or yours.

Each of these stakeholder categories requires some form of communication, and when a project addresses only client project management, there is potential for disruption and conflict with the other groups.

The project manager who limits communications to status reports and meetings is ignoring a variety of other communications mechanisms. The following list of types of communication indicates the usual intended audience:

- Status reports are intended for client project management, recipient groups, and your management.

- Team meetings are intended for the project team.

- Steering committee meetings are intended for client project management and client management.

- Newsletters are intended for client management, the client team, or users.

- "Town hall" meetings are intended for client management, the client team, or users.

- Teleconferences are intended for client management, the client team, or users.

- Videoconferences are intended for client management, the client team, or users.

- The Intranet Web site is intended for all client staff.

- The Internet Web site is intended for external stakeholders.

- The telephone hotline, which provides hourly updates at critical times, is intended for the project team, client project management, and the client team.

- Radio and television updates are intended for external stakeholders.

As the project manager, you need to prepare a communications plan. This document lists each of the communications types you intend to use during the project, then, for each type, it describes the purpose of the communication, specifies the target audience, identifies who is responsible for preparing and issuing the communication, and gives the frequency of communications. Exhibit 4.25 presents a form to help you prepare a communications plan for your project.

Exhibit 4.25. Communications Planning Form

Communications Planning Form

Project: _____ **Date:** _____

Manager: _____

Status Reports:

Purpose: _____

Audience: _____

Prepared by: _____ Frequency: _____

Team Meetings:

Purpose: _____

Audience: _____

Prepared by: _____ Frequency: _____

Steering Committee Meetings:

Purpose: _____

Audience: _____

Prepared by: _____ Frequency: _____

Newsletters:

Purpose: _____

Audience: _____

Prepared by: _____ Frequency: _____

"Town Hall" Meetings:

Purpose: _____

Audience: _____

Prepared by: _____ Frequency: _____

(continues)

Exhibit 4.25.　(Continued.)

Teleconferences:

   Purpose: _____

   Audience: _____

   Prepared by: _____ Frequency: _____

Videoconferences:

   Purpose: _____

   Audience: _____

   Prepared by: _____ Frequency: _____

Intranet Web site:

   Purpose: _____

   Audience: _____

   Prepared by: _____ Frequency: _____

Internet Web site:

   Purpose: _____

   Audience: _____

   Prepared by: _____ Frequency: _____

Telephone hotline:

   Purpose: _____

   Audience: _____

   Prepared by: _____ Frequency: _____

Radio and television updates:

   Purpose: _____

   Audience: _____

   Prepared by: _____ Frequency: _____

* * * *

THE PROJECT PLAN

The project plan is the culmination of all your activities so far. This is where your planning finally comes together in a comprehensive description of the project and how you will run it. As described in the introduction to chapter 4, the project plan is the final result of the planning process.

Writing the project plan should involve little more than assembling pieces that have already been prepared, from text describing the background and nature of the project to charts and diagrams produced from project management software. Many project managers write various sections of the project plan as part of the planning process, so that when the planning is done, so is the plan.

Exhibit 4.26 is a sample table of contents for a project plan. The details, including the Gantt chart, activity descriptions, estimates, and budget, are presented in appendices rather than in the body, which is almost entirely text and small tables. For example, Section 5.2.3, Estimate and Budget, simply states the estimate in workdays, perhaps by job classification, and the budget gives just three or four key amounts. The purpose of the body is to provide the reader with a general understanding of the project. The appendices provide the supporting materials for those who need to dig deeper.

The project plan table of contents includes several subsidiary plans for managing scope, risks, the schedule, the budget, communications, and quality. These may be physically included in the project plan or exist as separate documents that the project plan references. In either case, these subsidiary plans are also produced as part of your planning work.

The project plan is a working document; it is not deathless prose that will secure its author a place in literary history. It should be short and to the point. In particular, it should accurately reflect how the project will be carried out. The plan should be reviewed by peers who can spot holes and opportunities and help make a good plan even better.

Exhibit 4.26. Sample Project Plan Table of Contents

1.	**Introduction**
1.1.	Purpose of the Project Plan
2.	**Project Charter**
2.1.	Objective
2.2.	Scope
2.3.	Major Deliverables
2.4.	Business Need or Opportunity
2.5.	Financial Benefits of the Project
3.	**Completion Criteria**
4.	**Assumptions and Constraints**
4.1.	Assumptions
4.2.	Constraints
5.	**Workplan**
5.1.	Deliverables
5.2.	General Approach
5.2.1.	Work Breakdown Structure
5.2.2.	Schedule and Milestones
5.2.3.	Estimate and Budget
5.2.4.	Cash Flow Analysis
5.2.5.	Project Organization and Staffing
5.3.	Detailed Approach
5.3.1.	Major Steps
5.3.2.	(First Step)
5.3.3.	(Second Step)
5.3.4.	(Third Step)
5.3.5.	(Fourth Step)
6.	**Staffing Requirements**
7.	**Scope Management Plan**
7.1.	Purpose of the Scope Management Plan
7.2.	Project Scope
7.3.	Project Justification
7.4.	Project Deliverables
7.4.1.	Project Management Deliverables
7.4.2.	Project Deliverables
7.5.	Project Objectives
7.6.	Scope Changes
7.6.1.	Scope Change Factors
7.6.2.	Identifying Scope Changes
7.6.3.	Scope Change Procedures
8.	**Schedule Management Plan**
8.1.	Purpose of the Schedule Management Plan
8.2.	Project Schedule
8.2.1.	Potential Causes of Schedule Slippages
8.3.	Project Control Procedures
8.3.1.	Identification of Schedule Problems

(continues)

Exhibit 4.26. (Continued.)

14.   Invoicing Procedures
14.1.   Invoicing Type
14.2.   Invoicing Procedure

APPENDIX A: DETAILED PROJECT SCHEDULE
APPENDIX B: SOURCES OF RISK CHECKLISTS
APPENDIX C: WORK BREAKDOWN STRUCTURE
APPENDIX D: PROJECT STAKEHOLDERS
APPENDIX E: ASSUMPTIONS AND CONSTRAINTS CHECKLISTS

5

Running the Project

Do I understand the project justification?
Do I understand the background to the project?
Do I understand the project politics?
Do I understand who the players are and the roles they will take?
Do I understand the client's priorities?

Have I defined the project deliverables?
Have I established the scope—both system and project?
Have I determined how deliverables will be reviewed and approved?
Have I defined the structure and organization of the client team?

Have I defined the risks and developed plans to mitigate them?
Have I documented the project assumptions and constraints?
Have I developed a quality plan?
Have I developed a list of detailed project activities?
Have I defined the dependencies between activities?
Have I built a project estimate of the work required?
Have I assigned resources and leveled them?
Have I completed the schedule, complete with milestones?
Have I aligned the schedule with the client's requirements?
Have I developed a project budget?
Have I planned for implementation?
Have I planned for completion?
Have I planned for communications?
Have I prepared an overall project plan?

Am I building an effective team?
Do I know where I stand against the schedule, estimate, and budget?
Am I managing risks?
Am I solving schedule problems?
Am I managing requests for scope changes?
Am I managing for quality?
Am I micromanaging when needed and not elsewhere?
Are my subcontractors delivering on their commitments?
Do I understand the expectations of the client, and can I meet them?
Am I conducting regular team meetings, and are they effective?
Do I report project status and outstanding issues regularly?
Am I taking the time to reflect privately on progress?
Do I and my team celebrate our successes?

Running the Project

The difference between planning a project and running it is the difference between a library and a disco. Planning is concentration; running is chaotic. Planning involves a few people and deep, focused thought; running involves scores of participants, demands, crises, and problems. Planning is solo; running is teamwork. Planning takes place at a desk; running belongs in the hallways and meeting rooms.

Planning a project is linear. As with fixing a flat tire, one step follows after another; you can't put the spare on until you've removed the flat. With project planning, there are iterations, but they are iterations of sequential steps. If you execute the sections in chapter 4, "Planning the Project," one after the other, you will end up with a complete project plan. Running a project, on the other hand, is nonlinear, like driving. As you drive, you must simultaneously steer, keep in the right gear, stay in your lane, check your rear, watch your speed, avoid other drivers, and be aware of where you are and where you're going at all times. So it is with running a project—all the activities must be continuously carried out until the project is finished.

The sections in chapter 5, therefore, are not meant to be followed sequentially. Their order has no significance.

A Practical Problem

It is difficult enough for one person to master the skills required for both planning and running a project. What makes it harder still is the need to overlap them. In the world of theory, the project manager takes over a project, crafts the plan, nurtures it through approval, then, shifting gears, assembles the team and charges into battle. In practice, the team comes together and the turmoil of the work begins. At about this time (later for those who are unlucky), the project manager arrives and must complete the plan while also directing the team.

The project manager who is thrown into the melee of a project must make planning a priority. It is, sadly, not uncommon for the plan and the project to finish concurrently. The result is that nobody knows what is expected, the team spends much of its time thrashing about in different directions, and energy that could be used to move the project forward is wasted. About the only good thing that can be said of such a project is that it does not go off the rails. The rails were never laid.

Activities in Running a Project

Running a project consists of the following activities:

1. Building a team
2. Tracking project progress
3. Negotiating for resources
4. Controlling action items
5. Managing risks
6. Solving overrun problems
7. Managing scope changes
8. Managing quality
9. Microplanning
10. Managing subcontractors
11. Managing client expectations
12. Conducting team meetings
13. Reporting project status

14. Reflection
15. Closing the project

The following sections describe each of these activities.

* * * * *

BUILDING THE TEAM

Project managers do not build systems; teams do. Unfortunately, most projects are staffed not by a team but by a bunch of people who happen to be working on the same thing. There is a vast difference between a team and a bunch of people, not the least of which is performance. Some researchers have suggested that a team will outperform a bunch of people by a factor of seven. Building a team is therefore the most important aspect of running a project.

A team is a group of people who are *committed* to a *common goal*.

There are two concepts in this definition: a common goal and commitment. Your job as project manager is to secure both.

A Common Goal

The common goal for a project should be easy to define: It is the successful completion of the project. But what does that mean? Does it mean creating a system that has a high degree of sophistication and complexity, or one that is more modest? Does it mean designing a system that is intuitive, or one that requires substantial user training? Does it mean building a system with state-of-the-art technology, or with more conventional tools? Without a clear agreement on these and other issues, different members of the project team will define their own goals and then spend hours pressing their own points of view.

One of the most important steps in developing a common goal is to disclose it. There is nothing magical about a project goal; it can be stated as, "We will do [scope] by [schedule] within [constraints]." Problems arise when nobody tells the team members what the goal is. Understandably, they get confused.

Equally important is ensuring that all team members accept the goal. Everyone has an opinion about how systems should be developed and what they should contain, and some of those opinions will clash with the project goal. For example, if the client wants a low-cost system and is prepared to forgo some complex functions, some team members will be upset because the system will be functionally incomplete. If they do not accept the goal of a limited system, their discontent will either poison the team atmosphere or influence the team to overbuild. In either case, the costs will spiral and the schedule will suffer.

To get acceptance of the goal, there are four steps you can take:

1. Identify the problems that you know some members of the team will have. Say to them, for example, "I know some of you won't like the limited scope, but that's what the client wants."

2. Sell the project. Tell the team, "This project is important to us because. . . . As team members, you will learn. . . . I think this will be a good project because. . . ."

3. Ask the team to accept the goal, and put the onus on each person to object. Say, "I've described the scope, schedule, and constraints of the project. I'd like you to accept them as your own goals. If any of you have any concerns, please see me after the meeting." Do not ask people to raise their objections on the spot. The project goal is not open to debate.

4. Watch for furrowed brows, downcast looks, scowls, and other indications of discontent, then approach their owners after the meeting for a private discussion of the concerns.

When teams do not understand or commit to goals, it is usually because management chose not to disclose them unambiguously and consistently. Some managers feel that project participants should have no interest in the project beyond the work that has been assigned to them. In this view, team members are expected just to do their work. More detail would simply confuse them—or, worse, give them the notion that they might actually have influence.

The problem with this attitude is that work, particularly in systems, benefits from a knowledge of the context. Team members who understand how their assignments fit into the project or contribute to the final results will be better able to adapt what they are doing to the overall project. In other cases, management hides the goals out of the fear that if the team members really understood the project, they'd walk out. When projects are risky or the cost of failure is high, some managers believe that those who understand the risks will want to be far removed from the project so that they will not personally be associated with its consequences. If the company routinely punishes members of less-successful project teams, this fear is justified. However, in most companies, letting the team know the risks and the dangers focuses them and allows them to help keep themselves and one another on track.

As the project manager, it is your job to make sure that every team member knows the goals, background, and context of the project. Include a presentation of these in the project kickoff meeting, and make sure they are part of the orientation for new team members.

Building the Environment for Commitment

There is a difference between accepting a goal and committing to it. You accept a goal when you acknowledge it and agree that it would be nice to achieve it. You commit to a goal when you decide to make it so important that it has priority over everything else, or when you decide that failure to achieve it is intolerable, or when it becomes an emotional imperative.

Commitment is personal; each team member generates it internally. You cannot create commitment in others, but, as any motivational consultant knows, you can create an atmosphere. Your choice is whether that atmosphere will nourish commitment or poison it. In reality, you do not build teams, you build the environment from which commitment—and team-work—springs.

Building an environment for commitment requires that you commit to a few classic principles:

- **Lead by example.** People will commit to a difficult goal only if they see commitment from you. If you want them to put in extra time, put in extra time yourself. If you want them to produce quality work, make sure that your own work is unsurpassed. If you want them to treat the client with respect, treat the client with respect. Ensure that your actions reinforce your words.

- **Set specific expectations.** Make sure that all team members understand their assignments and delivery dates, and emphasize that you expect both to be honored. Many projects have been derailed when someone says, "I didn't know you wanted me to do that." Make sure that none of the team members can reasonably make such a statement to you; otherwise, they have nothing to which they can commit.

  Nothing is more important than setting expectations and demanding that they be met. Completed work is the measure of how a project is progressing, and work is completed by people meeting demands. Those who do not finish their assignments on time, or whose work is consistently late and riddled with errors, or who interfere with others on the team are poor performers. You have the right to remove them and insist that they be replaced by capable people. Not only will the others on your team not object, they will wonder what took you so long.

- **Develop leaders.** Make leadership fluid. Let it flow to those who deserve it. On any given issue, one person is more knowledgeable than the others, including you. When decisions must be made, let that person take leadership. You will get better-quality decisions, and you will send the message to your team members that you trust their abilities and judgment.

- **Walk the halls.** For many project managers, the safest place is the office, where there is so much work to do that it is easy to justify remaining desk-bound. The problem is that your desk will tell you nothing about what is really happening out there. You need to be available to your people—to be out among them, talking, listening, and involved. Otherwise, they will avoid you except to give you a distanced, sanitized, overoptimistic view of events and relationships that will leave you baffled and confused when the project comes crashing down.

- **Involve your team.** Let your people know how they are doing. Keep them up to date with status reports and reviews of plan versus actuals. They want to be successful, so they need feedback. More important, where problems emerge, such as a schedule slippage, solicit their advice and suggestions. Not only will you get a wealth of opinions, you will have their support for whatever actions they suggest.

- **Emphasize teamwork.** Teamwork means that work is divided among team members dynamically so that the burden does not fall unfairly on a few. If Fred is overworked and Mary has some spare time, bring Fred and Mary together to reallocate the load. If George gets sick, find out if his work can be distributed among the other members of the team. Above all, encourage an atmosphere in which each team member is willing to help others who are temporarily strained. Nothing can destroy a sense of teamwork more effectively than team saboteurs, those who undermine their colleagues to each other and to you. They particularly thrive off managers who support them. Be alert for team members who criticize others, especially if their comments are disguised by jollity. Then be absolutely ruthless in eliminating the behavior. If you do not, you will have a dispirited, antagonistic group of people—the opposite of a team.

- **Serve your team.** You want your people working on the jobs they have been assigned, not on peripheral activities. If the clerical staff has gone home and there is photocopying to be done or someone must tend to the fax machine, you do it. If someone must travel to the airport to pick up or send a package, you go. If a program needs debugging and the programmer is sick, you debug it. You make the coffee when the stuff in the pot congeals, and you order—and pay for—the pizza and the chicken when the team stays late. In other words, you do whatever needs to be done that would otherwise distract people from their assignments.

- **Defend your team.** There will come a time when members of your team will come under attack, from the client, management, external participants, or other team members. The quality of your team building will depend upon how you respond.

     Of course, if the attack is unjustified or the charges are mitigated by circumstances unknown to the attacker, you must defend the team member. However, the real test of your team-building skills comes when the attack is reasonable and you observe that, were you in the attacker's position, you would do the same. This is a test because in these cases, you must still defend the team member.

     When the charge is justified, your only defense may be to say, "I am not going to be pressured into acting prematurely. I will investigate this, but right now I'm not going to do anything until I have had the chance to check it out." Then investigate. If discipline is called for, apply it, but only to the extent that you believe is justified.

Defending someone who has made serious errors is not easy, but your reason for doing so is to maintain the integrity of the team. If, when someone complains to you about a team member, you agree with the complainant and confirm the criticism, you are committing two errors: You are condemning the person without a hearing, and you are setting an environment in which complaints are an acceptable means of dealing with others.

- **Remove obstacles.** What is interfering with the work? Is the temperature too high or too low? Is the room noisy? Is it smoky? Is the equipment archaic? You must be relentless in finding out what annoys and slows down the team. Then, to the extent of your ability, fix the problem or admit to the team members that you cannot fix it and that they'll have to adjust.

  Part of removing obstacles is finding them. Since most people will not complain, you must actively seek problems. Do so in public and in private. If the members of your team see that you are committed to making their lives better, they will give you their problems—and higher effort.

- **Praise in public.** When people do things right, let them know. Identify what they have done and why it is praiseworthy. Above all, praise in public. Everyone likes ego stroking, even the warm embarrassment that comes when others hear it.

  Praise everything that deserves praise. If someone looks especially sharp, praise. If someone has just completed a course, praise. If someone has been elected to the local school board, praise.

  The purpose of praise is to make people feel better. Such people will be far more willing to commit to the project than the person who, despite having put in fifty hours so far this week, has just been chewed out for coming in fifteen minutes late.

- **Correct in private.** Sometimes you will have to correct or discipline team members. The worst way to do this is to criticize them in front of others. Not only does this make an enemy, it reminds the others of the abyss between you, the manager, and them, the flunkies. Public criticism creates distance and builds isolation.

  Correct or discipline in private, and always follow three steps:

1. Describe the specific behavior that is a problem. ("On these three occasions, you committed to deliver something by a certain date, and you did not deliver.")

2. Identify the consequences of the behavior. ("On the first occasion, we could not start integration for a week and the integration team had to put in overtime to catch up. On the second occasion. . . .")

3. State what is required. ("You have now committed to deliver results by the fifteenth. I expect you to do whatever is necessary to get the work done or to let me know now if there will be a problem.")

Never criticize personality ("You're not forceful enough"). It's mean-spirited and probably wrong, and there's not much anyone can do about it anyway.

- **Facilitate communication.** One of the characteristics of a team is togetherness. Therefore, get the members together. If you cannot physically put them in the same place, make sure they can easily communicate with e-mail or voice mail. People will do what the structure of the workplace dictates: The harder it is to communicate, the less communication there will be.

- **Thank people.** Thank people liberally. Thank them for putting in extra time or helping someone else out or recommending a solution or telling you of a problem or taking a phone message or delivering a result or doing anything else that may help the project. Even thank them for doing the work they are paid to do. Why thank people? Why not? It makes them feel good, and it's free.

  One way to thank people is materially. Give them some time off. Buy a candy jar and keep it filled. Bring doughnuts to the team meetings. Take them out to lunch. Simple expressions of gratitude make it easier for people to want the project to succeed. Wanting success is the first step to commitment.

Another View of Team Building

Numerous studies have been done to find out what people want and how to motivate them. While the details differ, there are three benefits that today's workers, whether industrial, clerical, professional, or managerial, consistently value more than money: recognition, a sense of control, and appreciation.

You give recognition to team members by publicly acknowledging the benefits they have given to the project. You give them a sense of control by involving them in project decisions and by encouraging leadership. You give appreciation every time you make a person feel welcome and important.

There are three main reasons why managers do not give these valued benefits to their people. Some feel that their obligations end with the paycheck and that giving recognition, appreciation, and a sense of control invites staff to goof off or take advantage of the new corporate soft touch. Others simply do not think about these benefits or do not consider them important. These attitudes do not yield to arguments.

Other managers, however, would like to praise or thank staff but are reluctant to do so on the grounds that it seems manipulative, a con game with insincere platitudes. The solution is easy: Mean what you say.

You do not need to be effusive. In fact, if you force yourself into unnatural postures, you will indeed seem insincere. However, a simple "Well done," or "Good job," or "Thanks," or even "Not bad," when you mean it, is all that is required. With practice, you may even begin to look forward to praising and thanking.

What If?

There Are Team Members Who Openly Undermine the Team-Building Process

You will not have a team; you will have a set of factions. Work will falter; the project will fall behind schedule, and you will not be able to rescue it.

Actions

Identify the specific actions of the dissidents that have undermined team building. Document the effect on the team.

Confront the dissidents, describe what they have done and what the results are, and inform them that you expect the situation to improve. Set clear expectations, such as "I expect not to hear any more negative comments in team meetings" or "If you have any objections to the suggestions of other team members, I expect you to raise them professionally and to cease using ridicule.''

If the situation continues, request that the dissidents be replaced by more cooperative team members. Take this step even if you will lose a highly skilled participant. Nobody is irreplaceable, and the impact of this kind of behavior on your team is devastating. You cannot tolerate it.

You Have People Who Constantly Complain About Other Team Members

Unless you can stop the complaints, your team atmosphere will be poisoned by distrust and suspicion. If you actually take actions that support the complaints, you will foster the belief that you are not interested in your team and prefer political games to real progress.

Actions

If the complaint is offensive (for example, racially based), inform the complainant that you will not tolerate this kind of behavior and that you expect professionalism from your team. Your intent is not to support a cause, no matter how honorable, but to help build a team that is focused on the project goal rather than on each other.

When you receive a complaint, ask, ''Have you discussed this with the team member?'' If the answer is no, tell the complainant that you expect team members to work out difficulties among themselves and come to you only as a last resort.

If real frictions develop and worsen, you will have to become a mediator. It is reasonable to separate people who cannot stand each other or to structure the work so that one person does not feel exploited. However, make sure that your mediation is conducted with both (or all) parties present so that the results are as fair as you can make them.

A Client Demands That You Fire a Team Member

Such demands are typically about control and who wields it. You do. You cannot afford to defer to anyone else. If you accept the demand, you have yielded control of your team to the client and indicated to your team members whom they must please.

Actions

Recognize that the demand is never justified. It may be based on good reasons, and the client may be justified in stating his or her concern about a team member, but the team is yours, and nobody but you has hiring and firing authority.

State that you absolutely will not meet this demand but that if the client cares to withdraw it, you are willing to discuss any concerns.

If you had intended to remove the team member before the complaint, you are now in a difficult situation, but you cannot comply with the client's request. Tell the client that you do not intend to fire the person, that you cannot accept ultimatums, that the demand is unacceptable, and that you expect a more reasonable discussion in similar situations in the future. Tell the team member that you have concerns but that you are prepared to offer him or her a chance for improvement. Then, at some point in the future, unless the team member improves, you can quietly ask management for a replacement.

* * * * *

TRACKING PROGRESS

Running a project is simple: Meet all activity completion dates, and the project is on track; miss one, and you are in trouble. Keeping the project on schedule, therefore, means ensuring that all activities finish on time and that all milestones are met.

Tracking Activities

There are two approaches to tracking activities. You can keep your fingers crossed and hope that Fred's "Yeah, it should be done by then" is a commitment. Alternatively, you can use a formal tracking mechanism. One of the best known is the estimate at completion (EAC); unfortunately, this is so cumbersome that few companies implement it properly, if they use it at all. This chapter describes EACs and, because they are difficult to use, gives an alternative approach. Another formal mechanism is Earned Value, which is described later in this section. First, however, there are some principles that effective tracking approaches must follow.

Principles for Tracking Activities

During World War II, when Germany was suffering from a shortage of butter but a glut of manure, the Reich commissioned a project to convert manure to butter. At the first status meeting, the project manager reported, "In converting manure to butter, there are four problems: odor, taste, color, and texture. We've solved the problems of color and texture. We're 50 percent complete."

Regardless of how you track progress, here are some principles that will make you more effective:

- **Be formal.** When you want to find out how people are doing, never ask casually and never depend on an oral response. If you ask, "How's it going?" the answer you will deservedly get is, "Fine." If you ask, "Are we on track for next Friday?" you will predictably hear, "Yeah, it looks like it." There is nothing wrong with casual conversation, but when you really want to find out what is happening, there is only one effective way: Ask all team members for a formal weekly status report. If the report is oral, overtly write down what they say.

- **Be specific.** Make sure all team members understand that when they say an activity is complete, it is complete. No further time may be booked against it, no more work may be done on it, its product advances to the next stage of the project, and its staff members become fully available for their next assignments. "Ninety percent complete" is a contradiction in terms.

- **Be sensitive to language.** If you ask someone if the work will be done on time, only "yes" means yes. Answers such as "Yeah," "It looks like it," "I think so," or "I'll try" do not mean yes. They are evasions offered in the hope that you will stop asking. When you get such answers, ask, "Does that mean yes?" and persist until you get a flat yes or an admission that "Well, there may be a problem."

    In particular, look for statements such as "It will be virtually complete" or "It will be 95 percent done." Both mean "It won't be complete." As any techie knows, "virtual" means "not real," and, as any project manager can tell you, the last 5 percent takes as long as the first 95 percent.

The Estimate at Completion (EAC)

The EAC is the estimate, *during an activity,* of the effort the activity will have required when it is finished. It is the amount of work done to date plus the team member's estimate of the amount of work remaining. For example, if you have a six-week activity on which three weeks have been spent and the person responsible estimates that four weeks are needed for completion, then you know, halfway into the activity, that there will be a problem, and you will have time to act.

Generating EACs is an administrative headache. Someone must calculate the time already spent on each activity, collect estimates of time remaining, calculate the EACs, compare them with the original estimates, and compile a report of variances. Furthermore, to be effective, EACs must be generated each week for all activities that are in progress.

The easiest way to generate EACs is with an automated time sheet procedure in which everyone submits a weekly time sheet that shows the time spent on each activity. Team members record their time against activity numbers, which ideally are the WBS numbers. The time sheet is used by the time reporting system to calculate the effort spent to date. It should also include a place for people to estimate the time remaining for activities they have worked on.

Exhibit 5.1 is a sample time sheet. If the time sheet does not include space for the estimates, you will have to ask team members to provide them

Exhibit 5.1. Sample Time Sheet

Time Sheet

Project: _____   For Week Ending: _____

Name: _____

Activity Number	Description	Hours	Estimate
_____	_____	_____	_____
_____	_____	_____	_____
_____	_____	_____	_____
_____	_____	_____	_____
_____	_____	_____	_____
_____	_____	_____	_____
_____	_____	_____	_____
_____	_____	_____	_____
_____	_____	_____	_____
_____	_____	_____	_____
Total		_____	_____

separately. (Exhibit 5.1 does not provide for daily time reporting because, unless overtime is paid on a daily basis, there is no value in knowing how the time was distributed over the week.)

An assistant can enter the actuals and estimates into software, either a spreadsheet or the project management tool, that calculates the EACs and generates variances from the original estimates.

When more than one person works on an activity, each person should submit a separate estimate for his or her work remaining. The EAC is the total of all work performed to date plus the total of all estimates.

There are three great advantages of EACs: They provide the status of an activity while it is in progress, they force people to commit to an estimate in writing each week, and, since they capture time actually charged to the project, they can be used to track the budget as well as the schedule.

If you manage EACs properly, you will receive weekly reports on all activities that are in progress, with the risky ones marked for your action. However, to use EACs, you must have two major mechanisms in place: a time reporting system that will capture and report time by activity number, and a means of collecting estimates, calculating EACs, and producing variance reports. If your organization does not use such systems, it is futile to try to impose them as a general practice. However, you can set up this kind of time reporting for your own project, especially if it is large, with a full-time team. For those of you with smaller or multiple projects in which it would be an administrative nightmare to set up a separate time sheet system for each one (not to mention the resistance from people who are being asked to submit multiple time sheets), there is an alternative that is less demanding and easier to set up.

Progress Reporting

Progress reporting is a formal mechanism in which each team member prepares a weekly progress report. Exhibit 5.2 is a sample progress report form that consists of four sections. In the first section, the person lists all activities worked on. For each activity, the person enters the scheduled and projected completion dates. The projected completion date will be one of the following:

OK: The activity will complete on the scheduled date.

Date: The activity will complete on the stated date.

C: The activity is complete.

This process ensures that all team members are aware of their scheduled completion dates for each activity and that they commit to a completion date in writing each week. Other sections on the progress report form allow team members to report the progress they have made, problems they have encountered, and the progress they expect to make in the following week.

Collect these forms each week at a specific time, preferably Monday morning. This lets people include weekend work in their progress reports. By Monday at noon, you will have been able to review the forms, and you will know the current state of the project.

When you receive the forms, review the Activity section and meet privately with each person who reports a slippage. You want to identify the

Exhibit 5.2. Sample Progress Report Form

Progress Report

Project: _____ **For Week Ending:** _____

Name: _____

Activity	Scheduled Completion	Projected Completion
_____	_____	_____
_____	_____	_____
_____	_____	_____
_____	_____	_____

Problems Encountered

Progress Made

Progress Expected

reason for the slippage and find a solution. Then review the Problems Encountered section for new problems and the Progress Made section so that you can announce progress. Next week, compare the Progress Made section to this week's Progress Expected to ensure that each person actually achieved what you were told he or she would.

Tracking Milestones

Milestones are key points in the project at which certain deliverables will be ready or a set of activities completed. Milestones are easy to track because they occur on specific dates and mark the delivery of specific products. If the products are ready on or before that date, then the project is on schedule. If not, it is late.

Managing milestones differs from managing activities in two respects. First, you must ensure that milestones are obvious to the entire team. Everyone should be aware that next Thursday afternoon we will present the completed process model or the data entry prototype or the implementation plan, and everyone should be willing to help out wherever necessary to ensure that the milestone is met.

Second, you must establish that milestone dates are not negotiable. Some activities may slip, but milestones will be met.

As noted in chapter 4, in the section "Preparing the Schedule," there are two types of milestones: internal and external.

An external milestone is one that delivers specific results to the client. It may be argued that external milestones are the only true measure of project progress; if they are met, it does not matter how the individual activities fared. From the client's point of view, the external milestones are the only things that count. Client involvement in the milestones means that the meeting to hand over the material must be booked in advance and that it cannot easily be changed. It also means that the schedule must allow for any packaging that the deliverables require.

Internal milestones are less formal and may vary as long as the external milestones are not compromised. However, the lack of formality is a problem if team members equate informality with insignificance. One of your challenges will be to ensure that internal milestones are treated as seriously as the external ones.

What If?

Team Members Consistently Understate Their EACs

An understated EAC is an underestimate. The activity will not be done on time, and, worse, you will not find out that it is late until the date it is due. You will not be able to track activities accurately.

Actions

Recognize that consistently unmet EACs are less a problem of estimating than one of commitment. People who do not meet their own estimates have little sense that the estimates matter and a poor understanding of the consequences of not meeting them.

For each team member who understates EACs, compile a list of instances, then meet with the team member to present the list and its effect on the project.

State your expectation that EACs are to be met. Then review the team member's current activities, and ask for a date by which the work will be done. Make it clear that this estimate is a commitment and that failing to meet it will have serious consequences.

If the problem persists, escalate the issue to the team member's supervisor and, in extreme cases, ask that the person be replaced on the team.

Team Members Object to Filling Out the Progress Reports and Providing EACs

This objection usually arises in companies where time reporting is informal or nonexistent and the progress reports are a deviation from normal practice. However, without these details, you will find it impossible to track progress on all but the simplest of projects.

Actions

Describe the importance of accurate progress reporting and insist that the reports be filled out as you requested.

State that you will interpret the absence of detailed reports as a commitment to meet the scheduled activity completion dates. If the team meets all its dates, you can congratulate them. If not, insist that those who are late on any activity submit weekly progress reports.

* * * * *

EARNED VALUE

Here is a question. You are three months into a six-month project and you have spent 50 percent of the project costs. Are you on budget?

Here's another. You are three months into a six-month project and you have completed 50 percent of the effort. Are you on schedule?

The answer to both questions is the consultant's favorite: "It depends." In the first case, if you have spent 50 percent of the budget but completed just 40 percent of the work, you are over budget. In the second case, if you had planned to complete 60 percent of the work in the first three months but have completed only half, you are behind schedule.

These examples illustrate that being on track is a function of two things: where you had planned to be at this point in the project and where you actually are. If you are behind where you had planned to be, in terms of either the budget or the work completed, your project is slipping, regardless of where you are relative to your position on the project time line.

However, what does it mean to be "where you had planned to be" or "where you are"? It depends on whether you are discussing the schedule or the budget.

- For the schedule, "where you had planned to be" is the work that you had planned to complete by the current date, and "where you are" is the work that you've actually completed. But how do you measure "where you had planned to be" and "where you are"? For our purposes, we will use effort, so that, for the schedule, "where you had planned to be" is the effort you had planned to have expended by the current date, and "where you are" is the effort that you've actually expended.

- For the budget, "where you had planned to be" is the effort that you had planned to expend for the work that you have actually completed (*not* for the work that you had planned to complete), and "where you are" is the effort that you've actually expended, just as it is for the schedule.

You may be surprised that the budget is measured by effort. After all, budgets are usually monetary and consist of the labor costs plus any nonlabor expenses such as purchases or travel. Obviously, you need to measure nonlabor expenses in dollars, but using money to measure labor usage has several problems:

- The labor budget is the effort multiplied by some charge rate, which varies among team members. If Fred, whose rate is $50 an hour, is assigned to activities that total 1,000 hours, the budget for Fred's work is $50,000. However, if Fred becomes unavailable and is replaced by Mary, whose rate is $60 an hour, the project budget for the same work is now $60,000, an overrun of $10,000 because of a circumstance beyond the project manager's control.

- If, for internal fiscal reasons, the charge rates are adjusted upward by some amount, the project budget is exceeded, and again, the project manager has no control over the excess.

- Many organizations do not charge labor costs to projects and are therefore tempted to conclude that preparing a budget is irrelevant and managing one unnecessary. This is a mistake: Managing an IT project budget is, for the most part, managing effort.

For these reasons, this discussion on earned value uses effort, usually expressed as hours, so that when we refer to the "budgeted cost," we are referring to hours of effort. This is a departure from the traditional method of earned value, which uses dollars, but, since dollars are a direct multiple of effort, the components of earned value reflect the same thing regardless of whether the budgeted costs are in dollars or hours.

There is one final term that needs some explanation. The "value" in earned value has nothing to do with what the client perceives as the value of the project product. It refers to the contribution of an activity or set of activities to the overall project and is synonymous with the budgeted cost of that activity or set of activities, whether expressed in dollars or in effort.

Before we get to the formal definitions, let's look at a simple example of measuring progress. Assume that you have an activity that will take four weeks and require full time from Fred, giving an effort for the activity of 160 hours. At the end of week two, Fred tells you that the activity is 40 percent complete (more about percent completion later) and that he has worked for two full weeks on the activity. From this, you can determine the following project status:

- You had planned that at the end of week two, Fred would be 50 percent complete and would, therefore, have used up eighty hours of his budget.

- You also observe that 40 percent of the work should require 40 percent of the budget, or sixty-four hours.

- Since Fred has expended eighty hours to complete sixty-four hours of value, he is over budget.

- Since Fred has produced only sixty-four hours of value at the point that you had planned he would have produced eighty hours, he is behind schedule.

Now let's change one of the conditions: Fred has not worked full-time. Because he was ill for two days, he has spent only eight days instead of the ten you had planned he would have spent. Under this condition:

- You had planned that at the end of week two, Fred would be 50 percent complete and would, therefore, have used up eighty hours of his budget.

- You also observe that 40 percent of the work should cost 40 percent of the budget, or sixty-four hours.

- Since Fred has expended sixty-four hours (eight days at eight hours a day) to complete sixty-four hours of value, he is exactly on budget.

- However, since Fred has produced sixty-four hours of value at the point that you had planned he would have produced eighty hours, he is behind schedule.

Or consider another set of conditions: that Fred worked two weekends as well as the two weeks and is now 60 percent complete.

- You had planned that at the end of week two, Fred would be 50 percent complete and would, therefore, have used up eighty hours of his budget.

- You also observe that 60 percent of the work should cost 60 percent of the budget, or ninety-six hours.

- Since Fred has spent 112 hours (fourteen days at eight hours a day) to complete ninety-six hours of value, he is over budget.

- However, since Fred has produced ninety-six hours of value at the point that you had planned he would have produced eighty hours, he is ahead of schedule.

Now you may object that all of this is overkill, that the easiest way to determine your schedule status is to glance at the "today" line on your Gantt chart. If you are on schedule, all activities to the left of the line will be finished and all activities that it intersects will be in progress. However, if the preceding analyses seem excessive, that is only because we have applied the techniques to a single activity. In any project, you will have many activities taking place at the same time. Some of those will be ahead of schedule, some behind. How do you determine exactly where you are?

This is where the concept of "earned value" comes in. Earned value is a specific set of techniques used to determine project progress against the budget and schedule and to predict the final project duration and costs while the project is still in progress.

Earned value defines three variables that are used to measure project performance. As you may conclude from the previous discussion, two of them are "where you had planned to be" and "where you are." Remember the meanings of these phrases:

- For the schedule, "where you had planned to be" is the effort you had planned to expend by the current date.

- For the budget, "where you had planned to be" is the effort you had planned to expend to do the work that you've actually done.

- For both, "where you are" is the effort that you've actually spent.

In the following examples, we illustrate the variables with amounts from a single activity, but on a project, they are aggregate totals of the effort of all activities to this point in the project. The variables are:

- **The Budgeted Cost of Work Performed, or BCWP.** This is "where you had planned to be" for the budget: the effort that you planned to expend to complete the work that has actually been done. It is called the "earned value." In the last of the three preceding examples, it is ninety-six hours, or 60 percent of the total activity budget of 160 hours.

- **The Budgeted Cost of Work Scheduled, or BCWS.** This is "where you had planned to be" for the schedule: the effort that you had planned to expend at this point in the project. In the example, the BCWS is eighty hours because you had budgeted that amount for the first two weeks of the activity.

- **The Actual Cost of Work Performed, or ACWP.** This is "where you are": the effort that you have actually expended at this point in the project. In the example, it is 112 hours, the amount that Fred has actually used.

From these three variables, we can calculate measures that tell us how the project is doing. There are two variances and two ratios or indices. They are:

1. **Cost Variance, or CV.** This tells you whether you are over or under budget. It is the difference between what you had planned to expend for the work that has been done and what you have actually expended. It is the BCWP minus the ACWP. In the example, the CV is 96 hours − 112 hours = −16 hours.

   A negative CV means that the project is over budget.

2. **Schedule Variance, or SV.** This tells you whether you are ahead of or behind schedule. It is the difference between what you had planned to expend for the work that has actually been done and what you had planned to expend at this point in the schedule. It is the BCWP minus the BCWS. In the example, the SV is 96 hours − 80 hours = 16 hours.

   A positive SV means that the project is ahead of schedule.

3. **Cost Performance Index, or CPI.** This also tells you whether you are over or under budget. It is the ratio of what you had planned to expend for the work that has actually been done and what you have actually expended. It is the BCWP divided by the ACWP. In the example, the CPI is 96 hours ÷ 112 hours = 0.86.

   A CPI of less than one means that the project is over budget.

4. **Schedule Performance Index, or SPI.** This also tells you whether you are ahead of or behind schedule. It is the ratio of what you had planned to expend for the work that has actually been done and what you had planned to expend at this point in the schedule. It is the BCWP divided by the BCWS. In the example, the CPI is 96 hours ÷ 80 hours = 1.2.

   An SPI of greater than one means that the project is ahead of schedule.

In terms of information, there is no difference between the two variances and their corresponding indices, but the indices can be used to project what the final cost and schedule of the project will be if current trends continue. The calculations are:

1. **Estimate at Completion, or EAC.** This is the original estimated total number of hours for the project divided by the SPI. In the exam-

ple, the EAC is 160 hours ÷ 1.2 = 133 hours. This indicates that Fred will complete the activity at the point at which you planned that he would have spent 133 hours, which is just under three weeks, two days, instead of the four weeks you had planned.

2. **Budget at Completion, or BAC.** This is the original total project labor costs divided by the CPI. In the example, the BAC is 160 hours ÷ 0.86 = 186 hours. This indicates that this activity will require 186 hours of effort to complete instead of the 160 hours you had planned.

A point must be made about this example. Although Fred will complete ahead of schedule, he will accomplish this by working on weekends, not by being more efficient. In fact, his actual effort will be greater than the estimate. Nevertheless, he will be available for another assignment three days earlier than planned.

There are two other general points to note. First, the calculations for EAC and BAC make a large assumption: that the causes of the current project status, whether ahead of or behind plan, will apply consistently for the remainder of the project. Since this is rarely the case, these figures must be viewed skeptically. However, used carefully, they can provide an approximation to the final project results.

Second, most project management software provides earned value calculations and gives you the three variables—BCWP, BCWS, and ACWP—at any point in the project. Because the software is based on the traditional method of earned value calculations, it expresses these variables as dollar costs. If you do not charge labor costs to the project, there will be no such costs and no variables. You can resolve this by charging each resource at $1 per hour. Your reports will put a dollar sign beside these values, so you will have to remember that you are looking at effort, not dollars.

Exhibit 5.3 gives a summary of the earned value terms, their definitions, and, for the calculations from the three variables, their interpretations.

Determining Percent Complete

The BCWP, which is used in calculating both of the variances and both of the indices, requires knowledge of the percent completion of all activities. However, determining percentage completion is risky, as any project

Exhibit 5.3. Summary of Earned Value Terms

Measure	Definition	Interpretation
Budgeted Cost of Work Performed (BCWP)	The budget that you had planned to spend on the work that has been done at this point in the project	
Budgeted Cost of Work Scheduled (BCWS)	The budget that you had planned to spend at this point in the project, regardless of what work has actually been done	
Actual Cost of Work Performed (ACWP)	The actual costs to complete the work that has been done at this point in the project	
Cost Variance (CV)	BCWP − ACWP	<0: project is over budget =0: project is on budget >0: project is under budget
Schedule Variance (SV)	BCWP − BCWS	<0: project is behind schedule =0: project is on schedule >0: project is ahead of schedule
Cost Performance Index (CPI)	BCWP ÷ ACWP	<1: project is over budget =1: project is on budget >1: project is under budget
Schedule Performance Index (SPI)	BCWP ÷ BCWS	<1: project is behind schedule =1: project is on schedule >1: project is ahead of schedule
Estimate at Completion (EAC)	Total project hours ÷ SPI	Gives projected total hours for the project if current trends continue
Budget at Completion (BAC)	Total project labor costs ÷ CPI	Gives projected total costs for the project if current trends continue

manager who has been informed that an activity "is 95 percent finished" will attest. Some authorities have suggested that accuracy in calculating percent completion is less important in IT projects than in construction projects because of the difference in activity duration. It is rare that a work activity on an IT project takes more than a few weeks, but some construction activities, such as highway construction, can take years. It is far more difficult to know where you are in that kind of activity than in one where activities are short. Therefore, it has been suggested that percent completion be set at some low value, such as 25 percent, when the activity is started, and set at 100 percent when it is finished. This approach understates progress and has the potential to indicate that the project is slightly over budget or behind schedule when it's not, but it can serve as a good approximation of the status.

Another approach to determining percent completion is to use the "projected completion" for each activity from the project time sheet. (See Exhibit 5.1 for a sample time sheet). To illustrate, if the activity was originally estimated at three weeks, two weeks of effort have been spent, and the team member is indicating a projected completion date two weeks hence, then two things are apparent: that the activity has slipped by one week, and that it is 50 percent complete (the activity will take four weeks, of which two weeks have been spent). You will have to be careful that the activity has slipped because the team member has to do work beyond the estimate and not because the activity depends upon some other activity's completion. For example, if the projected completion date is two weeks hence because another activity has slipped but the bulk of the work will have been completed next week, then this activity is still two-thirds complete.

Exhibit 5.4 is a sample earned value spreadsheet. The activity ID, name, duration, effort, and start and finish dates are exported from project management software. The planned percent complete is calculated by comparing the activity start and finish dates to the reference date in the heading. The BCWS is the planned percent completion multiplied by the effort, and the BCWP is the actual percent completion multiplied by the effort. The actual percent complete and the ACWP are entered manually. The spreadsheet calculates the variances, the ratios, and the EAC and BAC.

* * * *

NEGOTIATING FOR RESOURCES

Your project will go nowhere without resources. This means that one of your primary jobs is to make sure that you have the people your project needs. In fact, there are three factors that you need to consider:

1. **You need a set of skills.** If your organization has just one network analyst, you have no alternative. If there are several network analysts,

Exhibit 5.4. Sample Earned Value Spreadsheet

Earned Value Report as of 26-Mar-04

ID	Activity Name	Duration (Days)	Effort (Hrs.)	Activity Dates Start	Finish	% Complete Planned	Actual	BCWS	BCWP	ACWP	SV	CV	SPI	CPI
3	Define requirements	5	40	28-Jan-04	03-Feb-04	100%	100%	40	40	44	0	-4	1.0	0.9
4	Identify qualified vendors	2	8	04-Feb-04	05-Feb-04	100%	100%	8	8	10	0	-2	1.0	0.8
5	Prepare and issue RFQ	5	40	06-Feb-04	12-Feb-04	100%	100%	40	40	35	0	5	1.0	1.1
6	RFQ issued	0	0	12-Feb-04	12-Feb-04	100%	100%	0	0	0	0	0		
8	Evaluate written quotations	5	40	12-Mar-04	18-Mar-04	100%	100%	40	40	50	0	-10	1.0	0.8
9	Conduct demos and presentations	10	80	19-Mar-04	01-Apr-04	60%	40%	48	32	45	-16	-13	0.7	0.7
10	Check references	2	8	02-Apr-04	05-Apr-04	0%	50%	0	8	4	8	4		2.0
11	Negotiate terms and prices	2	16	06-Apr-04	07-Apr-04	0%	0%	0	0	0	0	0		
12	Make final hardware selection	1	8	08-Apr-04	08-Apr-04	0%	0%	0	0	0	0	0		
13	Hardware selected	0	0	08-Apr-04	08-Apr-04	0%	0%	0	0	0	0	0		
15	Purchase and expedite delivery	1	8	09-Apr-04	09-Apr-04	0%	0%	0	0	0	0	0		
16	Install hardware and system software	3	24	10-May-04	12-May-04	0%	0%	0	0	0	0	0		
17	Conduct acceptance tests	1	8	13-May-04	13-May-04	0%	0%	0	0	0	0	0		
18	Train the project team	2	16	14-May-04	17-May-04	0%	0%	0	0	0	0	0		
19	System ready for development	0	0	17-May-04	17-May-04	0%	0%	0	0	0	0	0		
20	Conduct ongoing maintenance	1	8	18-May-04	18-May-04	0%	0%	0	0	0	0	0		
	Totals	40	304					176	168	188	-8	-20	0.95	0.89

Estimate at completion 318
Budget at completion 340

you may request the one you know and with whom you work best, but any of the available analysts will fill your requirement.

2. **You need an availability commitment.** If you need a network analyst full-time, your project will suffer if you can get one only half-time. A less obvious problem occurs when you need the person half-time and one is assigned to your project while also having other responsibilities. The problem is that the person may not be able to give you 50 percent of his or her time because of other commitments. It's hard to complain to a manager that you need more of Mary's time when she's already assigned to your project.

3. **You need a duration commitment.** If you need Mary for three months, it's of little use when her manager tells you that you can have her for one.

You will encounter two types of resource negotiation problem: getting the resources you need at the start of the project, and negotiating for resources as the project progresses.

Requesting Resources at the Start of the Project

The first step in negotiating for resources is to tell those who are responsible for assigning them what skills you need, along with the required availability and duration. As soon as your plans are complete, prepare a staffing request. Exhibit 5.5 is a sample. On it, you list the various skill sets you need, your preference for specific people if you have one, the dates each resource will be needed, and the percent commitment. If you will need a person half-time for a month, full-time for three months, and half-time for two weeks, you can use three lines on the staffing request for the same skill set.

You don't need to wait until the planning is complete to submit this request. As soon as you know what resources you will need at the start of the project, prepare the request; then, as the planning progresses and your understanding of your staffing requirements extends further into the future, you can submit revisions. The sooner you ask for resources, the better the chance you will have of getting them when you need them.

Exhibit 5.5. Staffing Request Form

Staffing Request				

Project: _____

Manager: _____

Skills Sets Required	Preferred Team Member	Dates Required Start	End	%
_____	_____	_____	_____	__
_____	_____	_____	_____	__
_____	_____	_____	_____	__
_____	_____	_____	_____	__
_____	_____	_____	_____	__

Negotiating for Resources During the Project

When the project is underway, you can face two kinds of resource negotiation: when you need a resource that is on someone else's project, and when someone else needs one of yours.

There are two main principles behind resource negotiation. First, the project managers within an organization need to adopt a "we're all in this together" attitude in which cooperation is the standard. This approach ensures that the organization benefits because its key people are working together and it also means that when you need a few days of effort from someone on another project, that project's manager will be more inclined to cooperate. Therefore, when someone asks you for some of Fred's time, your first response should not be a protective "No." You need to review your project's status, weigh the urgency of the request against that of your project, and seek ways to help out the requester. You may accede to the request, ask that it be postponed for a few days, offer someone else instead of Fred, or, if you honestly conclude that there is no way for you to meet the request, say so, along with your reasons. This last option is crucial. If your natural inclination is to be cooperative because you dislike confrontation, you risk that others who are not as constrained will take advantage of you. As a project manager, you must take an objective look at your project's status, and, if it would suffer, you need to suppress your normal tendency and refuse the request.

The second principle of resource negotiation is that the ultimate arbiter of a resource request is the interests of the organization. If those interests dictate that Fred should be reassigned for a few days, that is what should happen, even if the result will be a slippage in your project. In such a case, you need to ensure that your management understands that any slippage occurred because your project was deprived of a key resource at a critical time, and not because you or your team failed.

In both these principles, your primary tool is the project benefits statement. If you can tell your management or the other project manager what delaying your project will cost them in deferred benefits, you stand a much better chance of holding on to your people. Of course, if the organization insists on benefits statements for all its projects, it has a means to weigh competing requests for the same resource and to evaluate whether the request for the use of a member of your team should be honored.

Suspending the Project

There may come a time when your project becomes starved for resources and your people are being pulled off to work on projects that management has, formally or otherwise, deemed to be of higher priority than yours. In such cases, projects usually die by attrition, finally folding when there is nobody left to work on them. The problem with this, from the organization's point of view, is that the work that has been done is lost and the value achieved from that work is nil. You can rescue that situation by recognizing that your project is being shunted aside and by recommending that it be suspended.

Suspending a project means completing all activities that are almost done and documenting those that are not. By preparing a complete set of documentation on what has been accomplished, you make it easier for the organization to revive the project at some future time when conditions have changed, ensuring that the bulk of the work that you have done will be available for the new team to pick up. Suspending a project also means temporarily closing it when it is presumably on plan and when you can claim that the project has so far been a success. The alternative is the sour taste and aura of failure that surrounds a project that collapses from re-source starvation.

* * * * *

CONTROLLING ACTION ITEMS

Have you ever come away from a meeting with the comfortable feeling that issues were properly discussed, agreements were reached, and general goodwill prevailed—and yet you were not sure what was supposed to happen next? In such a case, you know that nothing will happen next.

All projects are the result of actions, and actions are carried out by individuals. It is hard enough to get people to do work that is assigned to them; it is impossible to get them to do work that is not. There are two types of work to assign: project activities and action items. Like project activities, an action item is a piece of work that is given to one or two people to be done by a specified date, but action items differ from project activities in that the latter are part of the project plan. Action items are generally small, but they have the ability to cripple a project.

For example, suppose you are managing a project to convert an application from one computer system to another. The manufacturer of the target system has just released a new version of the operating system that will be preloaded on all new equipment orders. You have reason to believe that the application will not operate on the new version without modifications, so you decide to order the target system with the older version.

Someone on your team has read that the new version is tied into the system's firmware and that the older version will not run on a new machine. If this is so, you have a problem, and you all agree that this should be checked out, but unless somebody actually picks up the telephone and calls the manufacturer, this little item will be forgotten until the new equipment arrives unable to run the version of the operating system that you need.

As soon as the issue is raised, you must create an action item. You may ask the team member, or the technology architect, or a programmer to call the manufacturer, or you may do it yourself. It does not matter who handles it. The only things that matter are that somebody does it and that you make note of it so that you can follow up.

Raising Action Items

Action items are raised continually throughout any project. They come up in meetings, in technical discussions, in client reviews, in hallway conversations, over coffee, and during private reflection. Action items arise from:

1. **Assumptions.** Someone says, "Well, I assume that . . ." or "I think that . . . is the case." Unless you have absolute certainty (and sometimes even then), you are hearing something that needs to be checked out. Create an action item and assign it to someone.

2. **Doubts.** You or some member of your team question whether a statement is true. You need to verify what has been said. Ask the doubter to investigate.

3. **Tasks.** An unplanned task arises. For example, you discover that a new interface card is available that would solve your graphics problem. Create an action item to have somebody check it out.

4. **Questions.** Somebody—you, your client, or a team member—asks a question that cannot be answered immediately. Create an action item to find the answer.

5. **Requests.** Somebody—you, your client, or a team member—makes a request for material or information or equipment. Create an action item to ensure that the request is honored.

6. **Shoulds.** You think to yourself, "I should. . . ." Create an action item or it will never get done.

Tracking Action Items

The only way to track action items is to write them down; you cannot keep them in your head. There are three places to write down action items:

1. **Meeting Minutes.** Since most action items arise from meetings or are assigned in them, they should be recorded in the minutes.

2. **Your Personal Calendar.** Any action items that you take on yourself must go into your personal calendar. You may also choose to note other people's action items so that you have a reminder to follow up.

3. **The Issues Log.** This is described below in the section "Reporting Status." The issues log is the central repository of all issues, large and small. Everything that needs attention goes into the issues log, otherwise you will lose track of items that you have identified as worthy of follow-up.

Action Items and Meetings

If a project meeting does not produce action items, you have probably wasted your time and that of everyone else at the meeting. Any discussion, except those that are purely informative, requires that somebody do something. During the meeting, you need to continually ask, "Fred, will you handle this?" or "Mary, could you check this out?" When you get their concurrence—if you don't, either insist or assign the action to somebody else—set a date by which you expect the action to be complete. If Fred or Mary are not at the meeting, do not assign them the action because the chances are that they will miss it. Instead, assign yourself the action to delegate the issue to Fred or Mary after the meeting.

When you prepare the minutes of the meeting, make sure that the action items are prominent. You may choose to intersperse them in the minutes so that each action is associated with its discussion, or you can summarize them at the end of the minutes, but make sure you document them prominently.

Each set of minutes should begin with a review of the previous meeting's actions and the results to date. Actions that are completed can be closed, while those that are outstanding should be repeated with the new minutes. If an action completion date has passed and the action remains outstanding, leave it in the minutes with the original completion date. Both you and the assignee need to be reminded that the action is late.

Lay out action items in a format similar to Exhibit 5.6.

In the following meeting, the minutes will reflect the results as shown in Exhibit 5.7.

In this example, Fred's action item will not appear in future meeting

Exhibit 5.6. Suggested Action Item Layout

Action Item	Who	When
Call the vendor to ensure availability of the new firmware.	Fred	July 26
Review the count of the users with the client.	Mary	Aug. 3

Exhibit 5.7. Suggested Action Item Layout with Comments.

Action Item	Who	When
Call the vendor to ensure availability of the new firmware. *Done. Firmware is available now.*	Fred	July 26
Review the count of the users with the client. *Outstanding. The client has not responded. See discussion below.*	Mary	Aug. 3

minutes, whereas Mary's will remain until it is complete. In this way, the action item is constantly visible and will arise at each meeting.

What If?

Action Items Remain Open Long After They Should Have Been Closed

If action items are not completed, the project is just as much at risk as if project activities are not done. You need to be insistent with both.

Actions

Determine why the action item is still open.

If the problem is that the team member dismisses the action as unimportant, make it clear that you require a resolution.

If there are other barriers to completing the action, identify how else you might get it done. Perhaps it should be assigned to somebody else. Maybe the team member is unsure how to proceed and needs some advice or assistance. One common type of problem arises when team members need to call someone external to the project. Many team members will not persist if the person they are calling does not readily return calls. When this happens, take on the action item yourself; you are paid to be persistent. You may not be able to handle the details of the call, but you can get the necessary parties together.

* * * * *

MANAGING RISKS

Risks, like a well-known comedian, get no respect. Project managers dutifully assess them at the start of the project, record them in the project plan, then forget about them until one of them lunges up to destroy any pretense that the project is on track.

You need to manage risks; they must be in the forefront of your concerns. Ensure that risks are an agenda item for the weekly team meeting (see the section "Team Meetings"), that risks are a heading in the project status report (see the section "Reporting Status"), and that risks are a topic in your weekly reflection (see the section "Reflection").

In the team meeting, briefly review with the team all outstanding risks (a risk is outstanding when there is a probability that it will occur) and ask the team to estimate whether each risk's probability has increased, has decreased, or is unchanged. Then ask if there are any new risks that anybody can think of. It may not be pleasant when someone says, "Oops, I forgot to mention my holidays." But you would rather hear it now than wonder, at a critical point in the project, where Fred is.

In the project status report, list all risks where the degree of risk has changed.

In your weekly reflection, review all risks, even those that have been eliminated. You want to prompt yourself to uncover new risks or those that have been reincarnated.

The purpose of overtly reviewing risks is, of course, to keep them in your awareness and to sensitize all team members to them. The reason for including them in the project status report is to prepare your management for the day when you will say, "You are aware, of course, of [risk]. Well, it has happened."

What If?

You Discover That Team Members Are Not Telling You of Risks That They Consider "Not Significant"

Most team members have a limited view of the project compared to yours, which is more global. Therefore, the fact that someone sees a risk as being insignificant means only that it is insignificant for one part of the project. It may be acute for the project as a whole.

Actions

When you find a risk that you have not been told about, raise it at a team meeting and point out why it is significant to the project.

Make it clear that assessing risks is your responsibility, not that of any other team member. One by-product of this stance is that when anyone suggests a potential risk, you must not dismiss it on the spot; if you do, you will not be offered any other risks.

Be persistent in reviewing existing risks and seeking out new ones.

Some Team Members Continually Raise Risks That Are Trivial

Other than the annoyance factor, this carries no consequences for your project. However, the team member's persistence probably indicates a degree of immaturity, combined with an enthusiasm that is worth nurturing.

Actions

Ask the team member to rate the risks according to the probability/impact model and to give reasons for each rating.

> Review the risk assessment and provide feedback on its accuracy and on the kinds of risk that you are looking for.

* * * * *

SOLVING OVERRUN PROBLEMS

At some point in the project, somebody will be late completing an activity. How do you recover, and how do you ensure that whatever caused the overrun will not recur in other activities?

There are three ways that a project can overrun its plan. It can slip its schedule, it can exceed its budget, or it can exceed its effort. In most cases, these are related: If activities take more effort than you'd planned, your project will probably slip its schedule and, if you are being charged for labor, it will exceed its budget. However, it is possible to have an overrun on one of the constraints and not on the other two. For example, your project may exceed its planned effort, but, by having your team put in overtime, you can ensure that it still meets the schedule.

Overruns come in two varieties: those you expected and those you did not. They require two types of action: corrective, to reduce the impact of the overrun, and preventive, to avoid similar kinds of incidents in the future.

Expected and Unexpected Overruns

An expected overrun is one you knew about before the activity was due to end. An unexpected overrun occurs when you discover on or after the activity's due date that it is late or that it required extra effort to complete.

The purpose of tracking progress is to find out in advance about potential problems, so an unexpected overrun is a project management problem with implications beyond a schedule slippage. You will want to know why you were not told of the overrun until it happened. Unless some unusual circumstances arose during the last few days of the activity, you must recognize that you were misled.

The sooner you know of a potential overrun, the sooner you can act.

You must make it clear to your people how important it is that they give you as much notice of problems as possible. They must understand that failure to report a problem is a worse offense than being late or over their budget. Unexpected overruns, unless mitigated by sudden events, are not acceptable, and if they are repeated or blatant, you will have to remove the offender from the team.

Corrective Actions

Corrective actions reduce the impact of the overrun, which can range from minimal if it is absorbed by slack time to severe if the activity is on the critical path.

Corrective actions apply to activities in the future, as well as to the problem activity while it is in progress. The range of corrective actions includes any combination of the following:

- **Add resources.** It is a cliché that you cannot recover from a schedule problem by "throwing more people at it." If the activity requires a high degree of knowledge about the application, the development environment, the project standards, or project components, the cliché is true. However, there are many activities that you can partition and assign parts of to newcomers with little disruption. If you have designed the project to keep activities independent so that new people can be readily added, you will now be able to capitalize on your forethought.

- **Request overtime.** Overtime presents a dilemma. If the company pays for overtime, people are generally willing to work it, but the project budget balloons. Conversely, if the company does not pay for overtime, the budget is protected, but it is harder to get concurrence from the team. People's willingness to put in overtime also depends upon the culture of the company. If management expects overtime, treats it as commonplace, and regards it as one route to promotion, people will be willing to comply, but if overtime is the exception or the company regards it as a refuge for those who are unable to meet assigned targets, they won't.

  If your company's overtime policies are lenient, be prepared for budget overruns. If they are stringent, recognize that you may have difficulty getting overtime work from your staff.

The best way to get willing cooperation for extra work, regardless of overtime pay policies, is to build a team. When your people are committed to the project's success, they will do whatever is necessary to ensure it. If they are not committed, they will do the minimum necessary to keep their jobs.

- **Get creative.** Are there shortcuts you could take? Might a different approach cut the work? Is it possible to reduce the effort by being creative? For example, you might reduce the time for integration by forming small integration teams to work on two or three components as they are developed, rather than integrating everything at the end. You may be able to cut development time by assigning a database specialist to code all database accesses, leaving others free to focus on business logic.

  Getting creative does not mean thrashing about in a panic. Creativity is applying your intelligence and that of your team to come up with new, time-saving approaches to the work.

- **Reduce the scope or extend the schedule.** If you have a project that will take longer than the time you have available, there are no more resources to add, your people are already working overtime, and there is no other way you can think of to trim the work, you have just two options: Reduce the scope or extend the schedule. Sometimes you can reduce the short-term scope, delivering limited functionality by the deadline and the rest later.

  The approach you choose, whether to reduce the scope or extend the schedule or apply some combination of the two, will depend on the client's priorities—which you identified when you defined the project, remember—and on whether the deadline or the functionality is stricter. When all other options have been exhausted, these are all that remain.

Preventive Actions

Preventive actions are those designed to prevent a similar overrun from occurring in other activities. They require you to know what happened here. Was there a one-time event that caused the overrun? Was the estimate too low? Did the estimator not understand the extent of the work? Was there a change of scope? Did a team member not perform as well as you expected? In particular, you must determine whether the overrun was an accident or a symptom of a deeper problem.

You cannot plan for accidental slippages; that is why you have a contingency. Hence, other than reviewing the project plan and the risks, there are no specific preventive actions to take. Symptomatic overruns, however, are a threat to your project. They have one of just two possible causes: Your estimates were wrong, or your people did not perform.

If your estimates were wrong, you miscalculated the amount of work needed. Now that you have a better understanding of the project, you can review the other activities to identify those that have also been underestimated. Revise the estimates to reflect what you now know.

If your people did not perform, it is either because they are underqualified or because they simply did not meet your expectations. If they are underqualified, you may need to replace them, shuffle work assignments to put them on easier or less critical activities, or get them some training. You can send them to a course, or arrange for on-the-job coaching by other team members, other company staff, or outside consultants.

A special type of underqualification occurs in projects that involve new technologies or unusual development environments. You may find that your team, including the most senior technical people, become overwhelmed and frustrated by a continual succession of problems. Do not hesitate to call for help, externally if necessary, from people who understand the tools you are trying to use. It is more cost-effective to pay for a few days of consulting time than to drag the entire team down for several weeks searching for elusive solutions.

If some people did not meet expectations, it is time for discipline. Meet with each person—in private—to find out whether there are any problems and to restate your expectations. Ultimately, if you have a consistently poor performer, you will have no choice but to remove him or her from the project. If you cannot get a replacement, redo the plan with the lower level of resources.

Your preventive action will probably lead to a revised plan, and the revisions will probably not shorten the project duration. You now have the unenviable task of informing management and the client that the project completion date is jeopardized. You will either receive approval for the extended schedule or be asked to bring the completion date back to where it was. In the latter case, you are once again dealing with an externally imposed date, and your job is as described in chapter 4 in the section "Aligning the Schedule."

What If?

The Schedule or Budget Slips Because Assigned Team Members Are Inexperienced

If the estimates assumed a reasonable level of experience on the part of the project team members and they do not have the needed background, you will not be able to meet the schedule, and you will exceed the budget.

Actions

Revise the estimates to account for the use of inexperienced people. Include a block of time for training and some time and costs for on-the-job consulting, from an external source if necessary.

Identify specific people from other projects who have the kind of experience you need. If there are external consultants capable of providing the skills, revise the project budget to include them.

Present management with the option of either accepting the extended schedule and budget or providing you with the skill levels you need from other projects.

You Devise a Corrective Strategy That Is Not Consistent with the Project Methodology

If the methodology cannot be violated and management applies it consistently, your ideas will not be acceptable and your scope for making alternative plans will be limited.

Actions

Identify any risks that would arise because of your departure from the methodology and develop plans for mitigating them.

Prepare two plans, one that uses the methodology and one with your new strategy. Present the plans and the risk assessment to management, and ask it to decide which approach it wants you to follow.

Determine whether the methodology can be "retrofitted" to the project. That is, it may be acceptable to develop some of the deliverables required by the methodology after the project is over. Do not forget to estimate the extra effort and costs.

✳ ✳ ✳ ✳

MANAGING SCOPE CHANGES

The biggest single cause of project overruns is changes in scope. It's what you did not plan to do that will sink you. Scope changes are insidious. If you do not manage them, your budget and schedule will be destroyed before you recognize that anything has happened. If you manage them well, your career as a project manager is ensured.

If you have defined the project properly, you know what is in and out of scope. Therefore, managing scope changes simply means identifying them and estimating their impact on the project. However, it bears repeating that before you can identify what is out of scope, you must know what is in. Put negatively, if you have not adequately defined the project, you will now pay the price.

Types of Scope Change

There are four different types of scope change that you will encounter:

1. **Uncontested Scope Changes.** These are scope changes that the client requests or agrees to while acknowledging that they are actual changes of scope. Your only job is to estimate the effect of the change on the project and to get the client either to accept the change or to reject it.

2. **Contested Scope Changes.** These are scope changes that the client requests but insists that they are not changes to scope and are to be included within the price or schedule. They present a problem, but not for you. If the project is internal, the dispute must be settled between department managers. If it is external, it's a job for the account manager. Your only role is to get the appropriate managers talking and to provide any background information needed to support your position.

   If the negotiations conclude that the scope change must be added, you will require written authorization, either from the client or from one of your own managers. As the keeper of the project plan, you alone are responsible for accepting changes to it.

3. **Scope Creep.** This is a term that is often used synonymously with scope change, but scope creep is actually an uncontested scope change that the client asks you to add outside the normal scope change mechanism because it is trivial. If your project team tells you that the change is anything but trivial, you can inform the client that the change is more complicated than it first appeared and suggest that he or she submit a scope change request. However, if the change really is trivial, you have two potential problems. The first is that a lot of trivial changes can soon add up to a significant impact on your project, and you'll find that you've given away substantial work, endangered the schedule, and exceeded the budget by tiny increments.

   The second problem is that a trivial piece of work may turn out to be more complicated than you had originally thought. By the time you find this out, your team, in a praiseworthy effort to be cooperative, will have put in the extra effort to incorporate what is, in fact, a significant change.

   Your best strategy for dealing with scope creep is to be stingy in what you give away, but if you do decide to include a minor change, make sure that your team members know that you expect them to put in no more than a few hours on it without notifying you.

4. **Constructive Scope Changes.** These types of change are misleadingly named because they are changes not to the project scope but to the agreements with the client on how the project was to be conducted. They do, however, lead to changes to the project budget and schedule. For example, if you have agreed with the client that deliv-

erables submitted for review will be returned within five working days, you have the basis for a constructive scope change when it takes two weeks. Similarly, if you have assumed (and documented your assumption) that your team will be allowed unrestricted access to the client site and the client denies access on weekends, you have the basis for a scope change.

Constructive scope changes can also be used when the client team approves a deliverable, only to return some time later noting a deficiency. If you have proceeded on the strength of the approval, you can now submit a constructive scope change to revise the deliverable and to modify any work that was based on it.

As you may have guessed, it is the project manager who submits constructive scope change requests, and, of course, they can be a source of conflict between you and the client. You will want to reserve their use for extreme situations in which it is clear that the client's actions have seriously affected the course of the project.

Origins of Scope Changes

Scope changes arise from four sources:

1. **Overt Client Requests.** The easiest scope changes to identify are those that the client requests. They are not always the easiest to deal with, since the client may not agree that they are changes, but they are always obvious.

2. **Covert Client Requests.** Many scope changes sneak in when someone on the client team makes an informal request to someone on the project team for "one more report," another type of inquiry, or a new area of functionality. Such a request becomes a problem when the team member acts on the request, building it into the system, without telling anyone else—including you.

   These changes are not usually conspiratorial; nobody is out to cheat the system. They are, in fact, a consequence of what you want to establish: good working relationships between the project team and the client, a climate in which team members are encouraged to exercise judgment, and a professional attitude aimed at providing value. Unfortunately, if all this legitimate goodwill is not tempered with some control, the project's scope will explode.

3. **Smuggled Requirements.** The most difficult types of scope change to detect are those that are introduced as part of normal information gathering. For example, your team is conducting a workshop to determine detailed requirements for the purchasing system, and among them is a set of requirements for calculating vendor payables. The scope of purchasing has just been expanded to encompass accounts payable.

   These types of scope change do not typically arise because user teams are intentionally trying to sneak in extra features. They happen because business functions overlap, and it is not always easy to determine where one ends and another starts.

4. **Project-Team Enthusiasm.** Scope changes often arise from the project team itself. It is commonplace for team members to create new requirements. After all, why not provide a sales analysis by customer first name; the client may want to know sales to people named Fred. You do not want to discourage new ideas from your team, but you also do not want them to act until you have talked to the client. In many projects, new features get added without the project manager's or the client's knowledge. They just seemed like a good idea to the team.

Identifying Scope Changes

You identify scope changes by following a few consistent practices that are designed to build in a sensitivity to change requests. For example:

- During the project kickoff meeting, state the scope and ensure that everyone on the team understands and accepts it.
- Make sure that the scope is visible to everyone on the team through mottoes, pinups, and other "advertisements."
- Ensure that the scope is included in orientation materials for new team members.
- During the weekly team meeting, conduct a separate roundtable to review scope change requests.

- Whenever you or your technical leaders need to make a project decision, ensure that the scope is included as one of the factors contributing to the decision.
- During your period of reflection, include scope as a subject for review.

Scope Changes and Justification

Your first question in reviewing any scope change request or suggestion should be "What position shall I take toward the change?" That is, will you support it and push for its approval, or will you argue against it? Your stance should be determined by the effect of the change on the project's justification. Since the entire purpose of the project is to provide some benefit, you must support only those changes that will increase the benefits or increase the probability that they will be realized. Once you have determined that that is the case, you will still need to estimate the cost of the change and compare that with the resulting benefits, but your first filter must be whether the change will enhance the project's benefits at all. If it will not, it does not belong in your project.

Dealing with Scope Changes

A change of scope must be approved by the client before you act on it. As part of project planning, you should have defined a procedure for dealing with scope changes, similar to that outlined in the section "Scope Change Mechanisms," in chapter 3, including a means to submit change requests to the client. Exhibit 3.3 is a sample scope change request form. In any scope change request, you should specify a date by which you require a response. The change may be easy to handle up to some point in the project but difficult or more expensive after that. For example, a functional change may be readily included only until functional design has been completed.

A strategy that some project managers recommend is to look for a small scope change early in the project and then to submit a change request, offering to include it at no additional cost. The purpose is threefold: to exercise the change-control mechanism, to give the client notice that changes will be scrutinized, and to demonstrate service by including the change at no cost.

What If?

The Team Has Accepted a Change Request Without Your Knowledge and Started Working on It

Unless there are unusual circumstances, this situation is symptomatic of problems in your control of the team. The scope changes will mushroom, and you will not know what is happening.

Actions

Reestablish control. Estimate the effect of the change request on the schedule and budget, and let the appropriate team members know what their generosity has cost.

Meet with the client to ensure that all change requests come through you and not to members of your team.

The Client Insists on a Change That Does Not Fit the Project Justification

The only reason for the project is to provide benefits. Work that does not meet this criterion is wasted, and you run the risk that the project will ultimately cost more than is justified by the benefits.

Actions

Determine why the client wants the change, and ask for an outline of how it would benefit the organization. If it enhances the original project justification, it may be reasonable to include it in the project.

If the change does not provide benefits or is unnecessary, it is your responsibility to go on record as opposing it. You may be instructed to include it, but you need to make your position clear.

Look for signs that the project is at risk. When clients start making unreasonable demands, you may be dealing with a project that has become an object of political tactics in the client organization.

The Original Scope Is Ignored on the Grounds That the Additional Requests Are Vital to the System

When a client rejects the original scope, you now have a project that does not have one. You will have no way of managing scope, and the project costs and schedule will balloon.

Actions

Determine what business conditions have arisen that have forced such a radical change of scope. If you cannot identify any, recommend that the original scope be maintained and that any enhancements be conducted as separate projects after implementation.

If you are overruled, state that since the original scope is no longer in effect, neither is the original project plan. Recommend calling an immediate halt to the project while it is rescoped and replanned.

If the client does not agree, you have two choices: Attempt to fit new requirements into the existing design, or announce that you cannot continue under these conditions.

Approved Scope Changes Become So Numerous That They Threaten the Integrity of the Original Design

The changes will ultimately lead to a compromised design—in the worst case, one that must be abandoned. The project now runs the risk of becoming a megafailure.

Actions

Call an emergency planning session with your key team members to review the scope changes, the probable future changes, and the current state of the project.

Review the design and identify the points where it is at risk.

Determine whether the system can be redesigned while retaining the majority of the work that has been done to date.

Prepare a plan to implement the redesign and present it to the client and to management, along with the reasons that the new design has become necessary.

* * * *

MANAGING QUALITY

Of all the aspects of running a project, probably the most difficult one to keep on track is quality—not because it is complicated but because project participants feel free to discard it when the crunch comes.

Quality in systems projects is based on reviews and walkthroughs (see the section "Planning for Quality," in chapter 4). Your role is to ensure that those activities occur and that no deliverable is considered complete unless it is accompanied by a walkthrough review worksheet (see Exhibit 4.8) indicating that a review has been conducted and that all revisions agreed to in the review have been completed. Insofar as your project is concerned, this is all that is required of you to manage quality. However, quality is long-term. It is long-term within a project because its benefits are not realized until late in the project and after the project is over. It is also long-term across projects in that the practice of quality in individual projects leads to improvements in those that follow. If you are to be successful in managing quality over the long term, you will have to sell quality to your team and to your management. You do that in two concrete ways: Gather ammunition, and compile statistics.

You gather ammunition by extrapolating from the completed review worksheets what each major uncovered error would have cost if it had not been detected when it was. For example, if a requirements review catches a previously unidentified need to record prices in fractions of a cent ("We buy cable at twelve and a-half cents a foot"), prepare a set of projections indicating what that requirement would have cost had it been discovered at various later stages in the project. For example:

At the *requirements stage*, it took one hour of effort to revise the requirements document.

At *systems design*, it would have taken one week of effort to revise screen, report, and file layouts.

At *program design*, it would have taken one month of effort to revise layouts and program specifications.

At *implementation*, it would have taken three months of effort to revise the entire system and documentation.

A few such examples should be enough to convince your most intractable opponent of the hard benefits that come from building in quality to the product through reviews.

As the project progresses, keep a set of statistics that reflect the impact of your quality plan on the project. If the client organization already has a statistical base, use the measures that it contains. If not, define a few of your own. Some examples:

- Time spent on unit testing as a percentage of time spent on coding
- Number of bugs per program discovered during integration
- Number of revisions needed to files or databases after completion of systems design
- Number of revisions needed to program specifications after start of program design

Over time, particularly if you work within the same organization, you should see these numbers decline. If you are successful, the last three will reach zero. On that day, you can approach your management and claim the kudos that are rightfully yours.

Managing Peer Reviews

The most important tool for building quality into a systems product is the peer review, discussed in the section "Planning for Qualilty" in chapter 4. Normally, the peer review is a technical meeting to walk through a deliverable and identify and document potential problems. However, like any activity that throws team members together, it has some potential problems that you can circumvent by following a few basic principles.

Participation Should Be Restricted to Technical Staff

Two groups that should not be present at a review are clients and management (including you). You want to exclude clients because they should not be involved in internal project meetings, particularly those that focus on errors and problems. You want to exclude management because the presence of managers will exacerbate any defensiveness the team member is feeling. It will also switch the focus of the review from a search for technical compliance to one of performance evaluation. The sole exception to this rule is that if the personalities involved will create problems, you should be present as a facilitator and, if necessary, as a defender of your people (see the section "Building the Team," in this chapter).

Peer Review Does Not Require Approval

The role of reviewers is strictly to point out problem areas and suggest improvements. Other than enforcing conformance to standards, they have no right of approval, and, when reviewers and the team member who produced the deliverable disagree about some aspect of it, the team member's decision is final: It is his or her product.

Comments Should Be Specific, Not General

The purpose of a review is to identify errors, not to redesign the deliverable. Therefore, the kinds of comments that are appropriate are specific, such as "Must handle return code 13" or "Add logic to deal with incorrect date format." Where comments become general, such as "Approach needs to be revised" or "Work is not at the expected level," the review has ceased to be a search for errors and has deteriorated into a battle over approaches or an exercise in intimidation. You will need to intervene and to reinforce with your team the kinds of comments you expect to see.

Peer Review Is Not Employee Evaluation

Peer review can be stressful, particularly for less secure team members. You must therefore emphasize that its purpose is not to evaluate work or punish team members but to identify sources of error. You need to be scrupulous in stamping out any attempts to use peer reviews to discipline or embarrass team members. You also need to make sure that reviewers do not use the process to impose their preferred approach on the deliverable.

What If?

Team Members Object to Conducting Reviews

Your quality plan will be dead, and you can expect the time for integration and systems test to balloon.

Actions

There are typically two reasons for objections: "I don't have the time to review someone else's work" and "I'm a professional, and I don't need someone looking over my shoulder." The specific cause may lead you to modify what you say, but the overall message must be the same: "The quality plan is not negotiable. We need it to succeed, and I expect you to follow it."

Examine your own position, and make sure that you are not conveying to your team any impatience with delays that are caused by reviews. If a deliverable is a week late because significant errors were caught, you should celebrate and congratulate the participants because the review has just saved several weeks or months of effort later. If, on the other hand, you express dissatisfaction with the delay, you have provided an incentive to your team to avoid reviews.

The Client Says That Your Team Is Spending Too Much Time in Review Meetings and Not Enough Time Working

The client is attempting to get you to scrap your quality plan. In particular, if the project is behind schedule, the client sees this as one way to catch up or at least to avoid falling further behind.

Actions

Recognize that the client is challenging your mandate to manage the project and that the issue goes beyond your quality plan.

Point out that quality reviews are not the cause of any slippage and that scrapping them would ultimately cause even more delays.

Finally, insist that the quality plan be retained and followed.

Your Management Questions Your Adherence to the Quality Plan

If your quality plan is scrapped, the time spent on subsequent phases of the project will increase beyond your estimates. You risk having to answer for later slippages that your plan would have helped you avoid.

Actions

If your management says something like "We're all for quality, but we have a schedule commitment, and right now, you are overdoing it—just get on with the work," point out that quality reviews are not contingent but an integral part of the plan, with benefits to be realized upon integration, systems test, and implementation.

If your management orders you to stop the reviews, comply, but re-estimate the project, adding on time for later activities. Point out that the revised work plan is a consequence of your management's demands.

Managers Request Review Worksheets to Evaluate Employee Performance

If team members believe that reviews are being used to evaluate performance, they will become even more reluctant to participate. If you have succeeded in building a supportive team, they may even tacitly agree not to document errors in order to protect one another. The benefits of reviews will be lost.

Actions

Point out to management that performance reviews should be based on results, not process. The only relevant issue is that the team member's deliverables are produced on time and are of good quality. The number of intermediate errors or revisions a team member makes should not reflect on his or her performance review.

Decline to hand over review worksheets to management. If you are required to do so, revise your work plan, removing all quality reviews and extending the time needed for later activities. Make it clear to your management that quality reviews work only if they are restricted to detecting and correcting errors. Any other use compromises their effectiveness, and there is no point in continuing with them.

Some Team Members Use Reviews to Intimidate or to Force Their Approaches on Other Team Members

Reviews are intended to find errors, not to define approaches. For example, the purpose of reviewing a program design is to identify its problems and shortcomings, not to redo it. In some cases, all team members may agree that a different approach would be better and that the deliverable would be improved as a result, but some team members, particularly those with seniority, may use reviews to impose their preferred approaches on others. In such cases, reviews will dissolve into acrimony or team members will cease to regard comments seriously.

Actions

This problem is often hidden because most team members will not complain to you. One way of uncovering it is to examine the review worksheets and look for a preponderance of general comments. Where you find such a trend, you probably have an overbearing reviewer.

Do some detective work. Ask team members where the general comments came from. Look for the one or two people who seem to be at the center of the problem.

Meet with the entire team and reinforce the purpose of reviews and the types of comments that should be made. Remind them that general comments or intimidation are off-limits.

Meet with the offenders and make it clear what you expect from them as reviewers.

Attend a few reviews as an observer, but be prepared to step in if the review does not stay on track. Justify your presence by pointing out that the reviews are important and that you want to ensure that all participants understand their roles.

The Work of a Team Member Is Riddled with Errors

Since the purpose of a review is not to evaluate performance, you will find it hard to justify intervening. However, as the project manager, you really do not have to explain yourself, and, in certain circumstances, you can be inconsistent. If the offending team member's work is as poor as it seems, the rest of the team will thank you for taking action.

Actions

Meet privately with the team member. Acknowledge that although the purpose of a review is not to evaluate performance, you cannot ignore the results you are seeing.

Point out that the team member seems to be relying on the review process to identify errors rather than finding them before the review.

Identify the kinds of review comments that concern you and that you believe should have been caught before the review.

Set expectations for future reviews in terms of number and quality of comments.

* * * * *

MICROPLANNING

It is possible to overplan. Activities can be broken down into successively smaller units to the point where each hour of each team member's day is planned to a level of detail that will fall apart before the project is a day old. Planning is concerned with weeks and with activities that are decomposed to a "reasonable size."

However, most projects encounter critical periods when day-by-day control is required. For example:

- Integration and testing, when a number of modules are completed at about the same time, may require tight control to ensure that modules are handed over to the integration team as they are needed.

- Prototyping, which is characterized by brief flurries of development interspersed with user reviews, may require a daily level of control.

- A high-intensity set of activities, such as a facilities move, may need hour-by-hour monitoring.

These types of occasions require microplanning, a process that focuses regular planning down to the daily and even hourly level. Microplanning is no different from normal planning. You decompose activities, determine dependencies, and level resources. The difference is only in the scale and degree of formality.

Microplanning is not a replacement for regular planning. You are zooming in on a small part of your project plan, transforming the scale of planning from months or weeks to days or hours. Microplanning, however valuable, belongs within the larger framework of an overall plan. Otherwise you have nothing on which to zoom in.

Keep microplanning informal. Use hand-drawn schedules, or make up a daily activity list on a word processor. These are rough, transient, temporary working papers that you will consign to the wastebasket once the crunch is over. Do not formalize a microplan. If you do, you risk, first, that your management will come to expect such detail; second, that you will become fully occupied in planning the minutiae of each team member's day; and third, that your team will crack because of the intense pressure that microplanning creates.

The pressure arises from tracking. You track a microplan the same way you track a normal one. However, just as the scale of a microplan is one of days, so is the frequency of status reporting. Suddenly, team members who have become used to weekly status meetings are required to report their status at least daily, and sometimes hourly. Such high-intensity bursts may be needed at critical points in the project, but they cannot be sustained over its normal life.

Microplanning can be seductive in the sense of apparent control that it gives. It is especially appealing to project managers who thrive on crises, since it emulates the intense, immediate-term focus that crisis management requires. The problem is that any project that is managed as a crisis soon becomes one, with strategies, context, and long-term value sacrificed to the headiness of the moment.

To summarize, microplan informally and infrequently. Resist anyone who attempts to standardize or institutionalize microplanning. Above all, before you microplan, make sure that this phase of the project work really requires it and that you have not succumbed to the temptation to replace leadership by authority.

What If?

Management or the Client Requests a Microplanning Level of Control Over All Aspects of the Project

This is a particular danger with organizations that love crises. The roll-up-the-shirtsleeves, full-speed-ahead mentality does not thrive when things are going smoothly, but as described earlier, you cannot sustain that level of control over the life of a project without creating a high degree of stress and friction among team members.

Actions

Separate *reporting* from *control*. When you are asked to give a current status, speak in terms of hours or days, not weeks. But when you are dealing with your team members, ensure that you provide them with an environment of calm within which they can work.

Resist all attempts to get you to prepare a plan that is detailed to any less than two weeks. However, if your client wants a daily update, provide a written, point-form outline of progress to date.

* * * * *
MANAGING SUBCONTRACTORS

To a project in trouble, a nonperforming subcontractor can be a blessing. It is hard to fault a project manager who says, "We were ready, but the subcontractor did not deliver." When equipment does not arrive on time or does not work, or software is late or incompatible with the hardware, or a consultant is not available, or a facility is not ready, who can blame the long-suffering project manager for events beyond his or her control?

Project managers are mortal and are not answerable for everything that might happen. If the truck carrying the new computer is hit by a landslide or the equipment being imported from Taiwan is tied up when a longshoremen's strike suddenly closes the port, it is probably unjust to reproach the project manager. However, most subcontractor delays can be avoided.

Managing subcontractors requires the same thing as managing your own team: visibility into what is going on. If the subcontractor is developing software, you need to understand the plan and the milestones. If you are to be accountable for subcontractor performance, you have the right to receive status reports, to attend reviews, and to participate in milestone activities. You need to know if the subcontract work is slipping before any deliverables are due, and you need to know in time to insist on corrective action. In short, you are a manager of the subcontractor, with all the rights of a manager.

Frequently, the subcontractor is a supplier, such as a hardware vendor. If you have ordered a computer and the sales rep assures you that it will be delivered by a specific date, you need to understand what must happen if the machine is to arrive on time. Is it in stock? Where? How and when will it be shipped? Must it be manufactured? If so, what are the steps in production that will let you know the manufacturing is on schedule? How can you be sure that the machine will not be diverted from the assembly line to a higher-priority customer? Again, you need visibility into the delivery—and sometimes the manufacturing—process. Your source for such visibility is the sales rep. What you really want are the names of people in the warehouse or the factory who can give you the status of your order firsthand. Failing that, you want the sales rep to provide you with periodic status reports.

A common supplier problem is software vendors that have provided release dates for software that your project requires. If you have developed a project plan that depends upon a software release by the published date, you have invited trouble; the delivery record of most software vendors is not promising. Furthermore, most software vendors deal with large markets and are immune from the actions of a single company. Unless you absolutely have no choice, do not base your plans on software release dates. If you must do so, ensure that the client and your management understand the risks.

For all subcontractors, ask, "What are the technical factors that will affect delivery?" Note their answers, then ask, "What are the operational factors that will affect delivery?" Note their answers, then ask, "What are the financial factors that will affect delivery?" You may file some of the answers for longer-term follow-up, while others may trigger immediate action. For example, if a hardware sales rep says, "Well, you guys haven't paid your last bill," call your accounts payable department to ensure that the bill will be paid, or at least that the supplier will not place you on credit hold.

Exhibit 5.8 is a list of potential risks in dealing with subcontractors. The list is short, but those who are creative in offering excuses for nondelivery will give you many new items to add.

The Legal Subcontract

The legal side of subcontract management is a discipline in itself, with formal contracts prepared by legal experts. You need to be aware of what the contracts say, but your primary concern is performance and delivery to a schedule. That requires that you understand and have the authority to monitor your subcontractors' internal procedures and plans.

Before a contract is signed, you should review it and ensure that it provides you with visibility or at least does not prohibit it. If the contract bars you from the visibility you need, make sure that your management understands that you are not able to monitor the subcontractor's progress and cannot be responsible for its performance.

Where possible, ask that a penalty clause for the late delivery be inserted into the contract. You may decide not to exercise it, but its existence provides you with a potent tool to persuade subcontractors to meet their commitments.

Exhibit 5.8. Potential Subcontractor Risk Areas

Technical Risks

The subcontractor will not assign adequate or capable resources.

The subcontractor is not familiar with some aspect of the project such as the technology or the application area.

The subcontractor does not follow a proven methodology.

The subcontractor does not use project management techniques that allow problems to be identified early.

Physical separation leads to technical incompatibilities: You cannot run what the subcontractor has produced.

Operational Risks

The subcontractor's staff goes on strike.

The subcontractor lands a higher-priority project and diverts key resources from your project.

The physical distance to the subcontractor leads to misunderstandings and confusion, as well as to reduced visibility.

Transportation causes problems. (The transporter is also a subcontractor and is subject to many of these risks.)

Customs regulations delay import into your country or export from the subcontractor's country.

Financial Risks

The subcontractor goes bankrupt.

The subcontractor holds up shipment because your company has not paid its last bills.

The subcontractor uses your schedule as a means to extract extra costs.

The subcontractor "baits and switches," replacing the high-quality resources that were proposed with less capable people.

The Demon of Distance

Your greatest enemy in dealing with subcontractors is distance. It is tough enough to be aware of what is happening across the street, but if your subcontractor is in Singapore, you have virtually no way to confirm the glowing status reports you will receive. Before you deal with remote subcontractors, pay particular attention to their references and to the experiences that other companies have had with them. The point, of course, is not that remote subcontractors are less trustworthy than those in your backyard but that distance makes them harder to observe.

Contingency Plans

If possible, create contingency plans to be used if the subcontractor's deliverables are late. Prepare your contingency plans in advance of the problem so that they can be triggered the instant you need them. For example:

- For equipment, arrange to use another department's or company's equipment in the short term, or arrange for a short-term rental if the vendor does not deliver on time.

- For packaged software, ask the manufacturer for a beta version if the release date slips. (Normally, you will want to avoid beta software, but if the urgency of the project exceeds the risk, it might be an option.)

- For custom software, identify short-term workarounds that you can develop that will allow your project to continue if the contractor is late.

- For consulting, identify other consultants that you can call on at short notice if the consultant you are provided proves not to be acceptable.

What If?

The Subcontractor Has Assured You That the Schedule Will Be Met Until the Very Last Minute

Assuming that you accepted the subcontractor's assurances in good faith, your project schedule is now at risk.

Actions

Establish a new delivery date and determine your degree of confidence in it. Identify what you think is the most likely actual delivery date.

If you were able to establish a contingency plan, put it in motion.

If there is a penalty clause in the contract, remind the subcontractor of it.

Notify your management of the impact on the project, and consult with it on steps that could be taken with the subcontractor.

When the deliverable arrives, treat it as a late activity and apply the corrective actions described in the section "Tracking Progress," in this chapter.

Document the subcontractor's performance as a guide to be used in assigning contracts for future projects.

You Have No Power to Get a Subcontractor to Perform

If you truly have no power, then you are at the mercy of the subcontractor. For example, if a software vendor is unreasonably late in releasing a version that you absolutely must have, you have no choice but to wait, and your project will suffer.

Actions

In your initial dealings with subcontractors, identify potential sources of power. These may be legal, economic, or moral, but you need to establish what will motivate each subcontractor to perform.

If you determine that a subcontractor is immune from any actions you may take, recognize that your project is exposed and identify that exposure as a risk.

* * * * *

MANAGING CLIENT EXPECTATIONS

Too many projects have been sunk by failing to deliver what the client expected, even when the results were defined. There is a difference between *definition* and *expectation*. If you produce an inquiry screen that displays a customer's name, address, phone number, and credit status, you will have met the definition. However, if the client says, "I didn't know it would look that cluttered," or "It takes too long," or "It's awkward to get to this screen," then you have not managed the client's expectations.

Problems in expectations are the direct result of two errors: failing to identify client expectations at the start of the project and neglecting the client while the work is in progress. If you did not take the time to uncover the client's vision for this system, you will now face the unpleasant experience of having the client disapprove what you have worked so hard to produce.

Neglecting the client means that not only have you worked on the system in isolation, you have forgone any opportunity to manage expectations. Managing expectations is not simply finding out what the client wants; it is guiding the client to expect what you can provide. The first rule of managing expectations is "no surprises." Whenever the client sees anything—a report, a screen, a document, or a program—it will be familiar; the client will have seen its precursor before.

This means that as a deliverable is in progress, you will show it to the client as it evolves. If the deliverable is a document, you will review the table of contents first, then each section as it is developed. If it is a screen, you will first demonstrate a mockup. Then, as the screen is developed, you will show it to the client at various stages. The client should be aware of how your menus work and should have seen some examples of navigation before you deliver a final result. In other words, the client will be intimately involved with the deliverables as you produce them.

However, in all of this "show and tell," remember that your purpose is to manage expectations. Your client will make valuable comments, which you will undoubtedly want to incorporate into the deliverable, but at the same time, you are establishing what your project will provide. If the client is concerned that navigation is awkward when it is as simple as the application will permit, you can simulate operations for the most frequently performed transactions or demonstrate that experienced users will not be impeded. By demonstrating your menu paths in advance, you will uncover the client's expectations and, you hope, adjust them.

Even when you cannot change a client's expectations, you will now understand where the problems will lie, and you will be able to act. Over the course of the project, you may find that your client's expectations change as familiarity with the system increases. By uncovering expectations sooner, you will be able to take action both to modify them and to meet them.

Make It the Client's System

If you successfully manage the client's expectations, the system you deliver will be the client's, not yours. When you deliver *your* system, you deliver something that may be acceptable and that probably works, but that is not exactly right. When you deliver the *client's* system, you also deliver a sense of ownership, an attitude that the system belongs to the client and is right for the application. Managing expectations converts mere acceptance into enthusiasm.

Managing the Right Client

Most problems in acceptance come about because those who accept the system are seeing it for the first time. Typically, they succumb to two temptations: to attack what is new and to justify their involvement by criticizing what they see.

One of the precepts of sales is "Sell to the decision maker." There is no point in trying to sell a product to someone who does not have the authority to buy. Similarly, you must manage the expectations of the decision makers. You do not want to discover that the person you have been working with and whose expectations you have shaped is not the person responsible for accepting the system. If the client's sociology denies you access to the decision maker, you had better prepare for an unpleasant reaction at acceptance time. To the extent possible, you should involve the people who will be responsible for approving the system and authorizing its implementation.

User Acceptance

For most projects, user acceptance is the ultimate test, the trial lurking like a beast preparing to shred the noble efforts of the team. User acceptance is a barrier that you know will be difficult to surmount. However, it will be even harder if you do not define what acceptance is. User acceptance is the process of demonstrating to the user that the criteria established for acceptance have been met.

Clearly, if the criteria for project acceptance were not defined during the project, it is not possible to demonstrate that they have been met. Acceptance then becomes a matter of negotiating the criteria and hoping that the outcome of the negotiation does not depart too far from what the project has already produced. On the other hand, if the acceptance criteria have been defined and agreed to, acceptance becomes little more than a formality.

The technical purpose of user acceptance is to transfer the system to the user and to get paid. However, user acceptance can be an opportunity to create enthusiasm. Why settle for mere acceptance when you can generate excitement? Smooth user acceptance requires that you insist on one of two options:

1. The system will be formally accepted by the client project manager and user team leaders who have been directly involved in the development of the system.

2. The system will be formally accepted by nonparticipating client representatives who will be bound by the recommendations of the client project manager and user team leaders who have been directly involved in the development of the system.

In both these options, the decision to accept the system is made by those who were involved in its development. *Nothing else is acceptable.* If you cannot get the client to agree to one of these options, treat user acceptance as an activity rather than a milestone. Decompose it into initial user demonstrations, substantial time for modifications, and final acceptance.

What If?

The Client Team Changes During the Project and the New Team Has Different Expectations

When there is a significant change in the members of the client team, particularly senior ones, you will probably be faced with a new set of expectations, with the result that you may have to redirect your project. The cost and schedule will probably be affected.

Actions

Determine why the team is changing. If it is because of internal transfers or promotions within the client organization, your job will be easier than if the original team members were replaced because of dissatisfaction with the conduct of the project.

As soon as possible, meet with the new client team members and orient them to the project as if they were new members of your team.

Present the project approach and the effort to date as positive achievements and steps toward attaining the benefits that the client expects.

If the new team insists on making changes, point out that they will be treated as scope changes, with impacts on the budget and schedule.

The Client Expectations Change During the Project

Assuming that the client's expectations had been clear, their changing is a sign of dissatisfaction with the project. The client either does not like what has been delivered or is not happy with the manner in which it has been delivered. In either case, the project is in jeopardy, and you are professionally at risk.

Actions

Initiate a heart-to-heart talk with the client, starting with a statement like, "You don't seem pleased with the way the project is going. Is there something wrong?" Then listen for the response. If you can identify some problems and agree on an action plan to resolve them, the issue will probably disappear.

Escalate to your management. Let it know that the client seems unsatisfied and that some higher-level intervention is needed.

The Client's Expectations Seem to Shift from Day to Day

When you reach acceptance, you risk the client's finding fault with much of the system, even components that were reviewed without comment. Final acceptance will be difficult and time-consuming.

Actions

Notify your management that you have a potential issue in acceptance.

Keep a log of the changes in client expectations. Make sure that you date each entry.

When the client changes an expectation, confront him or her. Say something like, "On August 17, we reviewed this screen, and we agreed that it was acceptable. What has happened to change that?"

* * * * *

TEAM MEETINGS

Team meetings are an essential part of team building. Properly run, they help develop a true, committed team spirit. Improperly run, they provide public validation of the attitude that it's them against you.

The purpose of a team meeting is to gather and disseminate information, not to discipline, solve problems, or identify the guilty. While there are forums for these activities, your team meetings are not among them. You want the complete cooperation of everyone present, rather than defensiveness or withdrawal from those who feel like targets.

The agenda of a team meeting (a sample is shown in Exhibit 5.9) is invariant and follows a simple pattern: Information flows from you to your team, then from your team to you. You tell your team how the project is going. Are we on schedule and on budget, or are we slipping? Have there been any major changes of scope or direction? What is the client's reaction

Exhibit 5.9. Weekly Team Meeting Agenda

1. Presentation of project progress and outstanding issues
2. Roundtable to determine progress last week, planned progress this week, achievements, and problems encountered
3. Roundtable to review outstanding risks and identify new ones
4. Roundtable to examine the scope and identify scope changes
5. Fun

to what we have delivered so far? What progress has been made on the major issues that are slowing the project up?

What you want from your team members is to know how they are doing. In a roundtable, ask each person in turn to describe last week's progress, next week's expected progress, and any issues or problems that have arisen. As you receive the reports, write them down. They will become part of your project status report.

Next, conduct two more roundtables, one to review the risks and one to identify scope changes. As part of the risk roundtable, briefly describe the outstanding risks, then ask each person in turn to comment on them or to raise any new risks. Most people will pass. You are looking for the nuggets of information that will alert you to a potential problem.

For scope changes, ask the team members to report any requests they have received that might constitute a change of scope. Again, most people will have no comment, but those who do will provide you with valuable indications that the project may be diverging from its original goals.

Once the meeting is over, identify those people who did not accomplish this week what they said last week they would. Some of these will not be a surprise: Fred was out sick for three days, Mary got pulled off on another assignment, and George attended a two-day convention on database technologies. For others, you will have no ready explanation. Invite those people in—one at a time—to discuss why they are late and why they believe they will meet this week's target. Your goal here is not to discipline but to gather information to support whatever actions, disciplinary or otherwise, you will want to take.

Above all, remember that team meetings provide you with a means for dealing with your people in an open, nonconfrontational atmosphere. Take advantage of this. Make the meeting an occasion to celebrate a success or recognize special effort. Bring doughnuts or muffins. Set aside part of the time to design a project logo or mascot. Take orders for T-shirts with some expression that will be meaningful to the team. Have fun. If you do not regard yourself as the fun type, appoint a "social director" and make sure that you participate in whatever foolishness arises.

What If?

The Client or Management Criticizes the Frequency of the Meetings

Team meetings are a primary source of information on project progress, as well as a means of monitoring the progress of your team building. Without them, your job will be tougher.

Actions

Inform the client or your management that this project is yours and that you will run it your way. Adopt whatever behavioral posture you deem appropriate, but make it clear that decisions on how the project will be run are yours alone.

Some Team Members Rarely or Never Attend the Meetings

Not only will you find it harder to get activity status from these people, but their attitude is a challenge to your authority, undermining your team-building efforts.

Actions

As soon as the pattern becomes apparent, notify all team members that attendance at the team meetings is not optional and that you expect them to be present, barring exceptional circumstances.

If the problem persists, confront the offenders and find out why they do not attend. Then examine the meetings to see if the criticisms are valid. Are the meetings too long? Do some members monopolize the floor? Is the status too frequent for the volume or quality of information that is exchanged?

If you determine that the meetings can be improved, make a commitment to improve them. In any case, insist on all team members' attendance.

Some Team Members Ask to Be Excused on the Grounds That They Have Work to Complete

As an occasional event, this request is probably reasonable, but if it becomes continual, you are undermining your own process and creating a special class of team member.

Action

If the request is infrequent and you know that the team member is on a tight deadline, grant the request. Otherwise, do not.

Team Members Criticize the Meetings as a Waste of Time

If team members do not see value in the meetings, they will find all sorts of excuses for not attending, and the purpose of the meetings will be lost.

Actions

Review the conduct of the meetings to determine if there is any validity to the charges.

Regardless of what you decide to do, recognize that the purpose of the meetings is to help you manage the project. If they are fulfilling that goal, continue with them. If, on the other hand, you determine that you concur with the criticism, change the meetings by reducing their time, their frequency, or both.

Determine whether the meetings can be restructured. For example, if you have two teams, one working on the technology architecture and one on business functionality, you may be boring half the people at any point in the meeting. It may make more sense to convene two meetings.

* * * * *
REPORTING STATUS

Project status reports are one of the nuisances of the trade. Few people enjoy preparing them; it is unpleasant to have to document your problems, and, too often, the reports are ignored or, worse, used as weapons against you. For many project managers, one characteristic of the ideal project is no status reporting, but if you find yourself in such a project, search for someone to report to or leave.

Managers who do not insist on status reports are saying, in effect, "Don't bother us with trivia [into which category your project clearly falls]." Such "managers" will not be available when you need help, nor will they be prepared to accept any responsibility if the project slips or fails. Organizations that do not require status reporting may have project management, but they do not have project control: the management of project managers. If you find yourself in such a company, make up status reports anyway and issue them to whomever you think should get them.

Status reports vary according to company requirements, but the simplest include the following:

- **Accomplishments Last Period.** This is a list of the project's major achievements in the status reporting period. Note that these are major achievements. If you report each tiny piece of work, you may end up with a lengthy list, but your management will probably assume that you are covering up a lack of significant progress with a lot of noise.

  When you report a piece of work as complete, make sure it truly is complete. Few things will undermine management's confidence in you as much as seeing the same work reported as a current achievement for two or three periods running.

- **Planned for Next Period.** This is a list of the major achievements that you intend to complete in the next status reporting period. Be conservative. It is better to overachieve than to miss the target.

- **Issues.** This is a list of current issues: those from previous periods that are still unresolved and issues that are new this period. Issues should be listed with expected resolution dates and the name of the person who is responsible.
- **Risk Review.** This is a list of the major outstanding risks, and should include new risks and those for which the severity or degree of riskiness has changed.

In addition to these sections, some status reports ask for other items that are valuable in assessing progress:

- **Achievement Against Plan.** This is a list of deliverables, with scheduled and actual delivery dates and an indication of variances from the plan. Since achievement against plan shows all project deliverables, it provides a snapshot of overall progress.
- **Performance Against Budget.** This section reports whether you are under or over budget. Budgetary performance is difficult to assess. You may be under budget, but if you are also behind schedule, you may not have enough budget to make up the lost time.

The frequency of project status reports can be an issue in some companies. For most management or steering committee purposes, monthly reports are adequate, but managing the project requires tighter control; a lot can happen in a month. If your company requires monthly status reporting, produce a report each week and use it to generate the monthly report. You will find that reporting weekly keeps you better able to discuss project progress on short notice. It also reduces the effort required to produce the month-end tome that your managers require.

The Issues Log

The issues log is a listing of all outstanding issues: those that have not been resolved. Each issue requires no more than a line or two describing it, along with an issue number, the name of the person responsible for resolving it, its status (open, deferred, or closed), and a due date. It is also valuable to include a "concern indicator" that gives the importance (high, medium, or low) that you attach to the issue. Include the issues log with your status report, and in tracking the progress of issues, add dated comments directly to the log. Exhibit 5.10 is an example of an entry in an issues log.

Exhibit 5.10. Sample Issues Log Entry

No.	Description	Imp	Status	Who	Date
7	**Compatibility of network software** The current version of the network software is not compatible with the middleware that has been selected. *Nov. 12 The middleware vendor has been contacted and is reviewing the situation. We expect an answer by Friday, Nov. 15.* *Nov. 14 The vendor has a fix, but it may affect the interfaces to the online systems. A test fix is on the way and will be here by Wednesday, Nov. 20.* *Nov. 20 The fix was received and tested. It works.*	High	Closed	Fred	Nov. 15

The main purpose of the issues log is to keep track of the problems that arise and must be addressed. Regardless of who is responsible for resolving any given issue, you need to be relentless in ensuring that people act. The reason you include the issues log with your status report is to bring client issues to the client's constant attention. By numbering them, you identify those that remain outstanding over time. Clients become uncomfortable when issue 17 is still open when issue 156 has just been closed.

The issues that you should consider include anything that affects the project's benefits. When you identify actions or events that you believe jeopardize or reduce benefits, raise an issue. The issues log ensures that the issue will remain active and visible as long as it is unresolved.

The Status Meeting

In most projects, you will need to report status to the steering committee. The meeting is a presentation of your status report and will follow its format. However, the status meeting is also your opportunity to help ensure that the project stays on track from the client's point of view. The most effective tool for accomplishing this is the issues log. When you have concerns about project decisions or actions, enter them in the log and make sure that you review the log during the meeting. Be aware that if the members of the client's team have consistently failed to meet their required dates, you could embarrass the client's project manager if the review of the log is improperly handled. Discuss the log with the client's project manager before the meeting so that he or she will be aware of the issues and can work with you to formulate a position. If you do not, you risk creating an opponent.

What If?

Management Ignores Your Status Reports

When problems arise in the project, even though they are described in the status reports or issues log, management will not be aware of them and will be surprised and annoyed when they affect the project. Furthermore, management will not be able to intervene to help out when necessary.

Actions

Early in the project, identify the degree of attention that your status reports receive from management. Casually mention an issue that you have reported and observe whether your managers know what you are talking about.

If you conclude that nobody is paying attention to your reports, make a point of meeting with one of your managers periodically to review the issues and the status.

Document critical issues in separate memos, and follow up face to face to ensure that management has received them.

A Major Problem Has Occurred and the Next Status Report Will Be Bad

If management has been receiving positive reports, the sudden appearance of a negative one may reflect badly on you. Management will want to know why this surprise has appeared and why it was not forewarned.

Actions

Forewarn management. Call each member of the steering committee and your management and let them know what has happened. A useful phrase to start the conversation is, "We have a problem." The advantage of this approach is that when you call a meeting or issue your status report, each person will have the equivalent of inside information, which usually creates allies. Furthermore, everyone will have had the chance to think about the problem and will be able to bring you suggestions rather than recriminations.

Client Staff Consistently Fails to Resolve Its Actions on the Issues Log

Issues that do not get resolved are dangerous to the project and can develop into serious problems if they are not dealt with quickly.

Actions

Consult with the client project manager either to create a sense of urgency in the client team or to determine whether the issues can be reassigned.

If you do not get satisfaction, ask the steering committee for guidance. Client members may be able to influence the offenders more easily than you can.

If the problem persists, announce that the issue is unresolved, that the project requires an answer, that you have made an assumption that resolves the issue, and that, if the assumption proves to be invalid, correcting it will be a scope change.

* * * * *

REFLECTION

Managing projects requires an immense devotion to detail, especially in a discipline where a misplaced period can turn success into failure. The ability to focus on the work to the exclusion of everything else is crucial.

However, the problem with being focused is that you tend to lose the context. You need focus to get the job done, but focus will not tell you whether the job should be done or whether some other job would be better. Many projects have failed because the project manager did not look up from his or her Gantt charts to ask, "Are we going in the right direction? Are we solving the problem that we were brought here to solve?"

Reflection is a procedure by which the project manager formally separates himself or herself from the hectic round of activities in order to validate the direction of the project and to survey the landscape for new dangers and opportunities.

Reflection is formal. Enter it in your appointment book as a weekly one-hour meeting. Treat it as a priority, rather than as a flexible spot in your schedule. Early in the morning is the best time because you are fresh and you have the rest of the day to act on whatever you decide needs action.

Reflection is solo. Arrange to be alone. Stay in your office only if you can see to it that you are not interrupted. Anybody seeing you alone will assume you are available. Call-forward your phone. If you have an open-door policy that encourages interruptions, congratulations, but make up a Do Not Interrupt sign and let everyone know that the only valid reason to ignore it is to yell, "Fire!"

Reflection is honest. You are the only person who will be aware of your meeting and its contents. You do not have to be concerned with justifying your decisions, explaining your position, or diverting accusations. If there are problems, the only relevant issues are the strategies and tactics to solve them, not the assignment of blame.

Reflection is structured. This is a meeting, and, like any other meeting, it needs an agenda such as that presented in Exhibit 5.11.

In this agenda, the words "in general" appear repeatedly. You are not at this meeting to handle specific problems, such as late delivery or a team discipline problem. The purpose of reflection is to get you above the day-to-day details. Those you are already handling by being focused. Reflection is designed to deal with an entirely different level of issue.

* * * * *

CLOSING THE PROJECT

One of the characteristics that distinguishes a project from other forms of business activity is that a project ends. Once its purpose has been satisfied,

Exhibit 5.11. Reflection Meeting Agenda

1. **Review of General Project Status.** What, in general, is our status? Are we solving the client's problem?

2. **Review of General Project Problems.** What, in general, are our problems? Is the staff motivated? Are staff members pulling together? Is the client responsive? How are client relations? How might they be improved?

3. **Review of Benefits.** How, in general, are we addressing the project benefits? Does the original justification still apply? Has the project's progress altered the cost-benefit analysis? Are we doing things that do not support or that detract from the realization of the benefits? How can we enhance the benefits?

4. **Review of Risks.** What, in general, are the risks? Do they lie in delivery? In technology? In application rules? In user acceptance? How have they changed in the last period? What new risks have emerged?

5. **Review of Scope Issues.** What, in general, are the scope issues? Is there pressure to expand the scope? How? From whom?

6. **Review of Management Relations.** What, in general, are the problems with my managers? Do they understand the issues? Are they responsive to the project problems? Do they accept my judgments and recommendations?

7. **Review of Team Building.** What, in general, can I do to improve team spirit? Is the team motivated? Are there general concerns I need to handle?

8. **Action Items.** What actions will I take to resolve the issues that I have identified in this meeting?

---

it is closed and becomes part of organizational history. Unfortunately, too many projects seem to drag on forever, coming to a grudging conclusion more by attrition than by design. Furthermore, even when projects finally end, it is often because people simply stop working on them: They die from neglect.

Just as there are proper ways to define, plan, and execute projects, so there is a right way to end them. Closing a project involves three major steps: gaining client concurrence that the project is over, capturing lessons learned during the project, and completing administrative closeout.

Gaining Client Concurrence

As noted in the section "Planning for Completion," in chapter 4, the best way to gain the client's agreement that the project is complete is to document, during the planning stage, a set of completion criteria with which you and the client agree. Once the completion criteria have been met, the project is finished and the signoff should be automatic.

One of the key acceptance criteria is the acceptance test that the client has defined during the project and will now execute. If you were wise, you have already run these tests as part of system testing and corrected any deficiencies, but it is still possible for client staff to discover errors that you overlooked. They may test a condition that you had not considered, or they may misread instructions and take navigation steps that you had not planned. For example, a tester may enter a foreign client with a different format for the telephone number or zip code. If the system expects national formats, the tester may generate an error by entering an international one. A client tester can also generate an unexpected event by backing out of a set of steps using a browser button rather than the buttons defined in your system.

When such errors occur, you will need to determine if they are the result of a change of scope, which you can request additional time and budget to add, or an oversight on the part of your team during design and development, which you may have to correct. However, if you have been thorough, the acceptance test will usually be successful.

Part of gaining concurrence is providing the client with comfort that he or she will not be abandoned once the project is complete. The best way to accomplish this is to satisfy the client that support is available, either through an applications maintenance group, a help desk, or some type of hotline. Make sure that you introduce the client to the managers of those groups and that they help satisfy the client that he or she is in good hands. When you hand over a project product, you are not simply handing over work, you are also passing on a relationship.

Capturing Lessons Learned

Some people have five years of experience, while others have one year of experience five times. The difference is that the former capitalize on the lessons of each year of experience, allowing them to avoid making the same mistakes over and over again. Just as an individual can learn from his or her errors, so can an organization. The purpose of capturing lessons learned is to help the organization benefit from its errors and advance to a higher level of project management.

Projects produce two types of lessons learned: the lessons relating to how the project was conducted and the lessons relating to the effectiveness of the product. You can identify these lessons with two separate procedures that follow a project: the post-project review and the post-implementation review. Both contribute to a database called the "lessons learned repository."

The Lessons Learned Repository

Lessons are valuable only when they are available for the next situation to which they apply. For this reason, many organizations have adopted a lessons learned repository, a database that contains lessons learned from previous projects and that project managers can use to help them avoid making the mistakes of their predecessors. The repository is a mechanism for organizational learning.

However, there are two problems with the repository. The first is that it requires project managers to make public their most egregious errors. The second is that as the repository grows, the probability that busy project managers will review it drops to near zero. The consequences of these problems are that the most valuable lessons never get recorded but that it does not matter since the repository is never consulted.

The first problem is addressed by ensuring that lessons learned are phrased as lessons as their name implies, and not as a litany of blunders. For example, on one project, the project manager became embroiled in a flurry of memos with the client concerning the training schedule. The client then approached the project manager's supervisor and asked to have him replaced because of his "lack of cooperation" on scheduling training. In reality, the lack of cooperation resulted from the project manager's inability to acquiesce to the client's demands. His position was reasonable, but by the time the dispute reached his supervisor, it was too late to salvage a positive result. In the postmortem, the project manager conceded that, rather than sending memos, he should have met with the client to discuss the schedule. The lesson that he learned was, "Never issue more than two memos on the same subject."

In the lessons learned repository, it is not necessary to record the gruesome details of what went wrong; you can simply note the lesson. Anyone who is curious can approach the project manager who entered the lesson and discuss privately what happened.

The second problem of a lessons learned repository—that as it grows, nobody will consult it—can be addressed by having a repository owner who is responsible for entering, cataloging, and extracting lessons. This is a valuable function for a project management office. With this process, any project manager who is starting a project can contact the repository owner with project details such as the project type, size, client, or technology, and the owner can extract relevant lessons and return them to the project manager. Since the project manager does not have to wade through pages of irrelevancies, it is more likely that he or she will take the lessons to heart.

The Post-Project Review

A post-project review is concerned with how effectively the project was executed. How well did we manage scope? Risk? Communications? Quality? The budget and schedule? A post-project review is conducted in a meeting of the project team, excluding the client, and is held as soon as possible after the completion of the project. A post-project review may even be held before the formal completion, after the end of some major step, such as integration, before most of the team moves on to other projects.

The post-project review meeting may be chaired by the project manager or by someone independent of the project, but in the latter case, be careful to ensure that whoever chairs the meeting does not use it as an opportunity to expound on how he or she would have run the project.

The agenda of the meeting is to review a list of questions as a checklist and to have participants offer their suggestions and comments. A suggested list of questions is given in Exhibit 5.12. The project manager documents these comments and uses the checklist to indicate which of the items has an accompanying lesson. The entire package is then passed on to the lessons learned repository.

The Post-Implementation Review

A post-implementation review is concerned with the effectiveness of the project's product and its implementation. It deals with questions such as whether the product fulfilled its purpose and whether the organization realized the benefits that it expected when it authorized the project.

A post-implementation review is held six months to a year after the

Exhibit 5.12. Post-Project Review Checklist

Post-Project Review Checklist

Project: _____ **Date:** _____

Manager: _____

Scope Lessons

What did we do well in defining scope?   __

What could we improve in defining scope?   __

What did we do well in controlling and managing scope?   __

What could we improve in controlling and managing scope?   __

Schedule and Budget Lessons

What did we do well in estimating?   __

What could we improve in estimating?   __

What did we do well to stay on schedule?   __

What could we improve to stay on schedule?   __

What did we do well in meeting the budget?   __

What could we improve in meeting the budget?   __

Team Building Lessons

What did we do well in developing a team spirit?   __

What could we improve in developing a team spirit?   __

What did we do well in gaining the commitment of team members?   __

What could we improve in gaining the commitment of team members?   __

Customer Relationship Lessons

What did we do well in managing customer expectations?   __

What could we improve in managing customer expectations?   __

What did we do well in using customer resources?   __

What could we improve in using customer resources?   __

What did we do well in gaining customer confidence?   __

What could we improve in gaining customer confidence?   __

What did we do well in achieving customer satisfaction?   __

What could we improve in achieving customer satisfaction?   __

What did we do well in handover of the product to the customer?   __

What could we improve in handover of the product to the customer?   __

Vendor Relationship Lessons

What did we do well in gaining vendor cooperation? —

What could we improve in gaining vendor cooperation? —

What did we do well in understanding vendor status? —

What could we improve in understanding vendor status? —

Internal Company Lessons

What did we do well in acquiring resources for the project? —

What could we improve in acquiring resources for the project? —

What did we do well in keeping management informed of project issues? —

What could we improve in keeping management informed of project issues? —

What did we do well in handover to production? —

What could we improve in handover to production? —

Quality Lessons

What did we do well in defining quality for the project? —

What could we improve in defining quality for the project? —

What did we do well in ensuring quality for the project? —

What could we improve in ensuring quality for the project? —

Risk Lessons

What did we do well in defining project risks? —

What could we improve in defining project risks? —

What did we do well in managing project risks? —

What could we improve in managing project risks? —

completion of implementation, when the product has had a chance to settle down. Any new process or system will generate resistance, errors caused by unfamiliarity, pining for the predecessor, or caustic comments on how the product should have been designed, built, or implemented. The reason for waiting before conducting the post-implementation review is to allow opposition to the product to disappear so that its evaluation can be conducted apart from the heat that accompanies change.

The purpose of the review is to help project managers and technical teams determine how they can better build products that fulfill user needs. It may seem unjust to criticize a project team for building a product that does not meet its purpose if they followed the client's specifications, but projects are not simply automated "do what the client says" agents; their job is to satisfy some real business need. If that means challenging what the client asks for, such a challenge is legitimate.

A post-implementation review may be held as a meeting or may involve interviews with members of the project team, including the project manager, and with those in the client organization. It is conducted by someone separate from the original project team, but the caution noted earlier holds: The review should never be used to advocate the reviewer's preferences in how to conduct projects.

The review focuses on four areas:

1. The scope of the product:
   - Does the product satisfy the original scope? If not, where does it depart? What lessons for future projects can we learn about identifying and managing departures from scope?
   - Does the product do what the client expected? If not, where is it deficient? What lessons for future projects can we learn about determining and satisfying the client's expectations and needs? Be careful to ensure that any "deficiencies" are departures from the original scope and not improvements that users have identified because they have become familiar with the product.

2. Implementation:
   - Was user training adequate? If not, where was it deficient? What lessons for future projects can we learn to ensure that training is adequate in the future?
   - Was implementation more disruptive than expected? If so, what were the causes of the disruptions? Could they have been reasonably avoided? What lessons for future projects can we learn about making our implementations smoother?

3. Documentation and support facilities:
   - Is the user documentation, written and online, adequate? If not, where is it deficient? What lessons for future projects can we learn to ensure that user documentation is adequate?
   - Is the technical documentation adequate? If not, where is it deficient? What lessons for future projects can we learn to ensure that technical documentation is adequate?
   - Are the support facilities, including the help desk, adequate? If not, where are they deficient? Could these deficiencies have reasonably

been avoided by the project? If so, what lessons for future projects can we learn about establishing adequate support facilities?

4. Benefits analysis:

- Did the product produce the benefits that the client expected? If not, where are they deficient? Could these deficiencies have reasonably been avoided by the project? If so, what lessons for future projects can we learn about defining and satisfying benefits?

Administrative Closeout

Projects attract a wealth of administrative details that need to be taken care of when they finish. Charge codes must be closed, equipment handed over to another project or to a general pool, and project information archived. Exhibit 5.13 is a checklist of items that you may need to take care of in order to ensure that the project is complete.

One of the key activities in project closeout is archiving project materials. You should gather the key project management documents of the project and bundle them into a file, either paper or electronic, depending upon your organization's standard. At a minimum, the archives should include the project proposal, the contract or other authorization to proceed, the project plan with any scope changes, project status reports, meeting minutes, the issues log, scope change requests, formal acceptance, lessons learned, and any memos, letters, or reports that dealt with substantive matters. The project archive should be indexed with details such as the project type, technology architecture, customer or customer industry, and application area so that future projects can open the archive and reuse some of its material.

What If?

During Acceptance Testing, the Client Adds New Tests

You risk that the new tests will not succeed because they are out of scope or because they deal with situations that you had not prepared for.

Exhibit 5.13. Project Closeout Checklist

Project Closeout Checklist

Project: _____ Date: _____

Manager: _____

Handoffs

The project has been handed off to and accepted by operations.   —

The project has been handed off to and accepted by maintenance.   —

The project has been handed off to and accepted by server support.   —

The project has been handed off to and accepted by database support.   —

The project has been handed off to and accepted by the help desk.   —

The project has been handed off to and accepted by the client.   —

Reviews

A post-project review has been conducted.   —

A post-implementation review has been scheduled.   —

Administration and Security

The project information has been archived.   —

All project charge codes have been closed.   —

All borrowed resources have been returned.   —

All project-specific network accounts and privileges have been terminated.   —

Project folders and files have been closed.   —

All project-specific vendor security accesses have been terminated.   —

All project-specific hardware has been disposed of.   —

All confidential information has been collected and safely stored.   —

The project sites have been cleaned and material disposed of.   —

Team member supervisors have been notified.   —

Actions

Insist that the acceptance test be terminated until you can evaluate the new tests.

Review the new tests to determine whether the system will pass them. If so, concur with them and resume acceptance testing.

If the system does not pass the new tests, present a change of scope. You have managed the project with a defined goal, which the client has now changed. The scope change will add the time and budget needed to modify the system to meet the new demands. If the client rejects the scope change, revert to the original acceptance test plan.

After a Successful Acceptance Test, the Client Still Does Not Sign Off

Project completion will be endangered.

Actions

Point out that all the completion criteria have been satisfied and that the client has agreed to sign off the project.

If the client still refuses to sign off, present a change of scope based on a departure from the original completion agreement. The scope change will add the time and budget needed to maintain the project team until the client signs off.

The Organization Does Not Have a Lessons Learned Repository

Lessons learned will not be available to the organization except informally, and mistakes will be repeated on subsequent projects, particularly when they are managed by a different project manager.

Actions

In this case, unless you are the manager of the project management office, you have little scope for developing such a repository. Nevertheless, holding the post-project and post-implementation reviews is still valuable. Forward the lessons to your manager, who can decide whether and how to disseminate them throughout the organization.

Regardless, maintain your own private lessons learned repository. You may share this with other project managers or not as you prefer, but by consulting it at the start of each project, you minimize the risk that you will repeat earlier mistakes.

* * * * *
PROJECT COMPLETION

Significant events have rousing conclusions. Symphonies, fireworks displays, and mystery novels all end spectacularly, signifying a clear, definable, and absolute finish. Projects, particularly those that are intense or that demand extreme effort, are significant events in the lives of all the team members. They require, no less than does a concert, a sense of finality and a celebration of achievement.

Most projects fizzle out. Even the successful ones wind down slowly as the level of work tapers off, until one day only a handful of people are left to wrap things up. Those who leave before the end of the project are removed from the team and transplanted elsewhere while the work to which they have committed themselves is still in progress. These people need a distinct point of transition and closure.

Some project managers attempt to bring the team together when the project is over, but the spirit and the chemistry are not the same. The people are now involved in different projects, and you will not be able to reconstruct the atmosphere of your project. It might be nice to get together, but it will be a reunion, not a celebration.

Therefore, celebrate the milestones. In particular, schedule a celebration for the completion of the point when many of your people will be dispersing. For example, once the development work is done and only the integration team will be left, hold a party. Call for nominations for the person who overcame the toughest problem, who showed the most tact, who was the best dresser, who maintained the best humor, who was most helpful, who bought the most muffins. Make sure that you let people know how proud you are of them. List and extol their achievements. Present them with project mementos such as T-shirts or pens with the project logo.

You may argue, "How can we celebrate when the project is not over? We still need to complete integration and implementation." But the project *is* over for many of your team. To deny them a chance to mark that completion is to withhold from them a valuable process whereby they can recognize their own achievement. "But what if the project is not a success? What if we're late and over budget?" Your choice is simple: You can send team members on their way with a sense of failure, or you can, while acknowledging the problems, recognize and make sure they understand the real achievements they made.

Private Celebration

At some point, the project really will be over. The team will have left, the deliverables will have been handed over, the final paperwork will be complete. It will then be time for you to recognize yourself. Take the time to sit down and do two things: Review and recognize your achievements, and document the lessons you have learned.

To recognize achievements, review the original project material and the client's situation when you started. Then examine where your client is today, and recognize that that progress is your doing. To your people, they were the ones who did the work, but you were the one who made it happen. Without your efforts, the project would have deteriorated into chaos and acrimony. You held it together and forced your team and the client to the conclusion. You now have the right to recognize the value that you brought to the project.

At the same time, you will have learned important lessons. When you review the project, ask yourself, "What could I have done here that would have been more effective? What cues did I miss that indicated an embryonic problem? How could I have been better?" Then write down your answers in a place that you can refer to when you start your next project. Please understand that the purpose of this exercise is not to club yourself with regrets. It is to help you learn so that, next time, the mistakes you make will be brand new and you will have progressed to a higher level in an honorable profession.

* * * * *

CONCLUSION

Project overruns are the norm. Rare is the company that consistently delivers projects on time, on budget, and fully functional. Rarer still is the company that overtly identifies the benefits it expects and actively pursues them.

It is hard enough to keep a project on track in those disciplines where the road has been traveled before, the activities are familiar, and the pitfalls are clearly marked. Modern systems projects, with evolving development technologies, changing methodologies, and novel applications, have created an environment in which each project is an exploration; not only is the plan difficult to follow, it is even harder to create with any degree of confidence.

If our industry is to mature to the point where it can routinely deliver what is required of it, one of the issues we must resolve is the shortage of qualified, experienced, professional, career project managers. We need to find and develop people who can work with the special ambiguities of project life, who can master the intricacies needed in project planning and execution, and who are powerful managers of themselves and their teams.

Such people are not common. Computer systems careers lead more readily to advanced technical expertise or line management. Project management is too often seen as a stepping-stone to "real" management or as a useful ancillary set of skills for technical leaders. Neither view is likely to produce people who are eager to make project management a lifetime career.

This book, like others that celebrate project management as a worthwhile vocation, is an attempt to describe the complex world of projects and the range of skills needed to manage them. Above all, I have two hopes: that organizations will recognize the significance of project management in their formal career streams and that project managers will emerge who embrace the challenges and rewards inherent in a needed, exciting, and fulfilling profession.

Index